Cross-Textual Reading of Ecclesiastes with the Analects

Contrapuntal Readings of the Bible in World Christianity

Series Editors: K. K. Yeo, Melanie Baffes

Just as God knows no boundaries and incarnation happens in shared space, truth does not respect borders and its expression in various contexts is kaleidoscopic. As God's church is birthed forth from local cultures, it is called into a catholic community—namely world Christianity. This series values the twofold identity of biblical interpretations that seek to engage in contextual theology and, at the same time, become part of a global and "many-voiced" conversation for the sake of mutual understanding. By promoting contrapuntal readings that hold contextual and global biblical hermeneutics in tension, this series celebrates interpretations in three movements: (1) those based on the biblical text that honor multiple and interacting worldviews (reading the world biblically/theologically); (2) those that work at the translatability of the biblical text to uphold various dynamic vernaculars and faithful hermeneutics for the world (reading the Bible/theology contextually); and (3) those that respect the cross-cultural and shifting contexts in which faithful communities are embedded, and embody, real-life issues.

International Advisory Board

Walter Brueggemann, William Marcellus McPheeters Professor Emeritus of Old Testament at Columbia Theological Seminary (U.S.)

Adela Yarbro Collins, Buckingham Professor of New Testament Criticism and Interpretation, Yale Divinity School (U.S.)

Kathy Ehrensperger, Research Professor of New Testament in Jewish Perspective, University of Potsdam (Germany)

Justo L. González, Emeritus Professor of Historical Theology, Candler School of Theology, Emory University (U.S.)

Richard A. Horsley, Distinguished Professor of Liberal Arts and the Study of Religion Emeritus, University of Massachusetts—Boston (U.S.)

Robert Jewett, Emeritus Professor of New Testament at Heidelberg University (Germany)

Peter Lampe, Professor of New Testament Theology, Heidelberg University (Germany)

Tremper Longman III, Robert H. Gundry Professor Emeritus of Biblical Studies, Westmont College (U.S.)

Daniel Patte, Professor Emeritus of Religious Studies, New Testament, and Christianity, Vanderbilt University (U.S.)

Volumes in the Series (2018–2019)

Volume 1: *Text and Context: Vernacular Approaches to the Bible in Global Christianity*, edited by Melanie Baffes

Volume 2: *What Has Jerusalem to Do with Beijing? Biblical Interpretation from a Chinese Perspective* (Twentieth Anniversary Edition), K. K. Yeo

Volume 3: *Chinese Biblical Anthropology: Persons and Ideas in the Old Testament and in Modern Chinese Literature*, Cao Jian

Volume 4: *Cross-textual Reading of Ecclesiastes with Analects: In Search of Political Wisdom in a Disordered World*, Elaine Wei-Fun Goh

Cross-Textual Reading of Ecclesiastes with the Analects

In Search of Political Wisdom in a Disordered World

Elaine Wei-Fun Goh

Foreword by Choon-Leong Seow

☙PICKWICK *Publications* • Eugene, Oregon

CROSS-TEXTUAL READING OF ECCLESIASTES WITH THE ANALECTS
In Search of Political Wisdom in a Disordered World

Contrapuntal Readings of the Bible in World Christianity 4

Copyright © 2019 Elaine Wei-Fun Goh. All rights reserved. Except for brief quotations in critical publications or reviews, no part of this book may be reproduced in any manner without prior written permission from the publisher. Write: Permissions, Wipf and Stock Publishers, 199 W. 8th Ave., Suite 3, Eugene, OR 97401.

Pickwick Publications
An Imprint of Wipf and Stock Publishers
199 W. 8th Ave., Suite 3
Eugene, OR 97401

www.wipfandstock.com

PAPERBACK ISBN: 978-1-5326-8147-9
HARDCOVER ISBN: 978-1-5326-8148-6
EBOOK ISBN: 978-1-5326-8149-3

Cataloging-in-Publication data:

Names: Goh, Elaine Wei-Fun, author. | Seow, C. L. (Choon-Leong), foreword.

Title: Cross-textual reading of Ecclesiastes with the Analects / Elaine Wei-Fun Goh ; foreword by Choon-Leong Seow.

Description: Eugene, OR: Pickwick Publications, 2019. | Contrapuntal Readings of the Bible in World Christianity 4. | Includes bibliographical references and index.

Identifiers: ISBN: 978-1-5326-8147-9 (paperback). | ISBN: 978-1-5326-8148-6 (hardcover). | ISBN: 978-1-5326-8149-3 (ebook).

Subjects: LCSH: Bible.—Ecclesiastes—Criticism, interpretation, etc. | Bible—Hermeneutics—Cross-cultural studies. | Confucius. | Philosophy, Chinese.

Classification: BS1475.2 G64 2019 (print). | BS1475.2 (epub).

Manufactured in the U.S.A. 09/30/19

Contents

Foreword by Choon-Leong Seow | vii
Acknowledgments | ix
Preface | xi
Abbreviations | xiii

1. Cross-Textuality and Ancient Literature | 1
2. Ecclesiastes and Political Wisdom | 37
3. The Analects and Political Wisdom | 91
4. Ecclesiastes and the Analects at a Crossroads | 137

Epilogue | 177
Bibliography | 179
Index of Authors | 199
Index of Subjects | 203
Index of Ancient Documents | 207

Foreword

THERE IS PROBABLY NO book in the Bible whose authority is as frequently called into question as Ecclesiastes. Its place as a document of the community of faith was disputed from the start. The rabbis of antiquity sought to remove it from circulation, partly because it seemed to be internally inconsistent and partly because they feared it might lead to heresy. Even though it did win approval as an inspired work at the famous gathering of rabbis at Jamnia in 90 CE, questions about its suitability for the general public continued to be raised for centuries thereafter. So Jerome reported in the fourth century that there were still some who tried to suppress it in his time. In the modern period, too, the book is more often than not viewed as one that stands at the periphery of the canon, at best a voice of protest.

Scholarly debates have continued to revolve around the tensions within the book and its apparent heterodoxy, and assessments of it have remained wildly contrastive. One interpreter argues that the author—known by his Hebrew pen-name, Qoheleth—was "a depressed workaholic," while another calls him "a preacher of joy." A majority of commentators regard the author as an unrelenting pessimist, constantly proclaiming that "all is vanity" (1:2), while others portray him as an unflappable optimist, who maintains that "there is nothing better for people under the sun than to eat and drink and be merry" (8:15). To explain the teachings of the book that seem idiosyncratic in light of the rest of the Bible, critics have argued that the author was influenced by skeptical traditions from Mesopotamia or Egypt or that his thoughts were shaped by various Greek philosophical schools. His perspectives are usually accounted for in terms of his intellectual background—most notably the putative foreign influences—or his personal disposition and predilection. Thus, Qoheleth is said to have been either a pessimist or an optimist because of his training and/or simply because "that was the way he was."

For all its difficulty, Ecclesiastes, especially in its opening poem about the cyclical nature of the world and its element (1:2–9), seems to resonate for many Asians. In fact, at the end of the nineteenth century, a scholar by the name of Emile Joseph Dillon found so many similarities between

Ecclesiastes and Buddhism that he argued that Ecclesiastes reflects a Buddhist influence. That theory is far-fetched, and hardly any scholar has followed Dillon's lead. Still, it is true that in Ecclesiastes, many Asian Christians will find much that is relevant, even inspiring.

In this book, Dr. Elaine Wei-Fun Goh introduces Chinese readers to the fascinating book of Ecclesiastes and its message for Asian Christians today. Dr. Goh's interpretation is deep and meaningful, for it is informed by the ancient world from which Ecclesiastes emerged. She draws on similar texts from elsewhere in the ancient Near East, and she reads the book against its sociohistorical background—a world of economic and political uncertainty that in some ways we find similar to our own world. Additionally, Dr. Goh brings Ecclesiastes to life for Asians by reading it cross-culturally, bringing the biblical text into conversation with classic Chinese literature. The result is a rich and exciting introduction to one of the "best kept secrets" of Old Testament Theology.

Choon-Leong Seow
Vanderbilt University
December 24, 2018

Acknowledgments

MANY PEOPLE HAVE PLAYED a part in the completion of this book. I am grateful to them for journeying with me during my doctoral pursuit and, subsequently, in the writing of this volume.

I wish to thank my academic advisor, Dr. Choon-Leong Seow, who is my mentor in biblical Wisdom Literature. He is a careful exegete and an exceptional scholar. He taught me Ecclesiastes, along with other Old Testament books, during my pursuit of the master of theology degree at Princeton Theological Seminary. Many thanks to him for encouraging me to search deeper in Ecclesiastes and to venture into cross-textual endeavor. His teaching and his commitment to Old Testament scholarship are qualities I seek to emulate.

In addition, I am grateful to Dr. Pan Chao Wee, Dr. Archie C. C. Lee, and Dr. Daniel See You Lay, who have sharpened my thoughts and arguments in many ways during my doctoral studies. I am learning to keep up with their proficiency in reading Chinese Classics in parallel with biblical texts. They have kindly affirmed my endeavor in cross-textual hermeneutics and, at the same time, have honestly challenged my ideas. Their critical comments on my research have certainly helped this book progress in a more constructive direction.

I am appreciative to Seminari Theoloji Malaysia (STM) for the support and encouragement in my research and writing. I am grateful that this book records one of the efforts and the commitments of the seminary to encourage research and writing. Many thanks to Wipf and Stock for the publication of this book and to K. K. Yeo and Melanie Baffes as series editors. They have been diligent and professional in the editing of this book; therefore, I claim responsibility should any mistake be found.

My heartfelt appreciation goes to my family. Words are inadequate to express my gratitude to my husband, Way Min, and to our daughter, Jolin. They have inevitably been brought together with me in a strenuous journey of research and writing. Now, to both of my loved ones, I dedicate this work.

Elaine Wei-Fun Goh
November 2018

Preface

VARIOUS CROSS-TEXTUAL READINGS HAVE been attempted between the Bible and Chinese literature. This study centers on the political wisdom of Ecclesiastes and of the Analects using an approach to cross-textual hermeneutics. It is the intention of this study to demonstrate that both texts offer wisdom pointers with regards to human survival amidst uncertain socio-political realities. In this study, a biblical text (Ecclesiastes) and a native text (the Analects) are read in the context of the author as a Chinese Christian reader. Chapter 1 introduces the vibrant interaction of biblical wisdom literature within the ancient Near East, where some of the political connections are highlighted. The openness of wisdom literature is then proposed to support this present effort of cross-textual research. Chapter 2 focuses on the reading of eight passages that communicate Qoheleth's political wisdom in Ecclesiastes. Chapter 3 centers on the Analects and the reading of some notable passages that relate to Confucius' political ideas. Chapter 4 seeks to demonstrate the dialogical dynamics between the two corpora, based on specific hermeneutical connections. At the conclusion, one's understanding is found to be examined, critiqued, and reclaimed by both biblical and native texts. There are distinctive *and* collective political insights of both wisdom texts. This study therefore suggests a contextual idea for living wisely when a reader stands in both one's faith and native traditions.

Abbreviations

AB	Anchor Bible
AEL	*Ancient Egyptian Literature: A Book of Readings.* Miriam Lichtheim. 3 vols. Berkeley: University of California Press, 1973–1980
AJT	*Asia Journal of Theology*
ANE	Ancient Near Eastern
ANET	*Ancient Near Eastern Texts Relating to the Old Testament.* Edited by James B. Pritchard. 3rd ed. Princeton: Princeton University Press, 1969
BDB	*The New Brown-Driver-Briggs Hebrew and English Lexicon.* Francis Brown, S. R. Driver, and Charles A. Briggs. Peabody, MA: Hendrickson, 1979
BHS	*Biblia Hebraica Stuttgartensia*
Bib	*Biblica*
BWL	*Babylonian Wisdom Literature.* W. G. Lambert. Oxford: Clarendon, 1960
CBQ	*Catholic Biblical Quarterly*
CBR	*Currents in Biblical Research*
CEAP	*Companion Encyclopedia of Asian Philosophy.* Edited by Brian Carr and Indira Mahalingam. 1997. Reprint, London: Routledge, 2001
COS	*The Context of Scripture.* 4 vols. Edited by William W. Hallo and K. Lawson Younger Jr. Leiden: Brill, 1997–2017
ECP	*Encyclopedia of Chinese Philosophy.* Edited by Antonio S. Cua. New York: Routledge, 2003
EOA	*Encyclopedia of Archaeology.* Edited by Deborah M. Pearsall. Amsterdam: Elsevier/Academic, 2008

HALOT	*A Concise Hebrew and Aramaic Lexicon of the Old Testament.* William L. Holladay. Leiden: Brill, 1971
ICC	International Critical Commentary
JBL	*Journal of Biblical Literature*
JCP	*Journal of Chinese Philosophy*
JCR	*Journal of Chinese Religions*
JQR	*Jewish Quarterly Review*
JSOT	*Journal for the Study of Old Testament*
LXX	Septuagint
NCBC	New Century Bible Commentary
NICOT	New International Commentary on the Old Testament
NKJV	New King James Version
NRSV	New Revised Standard Version
ODWR	*Oxford Dictionary of World Religions.* Edited by John Bowker. Oxford: Oxford University Press, 1997
OEANE	*Oxford Encyclopedia of Archaeology in the Near East.* Edited by Eric M. Myers. New York: Oxford University Press, 1997
OTL	Old Testament Library
REC	*RoutledgeCurzon Encyclopedia of Confucianism.* Edited by Xinzhong Yao. 2 vols. New York: RoutledgeCurzon, 2003
SBL	Society of Biblical Literature
SJOT	*Scandinavian Journal of the Old Testament*
TAD	*Textbook of Aramaic Documents in Ancient Egypt.* Bezalel Porten and Ada Yardeni. Jerusalem: Hebrew University Press, 1986–93
TDOT	*Theological Dictionary of the Old Testament*
TJT	*Taiwan Journal of Theology*
TWOT	*Theological Wordbook of the Old Testament*
VT	*Vetus Testamentum*
WBC	Word Biblical Commentary

I

Cross-Textuality and Ancient Literature

THE DISCOVERY OF VARIOUS ancient documents from the Near East has led to numerous comparisons of these documents to the biblical writings. Areas of comparison are vast, yet the comparisons have focused on the resemblance of biblical texts to the ancient literature.[1] Various interpretations have been offered. To account for the cross-cultural affinities, scholars speak of "cultural diffusion" (N. Smart),[2] "generic nominalism" (K. Sparks),[3] and "subconscious shared heritage" (J. Walton).[4] Whatever the label, it seems clear that there are genres that the biblical wisdom shares with these ancient wisdom texts.[5] Wisdom is didactic in nature. Wisdom is also dialogic and invites conversation. Furthermore, wisdom at times has to do with matters political. Despite the richness of literature, sapiential political counsel has yet to be investigated in any detail. These political counsels from the ancient Near Eastern wisdom texts are found to connect to each other. They usually concern courtly conduct and civil survival. The commonality is not surprising, since all wisdom texts originate within human societies, each with its own civic structures and issues. What is arresting, however, is the political wisdom generated in the interaction of the various forms of ancient literature.

This book holds two ancient sapiential texts together—one from the Bible and the other from Chinese Classics—in a cross-textual mode of

---

1. Areas of comparison have included instructions and admonitions, hymns and prayers, love poetry, rituals and incantations, prophecies, tales and novellas, as well as epics and legends and much more.

2. Smart, "Comparative-Historical Method," 571–74.

3. Sparks, *Ancient Texts*, 6.

4. Walton, *Ancient Near Eastern Thought*, 27.

5. A distinctive "generic matrix" marks the invention of distinctive texts to which the Hebrew Bible and Ancient Near East texts belong; see Sparks, *Ancient Texts*, 3, 10. Eight generic traits for his analytical generic approach are suggested: 1) content and theme; 2) language; 3) *Sitz im Leben*; 4) function; 5) form and structure; 6) material attributes; 7) mode of composition and reception; and 8) genre and tradition. See ibid., 13–21.

interpretation. The book of Ecclesiastes and the Analects both communicate pedagogic wisdom and insightful reflections in the areas of coping in life amid a chaotic socio-political backdrop. Both wisdom texts are didactic, dialogic and, in some measure at least, political. I propose that, with regards to the human quest for survival in a world marked by political uncertainty, Ecclesiastes and the Analects hold some things in common, complement each other, and enrich the understanding of one another. Not only do the texts demonstrate generic wisdom but also they offer practical counsel with regards to contemporary civic life.

The Relevance of This Study

This research takes place in an epoch marked by globalized interaction of cultures. Such an era enables diverse perspectives to be put into conversation. Therefore, some thinkers label the present one "a Second Axial Age," in which one finds discussions within a framework of a changing social environment.[6] They perceive the need to address some common subjects such as globalization, ecology, politics, gender, religious concerns, ethnic unity, and cross-cultural dynamics. While there are efforts toward globalization in some realms, there remain balkanization in others, not least those affected by religious ideologies. Presently, there is still much evidence of religious extremism (for example, the al Qaeda movement), violent confrontation (for instance, Palestinian suicide bombings), and intolerance (for example, the restricted use of the generic term for God, "Allah," in the national language in Malaysia). People live in an age where they should be coming together; instead, they are growing apart because they are parochial in their perception of different classics. One of our endeavors in this age, therefore, is at best to promote respect and awareness of the existence of other perspectives, other religions, various cultures and opinions. In the religious realm, different faith traditions have to realize the need to depart from claims of superiority and self-centeredness. People can welcome an exchange of religious ideas, comparative studies, cross-cultural dynamics, and

---

6. The First Axial Age or "axis age," an idea pioneered by German philosopher Karl Jaspers, refers to the period from 800 to 200 BCE, during which revolutionary thoughts appeared from many parts of the world that had had a profound influence on future philosophy and religion. During this axial age, humanity in general had a common concern for its existence and limitations and adapted a critical evaluation on life. Due to the effects of science and inventions since the twentieth century, intensified by the effects of globalization in recent decades, many thinkers follow Ewert Cousins' lead in naming the present epoch as the Second Axial Age. See Wang, *Jieshi, Lijie yu Zongjiao Duihua* [Interpretation, Understanding and Religious Dialogue], 1–3.

cross-textual interpretations. Putting doctrinal differences aside, religious representatives increasingly search for dynamics for working toward unity despite the diversity.[7] Therefore, an appreciative cross-cultural, cross-textual grappling with wisdom is surely salutary and timely. This book joins such endeavor with an anticipation of openness and mutual respect.

Dialogues have to be attempted between various religious and cultural texts. Such attempts will not only be transformative within particular faith traditions but also will be enriching in response to the challenges that come with a globalized reality. The dynamics are by no means simple. The interaction between Christianity and Confucianism, for instance, has been built on different models amid various challenges. The relation began with what has been called *a transcending approach*, namely, one that views Confucianism as having flaws that need to be corrected by Christianity.[8] Then, *a complementary approach* suggests that each faith tradition has some value to offer to the other.[9] A third, a *confrontational approach*, emphasizes the differences and then disables any interaction with one another.[10] A fourth, a *resolving approach*, consistent with post-liberal theological thought, syncretizes two different faith traditions in order to suggest a new one.[11] Fifth, a *comparative approach*, suggests one cross over to the faith tradition of another in order to understand, interpret, and practice faith from their perspective.[12] This comparative approach is an approach taken

---

7. During the time this research was written, there were proactive visits of Muslim undergraduates from Malaysia National University (*Universiti Kebangsaan Malaysia*, UKM) to Malaysia Theological Seminary (*Seminari Theoloji Malaysia*, STM), an institution where Christian workers and pastors are trained. This event happened despite increasing tensions between Muslims and Christians in the country. Likewise, various non-Muslims in Malaysia are coming together amid religious clashes involving Islamic fundamentalists. As such, associations such as Malaysian Consultative Council of Buddhism, Christianity, Hinduism, Sikhism and Taoism (MCCBCHST) are being formed. People have begun to see the need to put aside differences, seeking instead cultured means for working together.

8. The transcending approach was taken by most Christian missionaries from the sixteenth to nineteenth centuries. See Wang, *Jieshi, Lijie yu Zongjiao Duihua*, 75.

9. The complementary approach is observed and purported by Cobb in his *Transforming Christianity and the World* and *Christian Faith and Religious Diversity*; see D'Costa, *Christian Uniqueness Reconsidered*, 81–95.

10. The confrontational approach is maintained by Gernet, *China and the Christian Impact*, which discusses the experience of the Jesuit mission in China with an approach from an almost exclusively Chinese point of view.

11. Lindbeck, *Nature of Doctrine*; see also Wang, *Jieshi, Lijie yu Zongjiao Duihua*, 76–78.

12. The comparative approach is a branch of Christian comparative theology that studies religious diversity and compares traditions. See Clooney, *New Comparative Theology*, 191–200; see also D'Costa, *Christian Uniqueness Reconsidered*, 63–80.

by recent comparative theologians vis-à-vis faith dialogue in the Second Axial Age. It came about after evaluating models of the past, all of which had faced various criticisms. As a result of all these development between Christianity and the Confucian tradition, biblical scholarship has to consider undertaking a transition from monologue to dialogue. The dialogue thus far, however, has taken the Bible as the main text and the other as a subsidiary one. The relationship between scriptures from diverse faith traditions appears to be in need of reassessment.

While the comparative approach requires orientation and learning of other religious traditions through shared experience, this book takes a step further to engage a dialogical approach. It invites accommodation rather than mere comparison. This *dialogical approach* aims at cross-textual interpretation, where one treats two texts side by side so that they illumine each other. This approach generates new readings that are possible only if both are studied in parallel. In some ways, this approach is not new. Scholars who engage in different cultural traditions at present have frequently employed such a dialogical method. They study the Old Testament alongside other ancient Near Eastern texts to highlight affinities and differences between the two corpora. They often speak of the influence of certain ancient Near Eastern texts upon the Bible. At times, they even speak of how a foreign text illumines parts of the Bible. This chapter attempts to illustrate some of these affinities. There are some notable Ecclesiastes parallels in the discipline of cross-textual scholarship that focuses on political wisdom. Some definitions, however, need to be drawn beforehand.

Clarifications of the Title

Wisdom

The biblical adjective *ḥākām* ("wise"), and its noun *ḥokmâ* ("wisdom"), primarily signify one's skill or expertise (Exod 28:3; 35:25; 1 Kgs 7:14; 1 Chr 22:15, 28:21; 2 Chr 7, 13–14) in craftsmanship as well as in technical work (Isa 3:3; Jer 9:17–18). The term conveys also one's competence in administration (Gen 41:33, 39–40; Dan 1:20).[13] As such, goldsmiths (Jer 10:9), artisans (Exod 31:3–6), sailors (Ezek 27:8), homemakers (Exod 35:25), sanctuary construction workers (Exod 36:1–2), and idol makers (Isa 40:20) are considered "wise" because of their skills.[14] The term also is associated

---

13. Brown et al., *BDB*, 315.

14. Animals are sometimes called "wise" because of their survival instincts; for example, in Prov 30:24.

with people in religious affairs or in keeping faithfulness to the LORD (Deut 4:6; Jer 4:22; 8:8–9; Ps 107:43). Accordingly, political skills that associate with court advisers (Isa 19:11–12; 29:14), officials (Deut 16:18; 2 Sam 15:12), and kings (Prov 20:26; Isa 10:13; 1 Kgs 10:6) are regarded as "wise." Even political skills that involve less than benign aspects are regarded as "wisdom." As such, Amnon's friend, Jonadab, who taught Amnon a pretense to rape his sister, was said to be "wise" (2 Sam 13:3–5). Likewise was David's political counselor (*yôʿēṣ*), Ahitophel, who turned against David later (2 Sam 15:12; cf. 2 Sam 16:20–23). They were considered "wise" even though their motifs and effects were not necessarily salutary.

"Wisdom" in its essence is "the art of steering" and "the ability to cope."[15] The forms in which wisdom expresses itself are diverse. Gerhard von Rad, therefore, suggests a broad definition: wisdom has to do with human understanding and is a particular form of human knowledge and behavior.[16] James Crenshaw observes that, as a way of life, "wisdom" is the pursuit of means of the mastery of the world, and its knowledge is transmitted for future generations.[17] Crenshaw's observation is particularly insightful for pointing out that the genres of wisdom writing seem to share in an attitude and intention translatable into a characteristic literary pattern. Wisdom is an "art of living" in the broadest sense.[18] It is a knowledge that leads one to understand the essential meaning of life, at the same time suggesting the ways to carry out that meaning.[19] Such knowledge is articulated through collections of wisdom literature.

Politics and Political Wisdom

As *ḥakam* (the wise) is also *yôʿēṣ* (counselor) in the Bible, the wise were often court officials or political consultants. Proverbs and ancient Egyptian wisdom literature consist mainly of political advice, where some texts were explicitly about governance. *The Instructions of Ptahhotep*, *Instructions of Amenemhet*, and the like are good examples. Therefore, the word "politics" here generally relates to activities that engage the administration of public affairs in a country.[20] Politics in this sense is understood as the art of governing a constitutional entity, such as a state or nation, and the administration

---

15. Crenshaw, *Old Testament Wisdom*, 9.
16. Von Rad, *Wisdom in Israel*, 8.
17. Crenshaw, *Old Testament Wisdom*, 1 and 3.
18. Blanshard, "Wisdom," 322.
19. Swidler, "Christian Historical Perspective on Wisdom," 557.
20. Soanes and Stevenson, "Politics" and "Political," 1362.

or jurisdiction of its internal and external affairs. "Political wisdom," therefore, is a practical wisdom toward political order that concerns day-to-day management of political activities and, at the same time, the quest for ways to cope in terms of political survival.

At the same time, wisdom is broadly about steering in life. The political wisdom defined in this book is thus inevitably wide. It does, however, have discernible properties. Political wisdom in this book first refers to prudent pointers toward effectual administration, crisis prevention, people management, and competent governance. Political wisdom in this sense is direct, aiming to maintain order and general well-being in a political organization. This aspect of political wisdom is *prescriptive wisdom*, and is more discernible in the Analects. Besides this meaning, political wisdom in this book also refers generally to the wisdom of survival in royal court and, at the same time, the wisdom of coping with social disharmony and political tyranny in particular. Numerous experiential and conceptual political reflections, therefore, are political wisdom as well. Political wisdom in this sense is indirect and reflective. This aspect of political wisdom is *descriptive wisdom*, and is relatively more discernible in Ecclesiastes. Wisdom is didactic in essence. This didactic nature connects both prescriptive and descriptive aspects above. These two aspects are both communicated through the composition of the Analects and Ecclesiastes. Political wisdom, therefore, is not only communicated through instructions and admonitions but also through anecdotes, political satires, political rhetoric, social observations, and reflections.[21] Political wisdom in both its direct aspect (instructions and admonitions) and indirect aspect (observations and reflections) represents wise pointers in both the Analects and Ecclesiastes. In short, political wisdom is primarily an art for cultivating one's civic existence. In Ecclesiastes and the Analects, it is wisdom for coping in life within a socio-political system.

---

21. The anthology that conveys the prescriptive aspects of political wisdom has a purpose of imparting practical wisdom for daily living—in courts; survival abilities; political know-how; effective decision making; civic management; and so forth. This wisdom is reflected through counsels to the kings or from an official to the son. Their legacy is passed on by authority figures: kings in the royal court and scribes who wrote and copied the proverbial sayings under royal commands. Conversely, the compilation of texts that conveys reflective aspects of political wisdom aims to suggest ways for civic survival, especially amid social disorder and political uncertainty. These are handed down within the wisdom tradition that concerns life in the public sphere. Their legacy is passed on through sapiential figures to the next generation. As illustrated earlier, various concerns and subject matters are shared through literature that conveys political wisdom.

Cross-Textual Reading

Cross-textual reading is an interpretive endeavor based on a dialogical model of two written texts that communicate analogous thoughts. Archie Lee defines cross-textual hermeneutics in Asia as a way for Asians "to read their own classical texts and the biblical texts together, and let one text shed light on or challenge the other, so that creative dialogue and integration can take place."[22] Cross-textual reading considers the contextual and cultural influence from which a biblical reader originates. It also, at the same time, serves the present context in which a biblical text is understood. Wisdom is a common human phenomenon across cultures and history, hence Confucius' wisdom may relate to Qoheleth's wisdom in the areas of human experience. Their texts, Ecclesiastes and the Analects, belong to the wisdom genre. Both texts are didactic in their political instructions and social reflections. They are both still actively and widely read today, especially by people who hold two traditions—faith and culture—together. Thus, the fusion of their wisdom necessarily deepens the understanding of a reader who embraces both traditions.[23] By demonstrating further hermeneutical connections and conceptual links, the integration between the two corpora yields new understandings and new challenges in the present context of the reader.

Ecclesiastes as a Wisdom Text

The term "Ecclesiastes" is the Greco-Latin form of the Hebrew *Qoheleth* (Greek *ekklēsiatēs*, Latin *ecclesiastes*). Both the Hebrew and Greek terms are connected to the verb "to assemble," and so the author's pen-name is thought to signify one who assembles people for religious purposes, one who gathers wisdom, or one who attempts to sum up teachings.[24] This study uses the term "Ecclesiastes" in reference to the book and "Qoheleth" in reference to the author. Ecclesiastes denotes a type of wisdom that inclines toward descriptive wisdom, albeit containing prescriptive wisdom as well. Most scholars date Ecclesiastes to a Hellenistic period around 300 BCE, on the grounds that the book presupposes a time of great economic activity and social turmoil that fits its ethos.[25] Some place the book during the Ptolemaic

---

22. Lee, "Cross-Textual Hermeneutics," 61.
23. Ibid., 185.
24. Crenshaw, *Old Testament Wisdom*, 133; Murphy, *Tree of Life*, 49.
25. For example, Crenshaw, *Ecclesiastes*; Fox, *Qoheleth and His Contradictions*; see Murphy, *Ecclesiastes*, xix–xxiii; xliii–xliv.

empire when its author, Qoheleth, wrote and taught in Jerusalem.[26] The above dating, however, does not explain the absence of Greek nuances in Ecclesiastes, as Greek loan-words frequently appear in the inscriptions from that period. Based on this absence of Greek literary evidence, it is unlikely that Ecclesiastes was written in a Hellenistic world, as some have suggested. Rather, Persian influence on Ecclesiastes is noticeably found in the literary terms Qoheleth used. Choon-Leong Seow has pointed out that the literary style Qoheleth employed (loan words and rhetoric) may have been influenced by turbulent socioeconomic change and political malaise in the early Persian period.[27] Therefore, dating it back to the fifth or fourth century BCE during the Persian period seems likely. This dating is based on the socioeconomic background that shapes the linguistic features, distinctive terms used, and the overall outlook of the book. It was located at a time when the assumptions of traditional wisdom were being questioned and explored.[28] Due to the distinct way of conveying wisdom for living amid the perplexity of life, the book often poses a challenge to interpreters. Qoheleth's teaching, unlike in the past, has in recent years been considered as being laid out following intended structures. I follow the idea to suggest a discernible outline to the book. Therein eight political passages are given attention in my research: Eccl 3:16–17; 4:1–3; 4:13–16; 5:8–10 [Hebrew 5:7–9]; 8:2–9; 9:13–16; 10: 4–7; and 10:16–20.

The Analects 《论语》 as a Wisdom Text

Confucius did not write any treatise that systematically expounded his thoughts. Instead, he elaborated on them in educational and political activities.[29] The Analects is a record of his thoughts, teachings, political observations, and dialogues with his disciples, as well as others. Some of its wisdom articulations have characteristics like the prescriptive wisdom of the ancient Near East, while some others are reminiscent of descriptive wisdom. The Analects is generally considered the most important work reflecting Confucian thought. As one of the cornerstones of the Confucian school, it represents one of the most influential books to be studied as much in East Asian civilizations, most notably China itself.[30] Though the exact date of completion of the Analects cannot be ascertained, it is believed to have been

---

26. For example, Perdue, *Sword and the Stylus*, 198–255.
27. Seow, *Ecclesiastes*, 12–36 and "Linguistic Evidence," 643–66.
28. Seow, *Ecclesiastes*, 21–36.
29. Huang, "Confucius and Confucianism," 536.
30. Bowker, "Analects," *ODWR*, 61.

written around the early Warring States Period (around 400 BCE).[31] The interpretation of the Analects in this book thus reflects Confucius' social and political background: during the late Spring and Autumn Period to the early Warring States Period. The Analects contains twenty books grouped by individual titles. The contents of the Analects are wide-ranging. It contains philosophical and ethical ideas, daily activities, living concerns, social observations, political advices, cultural matters, observations, reflections, and even personal temperaments and preferences. Yet these contents can be encapsulated into one common theme: learning how to become a *junzi* (君子). On how to be a responsible, proper, and wise person, the Analects remarkably engages a great concern in civic spheres. The great amount of political ideas in forms of instructions, admonitions, and observations makes the Analects one of the best examples for exploring political wisdom. Among other equally important key concepts to be explored, its political ideas are given primary attention in this book.

A Disordered World

As it is a reality in every generation, both Ecclesiastes and the Analects reflect social locations affected by disruptive social relationships and unruly political conditions. There were opportunities for people to acquire position, land, wealth, and fame. Yet there were also injustices and oppression that came along with acquisition. Confucius observed the source of evil in his day as a decay of moral standards among the ruling class. The wicked yet powerful were set above civilians. Influential noble families often ruled over the state rulers, generating political chaos and social disorder. Therefore, Confucius advocated governance based on collective attributes and managerial competence. And *junzi* became such an exemplar. Qoheleth, by contrast, doubted the certainty and longevity of political power. He observed life under the sun and was perplexed to see oppression and injustice. Therefore, he advocated divine judgment wherein no human judge was found. Qoheleth also observed indulgence at high levels and warned against improper governance. For both Confucius and Qoheleth, civil spheres were confronted with political disorder, social injustice, and threats of survival. These social and political locations are taken from the perspectives of Ecclesiastes and the Analects in order to expound their political wisdom so that one can learn to cope with such challenges today.

---

31. Zhang, *Lunyu Pingxi* [Commentary on the Analects], 398.

The Scope of This Book

This book will focus on eight passages in Ecclesiastes that contain political sentiments: Eccl 3:16–17; 4:1–3; 4:13–16; 5:8–10 [Hebrew 5:7–9]; 8:2–9; 9:13–16; 10: 4–7; and 10:16–20. All these passages touch on realities in civil society. They are grouped into two broad categories. First, Eccl 5:8–10 [Hebrew 5:7–9]; 8:2–9; 10: 4–7, and 10:16–20 are political wisdom conveyed in forms of direct instructions. Ecclesiastes 5:8–10 [Hebrew 5:7–9] concerns the advantage of having a capable political leader when oppression of the poor and the violation of justice are realities. Ecclesiastes 8:2–9 speaks of obedience to the king despite the challenges of serving in royal courts. Ecclesiastes 10: 4–7 illustrates the reality of the reversal of sociopolitical roles and expectations. And Eccl 10:16–20 contains political satires on the success and failure in ruling a kingdom. Second, Eccl 3:16–17; 4:1–3; 4:13–16; and 9:13–16 represent political wisdom communicated in the form of social reflections and observations of political realities. Ecclesiastes 3:16–17 relates the presence of wickedness in places of justice and righteousness that troubles Qoheleth. Ecclesiastes 4:1–3 touches on social oppression in the hands of the powerful. Ecclesiastes 4:13–16 is an anecdote that speaks of a wise young king replacing a foolish old king, who is eventually replaced by yet another. Ecclesiastes 9:13–16 depicts another anecdote where a great king and a poor wise man are set in perspective for rhetorical purposes. The eight passages above communicate the wisdom of survival in political circumstances, much of which can be the subject of discussion in view of the Analects.

Various politically-related chapters in the Analects are to be in dialogue with the passages above in Ecclesiastes. Most chapters in the twenty books of the Analects are rather short. They often address an issue to a particular person in a special discourse. Because of the nature of its textual arrangement, passages in relation to political ideas are scattered randomly throughout the twenty books. However, some chapters will be more engaged in close discussion with Ecclesiastes, notably Book 2, entitled "On Governance," *weizheng* (为政), and Book 12, which is entitled "Yan Yuan" (颜渊).[32] To a lesser degree, other books also contain political observations, instructions toward proper governance and administration, advice for proper courtly behavior and for nurturing proper civic attitude. They are grouped into two broad categories. The first category conveys instructions and admonitions

---

32. Yan Yuan (颜渊) was one of Confucius' disciples who was purportedly the latter's favorite. His name became a title since it is the first word that appears in Book 12. This way of naming the titles of the twenty books is consistent in Analects. In this book, a large amount of political ideas are recorded.

on political involvement. The second category communicates reflections on socio-political reality and civic life. The working criterion of selecting political passages from the Analects will be detailed in chapter 3.

The Biblical and Ancient Near Eastern Political Wisdom

The linear connection between *The Instruction of King Amenemhet I for His Son Sesostris I* and 1 Kgs 2 has inspired a common interest in finding more of such connections between the biblical text and ancient Near Eastern texts.[33] Amenemhet represents ancient Near Eastern didactic texts that communicate political advice on how a ruler might handle the throne. The king, who has earlier survived an attempted assassination, here warns his son not to trust people easily because anyone could be a potential traitor:[34]

> Beware of subjects who are nobodies,
> Of whose plotting one is not aware.
> Trust not a brother, know not a friend,
> Make no intimates, it is worthless.
> When you lie down, guard your heart yourself,
> For no man has adherents on the day of woe.
> I gave to the beggar, I raised the orphan,
> I gave success to the poor as to the wealthy;
> But he who ate my food raised opposition,
> He whom I gave my trust used it to plot.[35]

This royal instruction, which narrates the speech of a dying ruler for the benefit of the successor, finds a parallel in the Bible. It echoes King David's final testament to his son Solomon, in 1 Kgs 2:1–9, on how to begin his reign. As Leo Perdue suggests, this succession narrative is a testament of David, and one that garners Egyptian influence.[36] David orders Solomon to "use his wisdom," namely, to engage in political deception to execute the

---

33. See *Instruction of King Amenemhet I for His Son Sesostris I* in Lichtheim, *AEL*, 1:135–38.

34. Ibid., 135. The instruction was initially thought to be written personally by King Amenemhet I after he survived an assassination attempt. A more recent view is that the king was in fact murdered sometime in the thirtieth year of his reign, and this text was written by a royal scribe who was commanded by his son, Sesostris I, on behalf of the dead king.

35. Ibid., 136; the words of Amenemhet I, "As my feet depart, you are in my heart," ibid., 138.

36. Perdue, "Testament of David," 79–96.

potential threats of Joab and Shimei.[37] This move repudiates David earlier principles of compassion and forgiveness:

> Do according to your wisdom, and do not let his old age descend to Sheol in peace. (1 Kgs 2:6)[38]

> And now, do not acquit him.
> Since you are a wise man, you should know what to do with him, and bring his old age down with blood to Sheol. (1 Kgs 2:9)

The juxtaposition of these two royal testaments prompts two observations. First, the biblical depiction of courtly affairs and kingly politics connects non-biblical literature. Like the instructions in Proverbs, rulers are taught to seek political stability and order.[39] Second, based on the commonality of political concerns, political wisdom appears to have been held in common across the ancient Near East. Many texts of Mesopotamia and Egypt have been unearthed from ancient palaces and temples. Some of these are wisdom texts. Much of this corpus has been translated into modern languages, and they have shed light on ancient wisdom thought. Based on the fact that some literary deposits have been found in Palestine (for example, fragments of the *Gilgamesh Epic*), and wording and phraseology that appears strange in Hebrew is clarified when read in light of parallel texts, scholars think that the biblical writers were familiar with earlier Mesopotamia and Egyptian canonical traditions.

Similarly, the wisdom thought of Qoheleth have been related to the ancient Near Eastern world in which he is supposed to have lived. Among the themes that have commonly engaged Qoheleth and authors of ancient Near Eastern wisdom literature, the political aspect has yet to be explored. By employing the term "political wisdom" here, I have in mind two aspects. First, political wisdom is direct instructions and admonitions for political leadership. Secondly, political wisdom is also indirect teachings in the form of socio-political observations, reflections, and conclusions. In short, "political wisdom" is understood in light of both prescriptive wisdom and descriptive wisdom, because wisdom is didactic in essence. Ecclesiastes communicates these two types of wisdom on civic concerns. These types of wisdom in Ecclesiastes will be compared with ancient Near Eastern wisdom

---

37. According to Perdue, this succession narrative is also a piece of skillful craftsmanship. The author intended an ambiguity over David's changed character; Joab was ironically repaid with betrayal in David's execution order to Solomon. Shimei was earlier given an oath of pardon by David, but now David evidently intended to kill this old enemy. See Perdue, "Is There Anyone Left of Saul?," 79.

38. All English translations of Hebrew texts are mine unless otherwise noted.

39. Perdue, "Wisdom Theology and Social History in Proverbs 1–9," 89.

literature in this chapter. The intent of such a comparison is to show that Ecclesiastes has notable continuities with writings in the ancient Near East. This further suggests that more attention should be given to engaging external, wider wisdom links to this book. Some of the comparisons may illustrate linear connections or the ways in which analogous texts that are not mutually dependent may nevertheless be mutually illuminating.

From Egypt: The Instructions of Ankhsheshonqy[40]

This collection of unusually long but partially damaged instructions consists of several hundred maxims that include instructions, statements, and proverbs. Ankhsheshonqy, a priest of Re, was imprisoned due to a false accusation against him of plotting the assassination of Pharaoh. The unfortunate incident resulted in the protagonist aspiring to educate his son through a written text. The plight of Ankhsheshonqy is also reminiscent of Ahiqar and biblical Joseph, as well as Daniel, all of whom are linked to wisdom court tales. These instructions offer practical advice set on political matters. Suffering from a politically-motivated false accusation, Ankhsheshonqy counsels his son while in prison:

> Do not scorn Pharaoh's business (9:7).[41]
> Do not say something when it is not the time for it (12:24).[42]
> Do not speak of Pharaoh's business when drinking beer (16:16).[43]

Ankhsheshonqy recounted his own experience and wrote to save his son from similar trouble in court. Therefore, one should not escape Ankhsheshonqy's political allusion in 8:17:

> The wealth of a town is a lord who does justice.[44]

Ankhsheshonqy communicates his plight of justice to a king who is supposed to be discerning. This sentiment has its parallels in Eccl 5:9 [Hebrew 5:8], "the advantage of the land is a king to a cultivated field." Also, *The Instruction of Ankhsheshonqy* has a textual parallel with Eccl 11:1 that has remarkably illumined the interpretation of the latter:

---

40. See Lichtheim, *AEL*, 3:159–84; Faulkner et al. *Literature of Ancient Egypt*, 497–529. See also Sparks, *Ancient Texts*, 72.

41. Lichtheim, *AEL*, 3:166.

42. Ibid., 169.

43. Ibid., 172.

44. Lichtheim, *AEL*, 3:166. Alternate translation: "Blessed is a city with a just ruler." See Sparks, *Ancient Texts*, 72.

> Do a good deed and throw it in the water;
> When it dries you will find it.[45]

From Mesopotamia:[46] The Counsels of Wisdom[47]

This courtly advice is given from a wise man to his son who will succeed him as vizier to the ruler. Each section of this collection begins with an introduction of a wise saying, "do/do not," followed by a list of related maxims set in the form of courtly advice. One wherein records these lines:

> Beware of careless talk, guard your lips;
> Do not utter solemn oaths while alone,
> For what you say in a moment will follow you afterwards.
> But exert yourself to restraint your speech.[48] (lines 131–34)

This courtly instruction appears similar to the careful speech advocated in Eccl 10:20, and it illuminates what could probably mean in the latter:

> Even in your thought do not curse the king,
> and in your bedroom do not curse the rich.
> For a bird in the sky will carry the voice,
> and a winged creature will make known the matter.

---

45. Lichtheim, *AEL*, 3:174; it has been pointed out in Seow, *Ecclesiastes*, 62.

46. There is a distinction between *Egyptian wisdom* and *Mesopotamian wisdom*. Central to *Egyptian wisdom* theology was *ma'at*, the harmony of order, truth, and justice established by God at creation. Those living according to *ma'at* were promised a blessed life, whereas failure and death awaited all others. On the other hand, *Mesopotamian wisdom* looks to *ME* (a plural Sumerian term rendered as *parṣū* in Akkadian) as the proper order of all things. Human success was achieved by living in harmony with the pattern determined by *ME*, failing which was to face the absence of the divine. See Sparks, *Ancient Texts*, 65–66.

47. The Akkadian scribes produced this collection of instructional admonitions, which has 160 lines of topically organized maxims. The topics range from cautions about choosing companions, proper speech, charity, sex and marriage to kindness, piety, and advice about friendship. See Pritchard, ed., *ANET*, 426–27; 595–96; see also Lambert, *BWL*, 96–107.

48. Lambert, *BWL*, 105.

The Aramaic Proverbs of Ahiqar[49]

This Aramaic papyrus, discovered at the Egyptian city of Elephantine, is usually purported to have had a Mesopotamian antecedent.[50] There are eight sayings on obedience to the ruler (column 6, lines 84–88, 89b, 91–92).[51] Certainly, this text is another proverbial collection of political counsels.[52] In both the *Proverbs of Ahiqar* and Ecclesiastes, similarities of individual sayings can be observed.

Numerical sayings:

> Two things are beautiful and (that) which is three (the third) is beloved by Shamash . . . (Ahiqar 12:187)[53]

> And if one might prevail against another, two will withstand one. A threefold cord is not quickly drawn away. (Eccl 4:12)

Relationship between kingship and the deity:

> A king is like the Merciful;
> Even his voice is high.
> Who is there who can stand before him,
> but he with whom El is? (Ahiqar 6:91)[54]

> I say, keep the command of the king as over the word of oath to God.
> Do not be dismayed before his presence and leave.
> Do not stand in a harmful matter, for he will do whatever he delights.

---

49. Porten and Yardeni, *TAD*, 36–37. See also Lindenberger, *Aramaic Proverbs of Ahiqar*, 81–86; Pritchard, ed., *ANET*, 427–30.

50. The discussion on this papyrus is thus separated from that of both Egypt and Mesopotamia. It has two parts. The first part narrates a tale of Ahiqar, in which he is introduced as an adviser, is later wrongly charged of treason, and is eventually vindicated. The story of Ahiqar is often thought of as a recollection of the biblical court tales of Joseph and Daniel, who also lived and served in royal courts and experienced life-threatening encounters. Some, therefore, consider the texts about these royal court heroes as having "wisdom influence." See von Rad, "Joseph Narrative," 468–80; and Talmon, "Wisdom in the Book of Esther," 419–55.

51. Porten and Yardeni, *TAD*, 37.

52. The papyrus contains also a collection of sayings covering topics such as loyalty to the prince, morality, appropriate speech, charity, piety, longevity, and purity.

53. Porten and Yardeni, *TAD*, 49. See also the paraphrase from Matthews and Benjamin, *Old Testament Parallels*, 304. Numerical sayings quoted, as also in the biblical proverbs, are in the form of "x, x+1."

54. Porten and Yardeni, *TAD*, 37. I take the liberty of omitting the parentheses for easy reading. Arnold and Beyer, *Readings from the Ancient Near East*, 191. See also the paraphrase from Matthews and Benjamin, *Old Testament Parallels*, 304.

As which the word of the king is power, and who can say to him, "what are you doing?" (Eccl 8:2–4)

A rhetorical question is found both at the end of Ahiqar 6:91 and Eccl 8:4 vis-à-vis the king's authorities. The literary contexts for the passages of both writings teach on obedience to the king (Ahiqar 6:84, 93; cf. Eccl 8:2), and they elaborate on kingly obedience in order to do no harm (Ahiqar 6:87–88; cf. Eccl 8:5).[55] Such obedience is indeed wise for survival in court. Elsewhere, Ahiqar's call for moderation parallels Qoheleth's call: "do not be overly clever, lest . . . be extinguished" (cf. Eccl 7:16).[56] Other similarities between *Proverbs of Ahiqar* and Ecclesiastes include "my son" designations (Ahiqar 6:80; cf. Eccl 12:12) and distinction between the righteous and the wicked (Ahiqar 7:103–104; 11:171; cf. Eccl 3:17; 7:15; 8:14). Careful speech is also important to one's survival in royal court. As such, a passage in *Proverbs of Ahiqar* recalls the courtly advice in Eccl 10:20:[57]

do not curse the day until you have seen the light,
do not let it come upon your mind,
since their eyes and their ears are everywhere.
. . . for a word is a bird and one who releases it is without sense.[58]

These many connections point to a possibility that Qoheleth might have been familiar with the Aramaic *Proverbs of Ahiqar*, given that Aramaic was the *lingua franca* at that time. The Jewish communities in both Elephantine and Palestine also corresponded with each other.[59] In short, the ancient Near Eastern wisdom texts are associated with Ecclesiastes in civic counsels. The social locations of royal court, the political sentiments, and the types of rhetoric suggest commonalities between the literature. The illustrations of the parallels above seem to connect Ecclesiastes to the ancient Near Eastern wisdom literature. They indicate that political wisdom from the ancient

---

55. For the *Proverbs of Ahiqar* version, see Porten and Yardeni, *TAD*, 37.

56. Porten and Yardeni, *TAD*, 45 (column 10, line 147); quoted and translated in Seow, *Ecclesiastes*, 63.

57. The caution of careful speech in court in Eccl 10:20 also echoes a similar idea in the *Instruction of Amenemope* 24:1–4:

Do not listen to an official's reply indoors,
In order to repeat it to another outside.
Do not let your word be carried outside.
Lest your heart be aggrieved.

See Lichtheim, *AEL*, 2:146–63, here 2:160.

58. Porten and Yardeni, *TAD*, 37 (column 6, lines 80–82); quoted and translated in Seow, *Ecclesiastes*, 63.

59. Seow, *Ecclesiastes*, 63.

world was connected and was well documented. This connection suggests that more cross-cultural and cross-textual undertakings should be expected in a larger wisdom worldview today.

Wisdom in Cross Cultures and Texts

The well-documented evidence found in the above parallels set a precedent for cross-cultural readings. The parallels point out some similarities, suggesting that political wisdom might have connected the ancient Near Eastern civilization. Understanding this wider wisdom connection, rather than in isolation within the Bible itself, is important for grasping the freedom and openness of wisdom texts. Therefore, a broader liberty of interactions with non-biblical texts is necessary. The biblical and non-biblical texts together suggest a dialogical approach to pursue political wisdom.[60] W. W. Hallo has also purported a "contextual approach" to outline the biblical text against its wider literary environment.[61] Cross-cultural readings, however, ought not to point only to similarities and differences. Rather, as in the principle of synergism, a comparison of texts from two different cultures might yield perspectives—new angles—not possible in the study of a single tradition.

People in various cultures of antiquity found themselves caught in the vicissitudes of life amid political uncertainty. As the human impulse to survive in life, one seeks guidance from the instructions and reflections of wisdom literature. Such pursuit is a common one. In East Asia, notably China, there are a number of texts that may be broadly regarded as sapiential on account of their didactic style. These include works of various genres. On philosophy, *Daode Jing* (道德经) and *Zhuangzi* (莊子)—linked together under the rubric of "the School of Dao"—and *Daojia* (道家) are made popular by sages Laozi (老子) and Zhuangzi (莊子) respectively. *Daode Jing* is also regarded as a religious text under the heading of Daoism (道教). Its idea of "influence based on non-action," *Wuwei* (无为), is often said to have influenced political articulations in other Chinese works like the Analects. Further, on mixed genre between philosophy and politics, *Mencius* (孟子) is a collection of political dialogues in the name of the sage Mencius. Its central teaching on account of human conduct is believed to be evolved from that of Confucius. Another important philosophical work

---

60. Biblical wisdom was written, wherein other texts existed in the knowledge of biblical writers. The pluralistic society during the post-exilic period in the Near East had also introduced notable Phoenician, Aramaic, Babylonian, and Persian influences. This wider environment introduces foreign influences to the biblical literature and makes it dialogic in essence.

61. Hallo and Younger, *COS*, 1:xi.

is *Mozi* (墨子). It teaches "inclusive love," *boai* (博爱), as an ethical and social principle. *Hanfeizi* (韩非子) is an important legalist text that regulates strict law and penalties as the state's reinforcement measure. In the genre of history, the Chinese *Classic of History* (*Shangshu* 尚书) is a collection of documents and speeches allegedly written by rulers and officials of the early Zhou period. Besides, *The Spring and Autumn Annals* (*Chunqiu* 春秋) is a historical record of Confucius' native state, Lu (鲁). It covers the period from 722 BCE to approximately 481 BCE, focusing on diplomatic relations among feudal states. Important political alliances and military activities, as well as births and deaths within the royal families, are therein recorded. On military science, Sunzi's *Art of War* (*Sunzi Bingfa* 孙子兵法) and *The Romance of Three Kingdoms* (*Sanguo Yanyi* 三国演义) represent famous ancient Chinese works on effective diplomacy.

Above all, Confucian works in particular have been of key importance to Chinese history and culture. *The Four Books* (namely, the Analects or *Lunyu*《论语》, the *Great Learning* or *Daxue*《大学》, the *Doctrine of the Mean* or *Zhongyong*《中庸》, and *Mencius*《孟子》, all canonized by Zhu Xi (朱熹) during the Song dynasty), and the *Five Classics* (namely, the *Book of Songs* or *Shijing*《诗经》, the *Classic of History* or *Shangshu*《尚书》, the *Book of Rites* or *Liji*《礼记》, the *Book of Changes* or *Yijing*《易经》, and the *Spring and Autumn Annals* or *Chunqiu*《春秋》, all compiled by Confucius himself) constitute the Confucian legacy. They were the center of the educational system and imperial examination since the Song dynasty.[62] The Analects represents the cornerstone of Confucian wisdom texts that inculcates Confucius' ideas, notably his political wisdom. A key term in the Analects is *junzi* (君子, exemplary person). This is a Confucian construct of an ideal personality. In many instances, the *junzi* represents the wise who serve as counselors to the ruler.[63] The term could mean literally "son of a king," and rightly so in a feudal society. Besides its moral conception, it should be emphasized that the term *junzi* is also a political term. *Junzi* is undoubtedly a goal for Confucius and his students to achieve. Some of Confucius' students were not only scholars but also soldiers, like Zi Lu (子路) and Ran Qiu (冉求). Furthermore, *junzi* represents one who is not only learned (*xue*学) and wise (*zhi*知) but also humane (*ren*仁), courageous (*yong*勇), and righteous (*yi*义).[64] These

62. The canonization by Zhu Xi during the Song dynasty in the twelfth century CE resulted in the primary status of *the Four Books* over *the Five Classics*.

63 Cua, "Confucianism," *ECP*, 132.

64. See Chan, "Chinese Philosophy," 149. There are, of course, some other virtues to qualify a *junzi*. Notably, honesty (*cheng*诚), trustworthiness (*xin*信), observing propriety (*li*礼), loyalty (*zhong*忠) and respect (*jing*敬) too are repeatedly mentioned in

aspects of being humane, courageous, and righteous only make sense if one lives in a community of people. Therefore, the ultimate goal of being a *junzi* is never for moral cultivation of the self per se, but to benefit society. It is a civic identity. This conception of *junzi* has always involved the public, and its concern includes the political realm. Confucius intended a society governed by people of virtue who, through moral cultivation, would affect the social order and bring about civic welfare.[65] The Analects concerns the shaping of such people for survival amid political chaos. This political relevance makes the Analects one among Chinese wisdom literature that is best compared with Ecclesiastes.

A Cross-Textual Suggestion and Research Methodology

An Engagement of Cultural Currency

William Theodore de Bary, a Western Confucian scholar who has devoted his life to the study of ancient Chinese literature, has called attention to the use of Asian resources "in ways that do justice to Asian classics" as part of process of civilization.[66] De Bary has also pointed out that there is a general lack of studies of the home-grown classics among Asians. These classics are close to the human heart, and they are of impressive depths that command the attention of generations of Asians.[67] De Bary's appeal suggests a need, especially for Asians, to engage the native texts that characterize their cultural currency.

The ancient cross-culture dynamics has suggested a necessity to engage external writings in the reading of biblical texts. This necessity is also true for biblical interpreters in Asia who face a plurality of cultural texts. According to Archie C. C. Lee, biblical interpretation from an Asian perspective has been through three stages of development.[68] First, the *text-alone approach* emphasizes the exclusiveness and normativity of the Christian Bible. In this stage, Asian cultural traditions and social political experience are overtaken by Judeo-Christian communities of faith that have shaped Christian Scripture. Second, the *text-context interpretive mode* considers honestly the biblical historical settings. This stage of interpretive measure attempted to grasp what the Bible meant there and then and to

---

the Analects.

65. Chan, "Chinese Philosophy," 150.
66. De Bary, *Finding Wisdom in East Asian Classics*, xiii.
67. Ibid., 1.
68. Lee, "Biblical Interpretation in Asian Perspective," 37.

apply henceforth what the Bible means here and now. These first and second stages have often been found to be inadequate in a rich cultural context like Asia. They are thought to have disintegrated culture and faith traditions into two different, unrelated fragments. Therefore, a third stage is necessary. This third stage is advocated by Asian scholars, among whom Archie Lee is a pioneer. It requires a *cross-textual hermeneutics* that affirms the historically conditioned nature of both cultural texts—the biblical text (which can be culturally distant for Asians) and the native text (which is local to Asians). Cross-textual hermeneutics endeavors to bring both cultural texts in "direct interaction or confrontation."[69] The purpose of this interaction is to supplement and enrich the texts of one another.

Cross-textual hermeneutics engages the texts that are native to and deeply engrained in Asia. It is Asianized hermeneutics. This book intends to engage such a journey. Critical biblical scholarship has informed us that there are different levels of meaning underlying the biblical text. By considering these various levels of meaning—and their possible linkage to the native culture—one holds faith-native traditions together in perspective. This will localize biblical hermeneutics. As such, Asian biblical readers become active participants of the message of the Bible. And this research aims to contribute intrinsically to the area of wisdom literature. The interpretation of the Bible requires this re-appropriation of local cultures.

The background upon which the biblical text is written is conditioned in ancient Near Eastern culture. Likewise, the environment in which a biblical text is read today owes its understanding to one's cultural formation. The composition and interpretation of the texts in literate societies thus are both related to its cultural currency.[70] Relating the Bible to Asian community, the Bible can be read alongside other scriptures.[71] This effort aims to invite dialogical partners. Biblical hermeneutics is necessarily dialectical. It is an active engagement of more than one culture to mutually address the same concern. It involves ongoing conversation between one's faith and ethnicity. By doing so, one employs "creative hermeneutics" that "attempts to convey the complexities, the multidimensional linkages, and the different levels of meaning that underlie our present task of relating the Bible to Asia."[72]

---

69. Ibid., 38.
70. Hart, "Imagination and Responsible Reading," 308.
71. Kwok, *Discovering the Bible*, 32–43, especially 36.
72. Ibid., 13. Through this idea, Kwok Pui-Lan points to the potential for interreligious dialogue through interscriptural engagements.

There is a life-giving textual tradition in any native culture, but earlier biblical hermeneutics may have overlooked this local element.[73] Placing the Analects in interaction with the Bible will engage Chinese culture in biblical hermeneutics. This will enrich the reading of the Bible with an Asian perception. It is "a journey of imagination," in which one transcends the boundaries of biblical particularity to engage with one's native culture, as the other text, "before finally returning to ourselves with our horizons broadened and our 'self' in some sense more rounded and complete through the venture."[74]

Working out the hermeneutics situation evoked by the encounter with native culture, according to Hans-Georg Gadamer, means acquiring the right horizon of inquiry.[75] Gadamer stresses that "historically effected consciousness," *wirkungsgeschichtliches Bewußtsein*, is primarily a consciousness of the hermeneutical situation.[76] Essential to the concept of situation is the concept of "horizon"—the range of vision that includes everything seen from a particular vantage point.[77] The task of native-cultural understanding, therefore, involves acquiring an appropriate native-cultural horizon: by acknowledging the existence of the other and "making it the object of objective knowledge."[78] Therein lays truth that is also valid and intelligible. The horizon of the present is continually in the process of being formed. Thus, following Gadamer's cue, by embracing the historical depths of Chinese self-consciousness, one becomes aware of Christian "otherness."[79] The understanding of both aspects is always the fusion of these horizons, combining into something that is of living value, without either being explicitly

---

73. This is an example of so-called "cultural alienation," which is a result of the evangelization of Western Christianity. See Lee, "Cross-Textual Hermeneutics," 39–40.

74. Hart, "Imagination and Responsible Reading," 316.

75. Gadamer, *Truth and Method*, 302; the citation follows the revised edition. "To have a horizon" means to not be limited by what is nearby but to be able to see beyond it. A person who has a horizon knows the relative significance of everything within this horizon. The term "horizon" comes into play when referring to the claim of historical consciousness to see the past within its own historical horizon. So "working out the hermeneutical situation" means acquiring the right horizon of inquiry for the questions evoked by the encounter with tradition.

76. Ibid., 301. Gadamer defines the concept of "situation" as "a standpoint that limits the possibility of vision."

77. Ibid., 302.

78. Ibid., 303–4.

79. Ibid., 304–5. Gadamer stresses "transposing oneself" into someone else's shoes, not out of empathy nor in subordinating of one individual for another; rather, it involves rising to a higher universality that overcomes not only one's particularity but also that of the other.

foregrounded by the other.⁸⁰ This nevertheless involves a tension between the native text and the faith text. The task of cross-textual hermeneutics involves a daring assimilation of the two without covering up any tension between them. Even if the new understanding brings about critical self-examination of Christian faith tradition, its purpose should be progressive rather than subversive.⁸¹ In short, through a constant interaction with a native text, one brings a fresh understanding to the biblical text. Engaging in such endeavor may also constantly put pressure on the boundaries of authority of the Bible. A biblical interpreter should nonetheless take on continual interpretation and re-interpretation of the Bible in light of new discoveries from these realms.

Entering proactively into a native textual world of the Analects—to appreciate its language and to grasp its message—is therefore imperative. Biblical hermeneutics that engages local elements empowers Christian interpreters to work within local languages whose unique rhetorical devices, metaphors and imageries are easier to connect.⁸² Cultural hermeneutics or "native hermeneutics," as R. S. Sugirtharajah calls it, fosters this awareness of homegrown traditions that are often sidelined in biblical interpretation.⁸³ With the native consciousness, a Chinese Christian approaches the Bible with values and understandings conditioned by this heritage. As this book will seek to demonstrate, Confucius' sayings illumine the sayings of Qoheleth. They uphold and enrich Christian faith without thrusting aside the indigenous dynamics. Hence, one may find that both "classics" speak something in common—and also additional—to one's faith and nativeness. It is therefore the intention of this book to invite biblical interpreters to commit to both faith scripture and native scripture. Through this endeavor one can be an active recipient of the biblical message, not a passive one, to discover the message meant for people outside the ancient Near Eastern tradition.⁸⁴

---

80. Ibid., 306.

81. Wang, *Jieshi, Lijie yu Zongjiao Duihua*, 52.

82. A Chinese's cultural linkage to Confucianism encompasses areas of the formal education system, family values, day-to-day conversations, social structures, social perceptions, responsibilities, moral principles, religious interests, and the like.

83. Sugirtharajah, *Asian Hermeneutics and Postcolonialism*, 14–18. Sugirtharajah advocates native hermeneutics as a way of post-colonial criticism.

84. In other words, when one values the interpretation of other texts, one grasps the biblical truth creatively.

A Cross-Textual Hermeneutics on Political Wisdom

To Chinese Christian readers who are heirs of two formative traditions, the Bible and Confucian classics are collectively involved in the formation of their identities. This book proposes the synergism from the intersection of two identity-forming texts, by bridging their historical contexts that were characterized by similar social and political situation. The authors of both texts have struggled with the political realities of power abuse. Such political realities shape the message conveyed through the Analects and Ecclesiastes respectively. While Confucius in the Analects was preoccupied with managing the situation, Qoheleth in Ecclesiastes was concerned with coping with such a reality. A general assumption is that Ecclesiastes and the Analects have little in common. Yet political wisdom represents an essential connection between the two corpora. Wisdom is essentially universal. The interaction of two wisdom texts, therefore, invites integration. Through this endeavor, this book attempts to "appropriate the Bible in the context of a multi-scriptural environment,"[85] and to contribute to the sphere of biblical hermeneutics, especially in the reading of Ecclesiastes.

This book thus holds a corrective aim: to revise the misconceptions and inadequacies of a self-sufficient, Bible-only reading.[86] This is not to say that biblical truth is flawed. Instead, this is to say that the biblical text is never read in a contextual cultural vacuum. In this case, the native-cultural text fills the contextual-cultural vacuity of the Bible. As Lee suggests, "the biblical text can be illuminated and the message embodied in it enriched."[87] To an Asian interpreter, the common human quest expressed in Ecclesiastes can be specifically identified in its engagement with the Analects. Cross-textual interpretation thus surpasses the concern to simply point out similarities and differences between the two texts; it also explores how both texts can enrich one's reading in view of each other. In this sense, the texts can be said to engage in genuine dialogue and mutual enrichment.

Cross-cultural readings are not strictly a modern phenomenon. Indeed, the biblical authors wrote with the consciousness of the existence of other texts. The parallels of biblical wisdom literature with ancient Near Eastern texts laid out earlier suggest a literary context in which wisdom thoughts were written. With regard to this comparability, the Analects—an exemplar of ancient Chinese wisdom—also displays political wisdom. Both

---

85. Lee, "Cross-Textual Hermeneutics and Identity," 179.

86. Lee, "Cross-textual Hermeneutics on Gospel and Culture," 40.

87. Through a cultural text, the human issues and the religious quest in the biblical text can be clearly underlined. See Lee, "Cross-textual Hermeneutics on Gospel and Culture," 41.

the Analects and Ecclesiastes come from the period between 800–200 BCE, "the Axial Age" when humanity in general adapted a common approach to living. To the sages, the approach of wisdom is to observe human experience and to draw insights on how to deal with surviving issues, such as political existence. These insights serve as pointers toward a wise way of human existence: how to live sensibly in a challenging political situation that requires decent conduct and wise behavior toward life. In the case of Asian interpretation of the biblical wisdom literature, the Analects and Ecclesiastes should be deemed as rich political resources in the common struggle for human survival.

Contextual Considerations

This book not only considers the rich cultural traditions of Asia but also the unique socio-political experience of Malaysia. As early as 1972, the Critical Asian Principle (CAP) was formulated for doing theology and hermeneutics in Asia.[88] Critical Asian Principle emphasizes Asian contextual considerations. It advocates that some common Asian features—people of various ethnic groups, social institutions, political organizations, and religions—have inevitably characterized a reader's interpretation of the Bible. Among the distinctive characteristics listed, one stands out among others: Asian interpreters seek to achieve authentic self-identity and cultural integrity in the context of the modern world.[89] They are in search of a form of social order that seriously considers the plurality dimension of the life experience in Asia. Following this direction, this book upholds that the Chinese Christian experience in Malaysia gives a unique perspective to the understanding of Ecclesiastes (biblical text) and the Analects (native text). Cross-textual hermeneutics indeed concerns matters of relating the context to text,[90] so that the Malaysian socio-political context may speak to both biblical and native texts.

In recent decades, the socio-political development that concerns Chinese people and Christian circles in Malaysia has commonly been observed. Like many parts of the Asian world, the ethnic tensions as well as political controversies are present. In certain incidents, Malaysian Chinese were recipients of some politically motivated sarcasm or religiously motivated operations.[91] In a few occurrences, churches were the targets of violent attacks

88. Nacpil, "Critical Asian Principle," 3.
89. Ibid., 4.
90. Lee, "Biblical Interpretation in Asian Perspective," 36.
91. For example, Malaysian Christians were threatened with hate speech; a few

and unjustifiable religious interventions.[92] In a multi ethnic and religious environment, some Chinese people in general strive to live out traditional teachings of ancient sages like Confucius. Chinese Christians, in particular, meet another challenge where their religious rights are often brought into question. This context provides a unique socio-political perspective for me—a Chinese Christian in Malaysia—to interpret the Bible. Such a perspective leads me to engage the local contexts in direct interaction with the biblical text. As Archie Lee puts it correctly, on one hand the cross textual hermeneutical task affirms the cultural-historically conditioned nature of the biblical text; on the other hand, Asian perspectives are brought in to shed light in the interpretation of the biblical text.[93] This book therefore subscribes to the idea that Malaysia socio-political realities necessitate a Chinese Christian to reinterpret the Bible. Chinese Christians are undeniably at the crossroads of Malaysian contexts and the biblical texts.

In conclusion, as a research methodology, this book suggests the following undertakings. First, the presence of plurality of texts in the rich culture of Asia is affirmed. These cultural texts are deemed as important resources for the interpretation and the reinterpretation of the Bible. Second, the cultural texts are used to put into the dynamic of reading the biblical texts, to illumine, supplement and challenge each other. Third, the present context of a reader is crucial, as much as the cultural-historically conditioned contexts of both biblical and Asian texts. The focal point to sum up the undertakings of all the above, is political wisdom. Not only are Ecclesiastes and the Analects understood in terms of how Qoheleth and Confucius handled their political realities in the past, but also both texts are read today in terms of how a Malaysian Chinese Christian can cope with the present socio-political realities.

---

religious figures as well as activists were abducted, and they are still regarded as missing persons after more than a year.

92. For instance, since the controversial court decision in Malaysia on December 31, 2009—in favor of *the Herald* (a Catholic-owned weekly newspaper), to hold government regulations prohibiting non-Muslim publications from using the word "Allah" as unconstitutional—a total of ten churches and a few mosques have been attacked or vandalized.

93. Lee, "Biblical Interpretation in Asian Perspective," 38.

Previous Research

Cross-Textual Hermeneutics between the Bible and Ancient Chinese Literature

There is a growing emphasis on the use of Asian resources for biblical interpretation in Asia. Exploring the cultural connection between the Bible and Chinese literature is not new either. The following are some of what I consider the more important ones. Archie Lee has written substantially in cross-textual hermeneutics for the past three decades.[94] His work includes a theological reading of Chinese creation stories of Pan Gu (盘古) and Nu Wa (女娲).[95] Lee suggests that *huntun* (混沌), the idea of chaos in *Zhuangzi*, is adopted by the Chinese translator of the Bible to communicate the Hebrew *bôhû* in Gen 1:2. This depiction communicates to Chinese readers the meaning of chaos and formlessness that constitutes the basic understanding of the creation story in the biblical text. As one has noticed from the folklores of Pan Gu and Nu Wa, the Chinese have their own creation stories. Here, Lee points out how the Chinese reading of the creation of heaven and earth and the creation of human beings identifies with that of the Bible. Lee's work, therefore, has opened the door to a theological dialogue about creation narratives. Yet one might further argue that the creation narrative in the Bible does not negate the Chinese creation stories. Rather, it suggests a different view point on the Chinese understanding of creation.[96] This entails theological reflections among Chinese Christians and suggests dialogues in the task of doing theology in the Chinese context.

Lee has also crossed the border between psalms of lament in the Psalter and a Chinese poetic corpus, *Shijing* (诗经), to reflect upon the concept of humanness.[97] According to Lee, amid the socio-political struggles of the psalmists, both texts reflect a common context of human experience. Troubled relationships give rise to common pain. Outcries are heard at both individual and community levels. The biblical psalms of lament, as well as the Chinese *Shijing*, commonly reflect a quest for divine intervention in desperate situations.[98] The God of the Bible, explicitly depicted as an all-powerful deliverer, is at the same time the psalmists' enemy. The deity in *Shijing*, *Tian* (天), is also perceived to be an adversary. *Tian* is often questioned in human

---

94. See his major works in Lee, "Cross-textural Hermeneutics and Identity," 179–204.

95. Lee, "Theological Reading of Chinese Creation Stories," 230–36.

96. Ibid., 235–36.

97. Lee, "Kuayue Bianjie" [Crossing Boundaries], 197–221.

98. Ibid., 205.

suffering.[99] A parallel reading has enriched both traditions in the perception of the divine being. While barely surviving in passivity, humans can stress moral conduct as an agent of change (from the reading of *Shijing*) or can find comfort in piety to trust God nonetheless (from the reading of *Psalms*).[100] Lee further applies the element of lament from both texts to reflect upon the common Asian cry over poverty and injustice. In short, Lee has united the biblical psalms of lament and Chinese *Shijing*. They jointly communicate a "tripartite understanding" among suffering people, the oppressing earthly rulers and the sovereign divine being.[101] As a result, theology is remarkably linked with contextual experiences of human suffering.

Elsewhere, Lee has presented his reading of the sons of God in Gen 6:1–4 and the tower of Babel story in 11:1–9.[102] On two counts, the Bible provides another lens for understanding the Chinese narrative. First, the Bible enhances the traditional Chinese belief that God does appear in human form (cf. Gen 6:1–4). Second, like the Chinese belief, the Bible depicts humans as searching for the attainment of immortality (cf. Gen 11:1–9). In my opinion, the Bible therefore affirms Chinese experience. Attaining immortality, for instance, has long been real in the Chinese quest for longevity. Here a Chinese biblical reader finds no stranger in the Genesis account. The Chinese experience, in return, can help a biblical reader grasp what is at hand: the dynamics between the divine-human continuum. The Chinese experience informs the biblical reader about the common human intention to become like gods. This experience influences the way one interprets the Babel narrative—the people in Gen 11 actually wanted to be like God.

In a separate paper, Lee illustrates Chinese struggles to translate the biblical names of God. According to Lee, the term for the deity, *Shangdi* (上帝), should not be limited to a standardized Chinese term for identifying the biblical God.[103] Lee has taken a broader understanding of God's revelation: God was at work in the ancient Near East, and God was at work as well in the ancient Far East—China. The biblical God is, therefore, the God mentioned in Chinese classics. In different circumstances, the name

---

99. Ibid., 205–6.

100. Ibid., 213–14.

101. Ibid., 221. Accordingly, Lee has also compared Ps 78 with *Shijing*. See Lee, "Recitation of the Past," 173–93.

102. Lee, "Cross-textual Hermeneutics on Gospel and Culture," 41–42. Lee suggests a guiding principle in cross-textual hermeneutics: affirming that "both the Christian text and the cultural text are equally significant and valid when they independently pose the same religious quest and address the similar human religious dimension of life."

103. Lee, "Naming God in Asia," 38; Lee writes, "The insistence on using one standardized Chinese term to name God will not work."

of this deity is translated as *Shangdi, Shen*, or *Tianzhu*.[104] Therein a Chinese term for God, *Shangdi*, does not please everyone who tries to apprehend the biblical deity.[105] Such debates have involved the entire task of Chinese translation until today. In view of the long-standing debates on translating God's names, and the ambiguity of the meaning of the plural form of *ĕlōhîm*, Lee asserts that any claim to absolutize the name of God will be in danger of greater confusion.[106] Such representation is not without problems, however. After all, the Bible emphasizes the revelation of the divine name, YHWH, as a decisive name in the history of salvation (Exod 3). Indeed, the distinctive name, YHWH, emphatically a revealed name, overwhelmingly outnumbers any other epithets for the God of Israel in the Bible by appearing 6,828 times, including the term "God" which appears 2,602 times.[107] A Chinese biblical reader may still need to insist on a personal name for the biblical deity. This God is not just any deity, but one who reveals his name and shows his distinctive identity to a particular people. A name, therefore, qualifies such a relationship. Still, Lee's careful study has called attention to a wider perception of the biblical God. A general revelation should be set in view of any cross-cultural venture. This notion is instrumental in my research, as the deity mentioned in Ecclesiastes is always *ĕlōhîm*, never YHWH. *'Ĕlōhîm* is a general term referring to God in the Bible, while YHWH is a covenant-specific term referring to the God of Israel. I therefore correspond the term *Tian*, (天) in the Analects to *'ĕlōhîm* in Ecclesiastes. I further suggest that, by engaging two sets of text—Ecclesiastes and the Analects—one may need to find out a common frame of reference for God to substantiate a genuine theological dialogue.

Similar cross-textual works by others also have been brought to notice in recent years. A notable early attempt, however, is worth mentioning here. In 1954, H. H. Rowley compared the Hebrew prophets and the Chinese sages. Rowley compares five prophets of the Old Testament—Amos, Hosea, Isaiah, Jeremiah, and Ezekiel—with three Chinese sages—Confucius, Mencius, and Mozi. Recognizing that the societies and the traditions between the Hebrew prophets and the Chinese differed remarkably, the proclamation of words to influence others seemed to connect both figures.[108] Besides, the Hebrew prophets and the Chinese sages were consulted on matters of state

104. Ibid., 24–26.

105. According to a monotheistic claim, *Shangdi* represents the Chinese god. This god is not the God of the Bible.

106. Lee, "Naming God in Asia," 39.

107. I am indebted to my mentor, Professor Choon-Leong Seow, for this insight during my research.

108. Rowley, *Prophecy and Religion in Ancient China and Israel*, 18–21.

and were regarded as reformers. According to Rowley, they were statesmen in their respective social settings who spoke on national policies, and they were both concerned with social injustice as well as the needs of a sound government.[109] Rowley seems to place Confucius and Mencius on higher ground than the Hebrew prophets by stating "a greater affinity" in spirit and in substance of the former.[110] Nevertheless, in Rowley's opinion, the Chinese sages fell short of the Hebrew prophets due to the lack of religious heritage.[111] This conclusion represents the basis of Rowley's comparison and has seemed to garner questions on Rowley's fundamental approach—the basic assumption that all expression of religion in ancient China was less valuable because practitioners did not know the biblical God.[112] Rowley is nevertheless correct to illustrate the common interest of the Hebrew prophets and the Chinese sages, specifically in their moral and social conditions. He, too, points out their dealing with the deity in personal terms and their circles of disciples who compiled their teachings at later period, yielding to the substantial prophetic books and Chinese classics respectively.[113]

Relating the pursuit of Confucius' ethics to that of the Hebrew prophets, de Bary has compared *junzi* to the prophets.[114] A true *junzi*, according to de Bary, speaks out against social injustice just like the Old Testament prophets. Tensions therefore resulted between *junzi* and emperors, reflecting the political dynamics between the prophets and the kings in Israel. Recently, Oon-Soo Ang also has researched the pursuit of value among the Confucian sages and the Hebrew prophets.[115] Beginning with intersections between the East and the West during the Axial Age, Ang finds support to account for his comparative study between the Confucian sages and the Hebrew prophets.[116] In this study, Ang reads the prophetic books of the Old Testament with the entire Confucian anthology. Ang affirms that the Chinese and Hebrew civilizations have dissimilar frames of reference, yet he insists also on their common ground. One dimension of common ground Ang explores is perceptions of the deity. In both anthologies of literature, the deity has shaped the distinct personalities of Chinese sages and Hebrew prophets respectively;

---

109. Ibid., 27–49, especially 35–36.

110. Ibid., 43.

111. Ibid., 144.

112. See Kramers' critique in *International Review of Mission*, 95.

113. Rowley, *Prophecy and Religion in Ancient China and Israel*, 24–25, 51–73, 122–23.

114. De Bary, *Trouble with Confucianism*, and its Chinese version, *Dibairui, Rujia de Kunjing*.

115. Hong, *Zheren yu Xianzhi* [Axiology of Confucianism and Hebrew Prophets].

116. Ibid., 3–6.

both the Chinese sages and Hebrew prophets were visionaries.[117] Further, Ang examines the ideas of *zhong* (忠; loyalty) and *xiao* (孝; piety) of Confucian sages. He then compares them with the idea of *ḥesed* professed by the Hebrew prophets.[118] Likewise, Ang relates Confucian humanness and righteousness (*renyi*仁义) to biblical judgment (*gongping*公平) and righteousness (*gongyi*公义). Social order according to Confucian *liyue* (礼乐) also is paralleled with prophetic covenantal duty. The area Ang has chosen to enfold, in my judgment, is too vast. Comparing all the prophetic books with the entire Confucian collection is challenging for any careful dialogical task. Therefore, reading different prophetic contents in view of various Confucian scholars, including Mengzi (孟子) and Xunzi (荀子), challenges the thoroughness of Ang's approach to the texts. Ang's study is therefore more for philosophical comparison rather than cross-textual hermeneutics.

In-depth research by K. K. Yeo to pursue a Chinese Christian theology is recent and notable. Yeo compares Confucius with Paul in the search for ethics and virtues professed in the Analects and the Letter to the Galatians. Naming his approach as "intertextual reading,"[119] he first examines the textual worlds of both corpora. Then, suggesting the idea of "theological ethics in a world of violence," Yeo compares Confucius' *Tianming* (天命) with "God's will" in Paul.[120] Related topics, notably the law in Galatians and the *li* (礼) in the Analects, share something in common.[121] "To be human" (in the Analects) and "to be holy" (in Galatians) are given closed examinations.[122] In this careful study, Yeo has taken cross-textual hermeneutics to a new horizon by presenting numerous detailed and in-depth discussions. For instance, Yeo suggests the ethical and theological tasks of Chinese Christians: being creatively faithful to living texts.[123] Yeo likewise asserts the beauty in diversity derived by journeying to others and self.[124] One of the aspects that is of special interest to my own research is his grasp of a Chinese Christian political ethic. Yeo gives an example, stating that his reading of the Pauline epistle is influenced by his Confucian presuppositions: "I interpret the issue in Romans 13 to be not whether a government is legitimate, but *how*

---

117. Ibid., 7–51.
118. Ibid., 52–95.
119. Yeo, *Musing with Confucius and Paul*, 53.
120. Ibid., 111–76.
121. Both notions occupy central attention in each book, and both affect harmony in the society. See Yeo, *Musing with Confucius and Paul*, 177–252.
122. Ibid., 253–303.
123. Ibid., 403.
124. Ibid., 405.

it is to be just and benevolent."¹²⁵ The cross-textual task Yeo undertakes is exemplary. Yet one may argue that, by asserting a Chinese Christian theology based on Confucian *Xin* (信) and Pauline *pistis*, Yeo appears to assume that the Pauline epistle—specifically Galatians—represents the entirety of Christian theology.¹²⁶ Nevertheless, in view of the growing cross-cultural endeavors, this sizeable work is commendable for a scholar raised in Asia, particularly Malaysia.

A scholar from China, Heng-Tan Shi, also has published a parallel reading of the Analects and the Bible. Naming his method as "an alternate reading to the Analects," Shi chooses his subject matter from the key concepts of the Analects, comparing them to selected passages from the entire Bible. "To love people as a virtuous person," for instance, is read together with "loving your neighbors as yourselves."¹²⁷ The *junzi-xiaoren* (君子-小人) rhetoric also is compared to the biblical contrast of righteousness and wickedness.¹²⁸ By calling attention to many other subjects—such as learning, filial piety, nobility, education, character building and the like—Shi has pointed out many contact-points between the Bible and the Analects. What is lacking in Shi's work, however, is an in-depth dialectical engagement of both texts. Shi merely reads two related passages in parallel without delving further into dialogical insights. Therefore, Shi's work does not appear to engage genuine cross-textual hermeneutics; rather, it suggests various points of contact.

Zhi-Ming Yuan also has written a parallel reading of *Laozi* and the Bible.¹²⁹ As one may expect, Yuan engages his main discussion on Laozi's key concept of *dao* (道), translated as "the Way." The saying of Jesus, "I am the Way" hence inevitably becomes Yuan's conversation partner. Yuan digs into the "dao incarnate" from both corpora, affirming the truth claimed by both texts. From Yuan's work, one can see a Chinese Christian who, grappling with both native-faith texts, endeavors seriously to reconcile both traditions. Yuan does not highlight the tensions between the textual traditions. Rather, he attempts to unite them. In this book, Yuan illustrates his mastery over Chinese literature, notably the teaching of Laozi. Yuan shows readers how a Chinese can use one's literacy to understand the biblical truth more easily. The combined traditions have intrinsically shaped the identity of a

---

125. Ibid., 174.
126. Ibid., 375–401.
127. Shi, *Dongfeng Po* [Alternate Reading on the Analects], 171–86.
128. Ibid., 221–36.
129. Yuan, *Laozi Vs Shengjing* [Laozi vs. the Bible].

Chinese Christian. And Yuan has successfully affirmed that one tradition should not necessarily negate the other.

More publications have, in recent decades, attempted cross-cultural reading of the Bible and various Chinese texts. Thus, Dao-Sheng Li compares the Bible with Chinese culture. He places an emphasis on the biblical message for humankind while standing firm in the cultural heritage from which he derives.[130] In the area of cross-textual readings with Ecclesiastes, Christopher Heard has used *Daode Jing* of Laozi and explores their common pursuit of social order;[131] not forgetting Timothy S. Dobe, who also has attempted similar endeavors between Qoheleth and Laozi.[132]

These works indicate that biblical literature contains identifiable correspondences with a larger written tradition. Therefore, a present study of biblical wisdom related to its larger context is imperative. This book is in line with the previous research, notably in cross-textual hermeneutics between the biblical and Chinese literatures. However, this book is different because the political aspect, evidently present in both biblical and Chinese wisdom texts, becomes the focus. The Analects has long been thought of by others as a wisdom text primarily for shaping noble character. This book will nevertheless point out its articulation of political wisdom. On the other hand, Ecclesiastes is chosen out of the biblical wisdom books precisely because its political dimensions are passed over by most scholars. This present work hopes to make a contribution by comparing the political wisdom of Ecclesiastes with that of the Analects. The political dimension appears to have escaped the attention of cross-textual hermeneutics thus far.

Comparative Studies: The Thought Worlds of Christianity and Confucianism

Cross-textual hermeneutics has a wider philosophical framework that shares its emergent emphasis. Attempts also have been made to compare two different religious beliefs, as those of Christianity and of Confucianism. This line of comparison is found in abundance. In her published work of 1977, Julia Ching compares Confucianism and Christianity by pointing

---

130. With a primary aim to communicate the gospel effectively to the Chinese community, Li, *Shengjing yu Zhongguo Wenhua*, locates the Bible alongside Confucian classics on one hand and, on the other, draws out similarities of both on cultivating attitudes.

131. Heard, "The *Dao* of Qoheleth," 65–93.

132. Dobe, "Qoheleth and the Lao Tzu."

out their early encounters and by examining their respective religious heritages.[133] By doing this, Ching has put the dialogue between Confucianism and Christianity into a historical perspective. In addition, Ching attempts to highlight the Confucian religious dimension in light of Christian theological understanding. Ching argues in favor of Confucianism as a partner in dialogue with Christianity after surveying their commonalities and differences. By suggesting that Christianity, rather than replacing other religions, may learn from them or even be challenged by them, Ching has ushered in an important Christian development of religious dialogue. In another similar attempt, Ching has co-authored with Hans Küng to advocate further inter-religious dynamics.[134]

Christian scholars and Chinese philosophers in Asia also have contributed valuable effort toward similar endeavors. From the circle of Christianity, Jia-Lin Liang has examined how Christianity gained its footage among Confucian-educated Chinese.[135] Liang surveys some important periods of church history in China and has observed various models of religious crossroads over and above their failures. His finding invites Chinese churches to reflect on their lives and traditions facing Confucian values. Qing-Xiang Guo, too, based on the observation of Christian-Confucian dynamics during the era of the Republic of China, points out conflicts and integrations between the two thought worlds.[136] Guo pays special attention to their approach to ethics. Another study by Xin-Fu Yao advocates a dialogue between Christianity and Confucianism in search of a confluence of meanings.[137] Elsewhere, Cong-Lin Dong presents more general work in comparing Christianity and Chinese traditional culture.[138] In a similar attempt, Ming-Chieh Wu has established points of contact between Christianity and

133. Ching, *Confucianism and Christianity*.

134. Küng and Ching, *Christianity and Chinese Religions*. This stimulating book came from a series of lectures at the University of Tübingen in 1987. In this work, Hans Küng aims to present Christianity in light of Chinese religion to avoid exclusivism and, at the same time, reject uncritical syncretism. Julia Ching, on the other hand, introduces four Chinese religions: Chinese folk religion, Confucianism, Daoism, and Buddhism, underscoring their contribution to shaping the religious dimension of the Chinese.

135. Liang, *Paihuai yu YeRu Zhijian* [Hover between Christianity and Confucianism], 254–68. In this book, Jia-Lin Liang explores also distinctive adaptations toward Christian values taken by some notable Chinese thinkers.

136. Guo, *YeRu Lunli Bijiaoyanjiu* [Comparative Study on Ethics of Christianity and Confucianism].

137. Yao, *YeRu Duihua yu Ronghe* [Dialogue and Integration Between Christianity and Confucianism].

138. Dong, *Long yu Shangdi* [On Dragon and God].

Chinese culture.[139] Wu begins with a comparison of Confucian orthodoxy and Christian orthodoxy, yet he also concludes in favor of Christianity, that "Confucian orthodoxy can be considered as a tool for the spread of Christian orthodoxy."[140] Wu's method of establishing such points of contacts, however, is one that heightens the evangelism goal to the disadvantage of the other. It should best be avoided in view of the biases one may bring in any comparative study between Christianity and Confucianism.

From the side of Confucian scholars, positive efforts have been attempted toward meaningful encounters. Peter K. H. Lee has edited a notable volume on Confucian and Christian encounters after an international Confucian-Christian conference at the Chinese University of Hong Kong in 1988, and it includes the works of various scholars, notably, Xiao-Feng Liu, Yi-Jie Tang, Pei-Rong Fu, John Berthrong, William Theodore de Bary, and Julia Ching.[141] Among Confucian-Christian encounters, the theme on *ren* in Confucianism often is related to the *agape* of God in Christianity.[142] A similar comparative study between *ren* and *agape* also is established by Christian scholars in pursuit of a contextual theology.[143] Furthermore, the Chinese understanding of dao with respect to a Christian understanding of *logos* has been the subject of research in a work compiled by Xiao-Feng Liu.[144] In short, the research in line with these comparative studies is vast and is impossible to contain altogether in this book. What is important though is apparent: cross disciplinary research between the Bible and Chinese culture in Asia will continue to occupy more and more emphasis in years to come.

Research Approaches

This book has briefly suggested so far that various comparative studies and cross-textual hermeneutics have been attempted between the Bible and Chinese literature. The attention to political elements in the wisdom texts of both traditions, however, has been notably inadequate. On this ground, this book suggests a cross-textual reading between Ecclesiastes and the Analects. Chapter 1 represents an introduction. The earlier part of this chapter has demonstrated that biblical wisdom actively engages with other cultures

139. Wu, *Jidujiao yu Zhongguo Wenhua* [An Encounter of Christianity and Chinese Culture], 23.
140. Ibid.
141. Lee, *Confucian-Christian Encounters*.
142. For example, Whaling, "Jen and Love," 255–73.
143. Luo, "Lun Rujia de Ren [On the Theme of *Ren*]," 125–42.
144. Liu, *Dao yu Yan* [Way and Word].

within a wider world of the ancient Near East. This chapter asserts the importance of a dialogical approach to cross-cultural and cross-textual reading. Key concepts, as well as the scope of this research, are defined in this chapter. Using the evidences of cross-textual reality in ancient Near Eastern wisdom texts, this chapter has illustrated notable political coherences to necessitate cross-textual research. Eight passages in Ecclesiastes and politically related passages from the Analects also are set in perspective. The *Forchungbericht* follows to sum up previous related research.

The remaining chapters of this book illustrate how a biblical wisdom text may be read cross-culturally with a wisdom text from East Asia. Such endeavor entails a dialogical endeavor that interweaves three hermeneutical "worlds." *The world behind the texts* reveals a wider, open-ended, and vibrant wisdom textual interaction among various cultures. The world behind the texts of Ecclesiastes and the Analects is the world of wisdom. There are historical indicators and socio-political factors in Ecclesiastes and the Analects that have shaped their wisdom ideas. Therefore, these backgrounds first will be drawn out prior to the interpretation of selected passages from both primary texts. *The world of the texts* is the literary composition in Ecclesiastes and the Analects. The interpretation of Ecclesiastes and the Analects accordingly constitutes two different chapters in this book. Thus, chapter 2 details the structure, theme, and message of Ecclesiastes. The socio-economic and political background of Ecclesiastes that yields its message and theology is explored. Eight passages that communicate Qoheleth's political wisdom are selected. The translations and expositions of Eccl 3:16–17; 4:1–3; 4:13–16; 5:8–10 [Hebrew 5:7–9]; 8:2–9; 9:13–16; 10: 4–7; and 10:16–20 are laid out. A political reading based on those passages concludes the chapter. Chapter 3 communicates briefly the structure, theme, and message of the Analects. The chapter likewise explores its social location and political background. Notable passages related to Confucius' political ideas are explored, translated, and interpreted according to distinctive subject matters. This exploration yields key concepts with regards to practical wisdom based on the Analects.

In an exploration of *the world in front of the texts*, the reader, culturally conditioned and biblically convicted, interprets the two primary texts in reciprocity to create meaning. Such endeavor is the goal of chapter 4. This final chapter seeks to discover the dialogical dynamics between the political sayings of Confucius in the Analects and the political ideas of Qoheleth in Ecclesiastes. This chapter demonstrates some of their hermeneutical connections. At the heart of the book, this chapter illustrates how one's reading can be illumined, challenged, and enriched by another. The research seeks to discover distinctive *and* collective political insights in a disordered world.

Based on the findings revealed when the two texts intersect, a contextual idea of living wisely in the present socio-political world of the reader also is suggested.

2

Ecclesiastes and Political Wisdom

POLITICAL AND JUDICIAL SAGACITY naturally come under the trajectory of wisdom.¹ In the Reformation Era, in the eyes of Martin Luther, Philip Melanchton, and Johannes Brenz, Ecclesiastes is basically a book that is progressive about civic life.² Luther reads Ecclesiastes as "a book about politics and the family, about human existence in the context of creation order," and Qoheleth as "a political figure deeply concerned about social life."³ Believing that wisdom contains ideology, Walter Brueggemann asserts that the ideological dimension vis-à-vis social control and a concern for stability are articulated in Ecclesiastes.⁴ This chapter seeks to uphold Qoheleth's political wisdom for survival in socio-political challenges. Qoheleth advises on courtly behavior, shares his perspective on political leadership, and suggests ways to deal with the wickedness that exists within the power structure of society. Such insights in the socio-political dimension have been largely ignored by interpreters, giving way to hermeneutics on literary structures, genres, authorship, language, perspectives on life and death, religious views, and theology. This book asserts that a significant part of Ecclesiastes ad-

---

1. Whybray, "Sage in the Israelite Royal Court," 133.

2. The positive reading of Luther on *Ecclesiastes* comes as a pleasant surprise and is far from recognized. Unlike the allegorical and Christological reading of Jerome that had influenced the interpretation on *Ecclesiastes* for a millennium in the past, the reformers held faith and politics intact, thinking that Qoheleth (still believed to be Solomon by the reformers then) wrestles with poor leadership issues, which was also a problem of the reformers' larger environment. See Kallas, "Ecclesiastes: Traditum et Fides Evangelica; Bartholomew, *Ecclesiastes*, 31–32.

3. Bartholomew, *Ecclesiastes*, 32.

4. Brueggemann, "Social Significance of Solomon," 129. In the ancient Near East, kings and rulers are associated with the attribute of being wise in terms of choices of moral conduct and also administrative skills and leadership competence. Isaiah 11:2 describes an ideal king as one who associates with wisdom: he has the "spirit of wisdom and understanding, the spirit of counsel and might, the spirit of knowledge and the fear of the LORD." Besides, kings make important decisions and military policies by consulting their advisors who display attributes of wise counsel. See Whybray, "Sage in the Israelite Royal Court," 134.

dresses the political concern and that Qoheleth, a wise court official, articulates far-reaching political wisdom.

Ecclesiastes at a Glance

There are apparently two voices of Qoheleth heard in Ecclesiastes, primarily in the first person and remarkably less in the third person (only in Eccl 1:1–2; 7:27; and 12:8–10). The shift from third-person pronominal reference to the use of first person between the prologue-epilogue (frame-narrative) and the main body of Ecclesiastes has long been acknowledged. This shift however, especially in the epilogue, stands in harmony with the rest of the book.[5] The shift of personal pronoun entails a common disagreement in the scholarship of Ecclesiastes as to whether the book as a whole is written by one author, namely Qoheleth. Suggestions are either of an editorial authorship responsible for the frame narratives in Eccl 1:1–2 and 12:9–14[6] or an anonymous author who dialogues with Qoheleth's original text synchronically.[7] This book uses "Qoheleth" as the author who communicates the total content of the book. This follows Michael V. Fox's assertion that similar framing techniques (1:1–11, 12:9–14) are found among ancient Near Eastern texts without necessarily denoting a different persona or perspective.[8] In fact, from the Egyptian parallels, even if a different person had compiled and edited Qoheleth's material as a frame narrator, it does not change the message and outlook of the entire book.[9] Thus, the shift in epilogue as a whole should be noted as part of the rhetoric to authenticate Qoheleth's contribution as a sage. This is reminiscent of many epilogues found in ancient Near Eastern parallels. In short, the reading of Ecclesiastes in this book regards it in its entirety without assuming a departure of the frame-narrative from its

---

5. Seow, "Beyond Them, My Son, Be Warned," 141.

6. For example, Longman, *Book of Ecclesiastes*.

7. For example, Perry, *Dialogues with Kohelet*.

8. Fox, "Frame-Narrative and Composition," 83.

9. Seow, *Ecclesiastes*, 38. Based on the point that the call to obey God's command only occurs in Eccl 12:13a–14 and nowhere else in Ecclesiastes, Seow in his "Beyond Them, My Son, Be Warned" (138–41), treats Eccl 12:13a–14 as a postscript. Nevertheless, separating Eccl 12:13a–14 from the epilogue may not be unnecessary. In fact, one should foresee the call to obey God's commandment since Qoheleth does not estrange himself from the teaching of the Torah. Qoheleth advances lengthy remarks upon religion in Eccl 5:1–7 by referring to the temple, sacrifice, and making a vow (5:1, 4); he too differentiates the religious from the non-religious based on whether one gives sacrifices or not (9:2). As Seow has also pointed out, the content in Eccl 12:13b–14 is not contrary to the rest of the book.

main body. Before getting into a major discussion of the texts, a perception of Ecclesiastes' structure and theme will be laid out first. These aspects are important to yield an interpretation of the texts.

Structure and Theme

Ecclesiastes has a tripartite division consisting of prologue-body-epilogue.[10] The main crux within the body of the text contains a substructure in which crucial subject matters are surveyed. Hence, the main body of texts within Ecclesiastes (1:12–12:7) is outlined aside from the introduction (1:1), prologue (1:2–11), as well as the epilogue (12:8–14). Within the main body of texts (that is, 1:12–12:7) is a two-part division: the first half (1:12–6:12) and the second half (7:15–12:7). A set of transitional proverbs (7:1–14) links both of these parts. The first half (1:12–6:12) represents Qoheleth's personal encounter. This first half is further divided into two main segments: four counts of his self-experiments (1:12–2:26) and seven counts of his observations (3:1–6:12). The transitional proverbs (7:1–14) signify a transition from personal experience to Qoheleth's advice. These proverbs communicate the value of wisdom. The second half (7:15–12:7) of the body is Qoheleth's seven counts of advice. They include advice against extremes, advice against foolishness, advice for proper courtly behavior, advice about the righteous and the wicked (where a chiastic structure is discernible), advice on proper response to life's absurdity (that has seven counts of proper attitudes), advice on carpe diem and on optimizing youth. Despite a few suggestions that Ecclesiastes does not appear to have a structure or an order, this book is in favor of the idea that a clear outline is evident and that a thought pattern is discernible in the book.[11]

---

10. Ecclesiastes 1:1 is outside this tripartite structure. Longman suggests a three-part structure of prologue-body-epilogue in Ecclesiastes, whose narrator's voice framed the main literary unit, linking Ecclesiastes to three similar Akkadian texts: *The Cuthacan Legend of Nurum-Sin*, the *Sin of Sargon Text*, and *Adad-guppi Autobiography*. See Longman, *Book of Ecclesiastes*, 8 and 19.

11. Although differing vastly in approaches, most recent scholars support the idea of a discernible outline in Ecclesiastes.

Ecclesiastes: An Outline

1:1	Introduction	
1:2–11	Prologue	
1:12—6:12	**Qoheleth's Personal Encounter in an Elusive World**	
1:12—2:26	Qoheleth's Self Experiments	
	1:12–18	on Wisdom
	2:1–11	on Material and Sensual Things
	2:12–17	on Folly
	2:18–26	in Toil
3:1—6:12	Qoheleth's Observations on Human Endeavor	
	3:1–15	time and event
	3:16–22	the presence of wickedness
	4:1–16	relative good
	5:1–7	religious practices
	5:8–9	the presence of oppression
	5:10–20	acquisition of wealth
	6:1–12	life momentariness
7:1–14	**Qoheleth's Proverbs on Wisdom**	
7:15—12:7	**Qoheleth's Advice on Living in an Elusive World**	
	7:15–22	against extremes
	7:23—8:1	against foolishness
	8:2–9	proper courtly behavior
	8:10—9:10	about the righteous and the wicked
		8:10-14 absurdity in their retributions
		8:15-17 recommendation for enjoyment
		9:1-6 the certainty of their death
		9:7-10 recommendation for enjoyment
	9:11—10:20	response to life's absurdity
		9:11–12 the right time and chance
		9:13–16 the value of wisdom on kingship
		9:17—10:3 proverbs about wisdom
		10:4–7 prudence toward the authority
		10:8–11 the reality of occupational hazards

	10:12–15	proverbs about the wise vs. the fools
	10:16–20	proper governance and courtly conduct
11:1–6	carpe diem	
11:7—12:7	optimizing youth	

| 12:8–14 | Epilogue |

Ecclesiastes 1:1 is the introduction to the entire book. It claims the book as the words of Qoheleth, who is a son of David and a king in Jerusalem. The content of the book is then framed by a prologue (1:2–1:11) and an epilogue (12:8–14), both beginning with *hăbēl hăbālîm 'āmar qōhelet hakkōl hăbēl*, "vanity of vanities, says Qoheleth, all is vanity." The prologue has a repetitive *hăbēl hăbālîm* ("vanity of vanities") for an emphatic purpose. With such an emphatic tone of *hăbēl hăbālîm*, Qoheleth sets out to illustrate his observation toward a repetitive exchange of cosmic order while nothing really new take place (1:2–11). The prologue leads one from a universal experience to Qoheleth's personal reflections, thus shifting focus to the first half of the whole book (1:12–6:12). The first half of Ecclesiastes sets a tone for *hebel ûrĕ 'ût rûaḥ*, "vanity and a pursuit of wind" (1:14; 2:11, 17, 26; 4:4, 6; 6:9). It consists of two main descriptive wisdom materials: Qoheleth's four depictions on self-experiment with life (1:12–2:28) and his seven observations on human endeavor in an elusive world (3:1–6:12). The four depictions of Qoheleth's self-experiment denote Qoheleth's success in all possible areas of life. Each of the four depictions ends in an expression of *hebel ûrĕ 'ût rûaḥ*, "vanity and a pursuit of wind," except for 1:17–18, which has *ra'yôn rûaḥ*, "a chasing after wind."[12] These four depictions of Qoheleth's self-experiment speak of Qoheleth as one who has had wisdom (1:12–18), has taken material possessions and life enjoyment (2:1–11), has preferred wisdom over folly (2:12–17), and has labored in toil (2:18–26).

With the consistency of a sigh, *hebel ûrĕ 'ût rûaḥ* (in 4:4, 6; 6:9), Qoheleth recounts his seven observations on human endeavor (3:1–6:12). Each of these observations ends with his concluding remarks (3:14–15; 5:9; 5:18–20) or questions (3:21–22; 6:11–12) or both (4:11–12; 5:6b–7 [Hebrew 5:5b–6]). These seven observations are each marked with the word *rā'â* ("see"),[13] except for 5:1–7 [Hebrew 4:17–5:6], which is actually an

---

12. One can maintain that the lack of *hebel ûrĕ 'ût rûaḥ* in Eccl 1:17–18 recalls the *hebel ûrĕ 'ût rûaḥ* of 1:14 in the same discourse.

13. Mostly as first-person pronouns, except 5:8 [Hebrew 5:7] in the second-person pronoun, in a form of stipulation.

advice itself.[14] The first half of Ecclesiastes contains large blocks of observations and the second half, instructional material.[15] But the first common singular (1cs) form of rā'â occurs throughout the book. This occurrence entails a consistency in Qoheleth's observation in the whole book. As such, Qoheleth's advice in the first half of the book is interwoven with his central observations. Likewise, his observations are detectable within his prevailing advice in the second half of the book.[16] Nevertheless, the governing idea in the first half of the book is still largely observations. Thus, there is first an observation of time and event, expressed through fourteen sets of parallelism, before concluding with an observation of God's sovereignty in time and event, as well as in human toil and enjoyment (3:1–15). Qoheleth observes too the presence of wickedness in place of judgment and righteousness. He affirms God's judgment in due time, points out the ultimate destination of humans, and concludes with his perception to enjoy one's work and toil (3:16–22). These observations end with a rhetorical question in 3:22. From here, Qoheleth continues to observe the relative-good experiences through a series of "better-than" sayings (4:1–16). He advises on religious practices (5:1–7) and observes an oppression from the powerful to the poor (5:8–9), acquisitions of wealth through economical activities (5:10–20) and life momentariness (6:1–12).

Before Qoheleth engages further his advice and observations in the second half of the book (7:15—12:7), he shifts to his traditional proverbial wisdom teaching (7:1–14). Qoheleth is a sage who teaches in the wisdom tradition. Therefore, it is no surprise for Qoheleth to utter proverb-like sayings here distinguishing wisdom and folly. The poetic structure in 7:1–14 stands in a strategic location as it bridges Qoheleth's prevalent observations in the first half of body text to Qoheleth's overarching advice in the second half. Rather than interrupting Qoheleth's argument in the book, as George Barton has suggested, the sayings indicate Qoheleth's traditional wisdom background.[17]

---

14. The shift in tone from the indicative to the imperative beginning in Eccl 5:1 [Hebrew 4:17] has been noted by Seow, *Ecclesiastes*, 46, hence marking the transition from the previous textual unit to the next, as Seow suggests.

15. Longman, *Book of Ecclesiastes*, 19.

16. In fact, the word *rā'îtî*, which is characteristic of Qoheleth's observation, occurs throughout the book (Eccl 1:14; 2:24; 3:10, 16; 4:15; 5:12, 17; 6:1; 7:15; 8:9, 10; 9:13; 10:5, 7). Qoheleth's observations and instructions are intertwined throughout the book, although his observations are more prevalent in the first half of the book and his instructions more prevalent in the second half.

17. Barton, *Critical and Exegetical Commentary*, 46. Barton believes that here Qoheleth has added the sayings of others to his main argument in the book.

Qoheleth proffers seven pieces of advice in the form of instruction. To begin, one should guard against extremes, including that of righteousness and wisdom (7:15–25). Besides, one should evade foolishness because it leads one to destruction (7:26—8:1). Changing the subject matter to courtly behavior, Qoheleth cautions about living under the situation of despotism. He advises on proper conduct in order to be safe (8:2–9). Qoheleth further recommends the righteous lifestyle over the wicked (8:10–9:10). Here a chiastic structure is discernible with regards to retributions and the death of both the righteous and the wicked.[18] Qoheleth next advises on the proper response to life's absurdity with preference to wisdom (9:11–10:20). This unit can be further divided into seven sub-categories. As proper responses to life's absurdity, one should discern the right time and chance (9:11–12). Further, one should know the value of wisdom on kingship (9:13–16), choose wisdom over folly (9:17—10:3), be prudent toward those in power (10:4–7), acknowledge the reality of occupational hazards (10:8–11), see the ending of fools (10:12–15), and grasp a proper courtly conduct (10:16–20). In addition to the prevailing advice, Qoheleth recommends a carpe-diem attitude, despite an unknown future (11:1–6). Finally, there is an instruction for optimizing one's youth, to act following one's heart and to fear God since everything is elusive (11:7—12:7).

The epilogue (12:8–14) forms an *inclusio* with the prologue, returning to Qoheleth's declaration that begins with *hăbēl hăbālîm* (12:8; cf. 1:2). The epilogue is set in a positive tone compared to the prologue. In the prologue, Qoheleth intends to invite readers into his view of an elusive world. In the epilogue, however, Qoheleth seals his concluding imperative to fear God nonetheless.

Based on the above outline, it appears that Ecclesiastes exhorts living pragmatically in a disorderly world. The motif often is claimed to be one with a negative tone because of the recurrent *hebel* throughout the book, occurring thirty-seven times altogether. Yet the underlying theme of the book is largely constructive. Eunny P. Lee is right to view Qoheleth's commendation to enjoyment constructively.[19] Enjoyment of life, according to Lee, lies at the heart of Qoheleth's vision of piety, which can be described as ethic

---

18. The chiastic structure I propose is as follows:
    A 8:10–14 absurdity in their retributions
        B 8:15–17 recommendation for enjoyment
    A' 9:1–6 the certainty of their death
        B' 9:7–10 recommendation for enjoyment

19. Lee, *Vitality of Enjoyment*, 32–82, 123–40. Lee explores the interplay between the commendation of enjoyment and the injunction to fear God in Ecclesiastes and suggests that both are positively correlated.

of joy and social responsibility.[20] This book affirms that there is a positive undertone of Ecclesiastes based on three factors.

First, the recurrent 'ĕlōhîm ("God") in Qoheleth's articulation is remarkable. Based on the verbs associated with the term, 'ĕlōhîm in Ecclesiastes is "a very active God."[21] God is the subject of two frequent verbs employed in the book: give, nātan (1:13; 2:26; 3:10,11; 5:18–19; 6:2; 8:15; 9:9; 12:7) and do or make, 'āśâ (3:11,14; 7:14, 29; 8:17; 11:5). God is also the one who judges (3:17), is angry (5:6), and who brings all human things into judgment (11:9). Therefore, Qoheleth affirms the divine actions and sovereignty. This view of God differs from most that see God as playing a passive role in Ecclesiastes, simply based on the ground that God's actions are incomprehensible and unpredictable.

Second, 'et-hā'ĕlōhîm yĕrā', "to fear God," is the motif behind Qoheleth's quest for meaning. This similar phrase appears throughout the book (5:6, 12:13; cf. 3:14; 7:18; 8:12).[22] This fear of God stands in the sapiential tradition, embracing godly behavior.[23] Moreover, Qoheleth advances lengthy remarks upon religion in 5:1–7. He solicits reverence and faithful implementation of one's covenants with God. His impression of God appears to be distant, yet such religion as he has is sincere.[24] People are thus advised to fear 'ĕlōhîm eventually in all that they do.

Finally, and most significantly, Qoheleth looks at human life through the lens of exception. Traditional teachings distinguish clearly between rights and wrongs, but Qoheleth points out their exceptions. Such a perspective is not pessimistic but critical and realistic. For example, like the other sages, Qoheleth affirms 'ĕlōhîm as one who is powerful in 3:14–15. But Qoheleth acknowledges also that God keeps humans in ignorance at times (3:10–11). Similarly, God controls the details of human life, but Qoheleth professes that God is also distant in human affairs (6:1–2 cf. 6:11–12). Furthermore, in Qoheleth's articulation, wisdom is asserted like the traditional teaching, but wisdom at times also is belittled (1:18; 2:15–16, 26; 8:16–17 cf. 2:13; 7:11–12, 19; 8:1). These exceptions are perceived in the past to be contradictions and inconsistencies that have raised questions of integrity and authorship. However, they also raise the possibility of an intended dialectical

---

20. Lee, *Vitality of Enjoyment*, 129–34.

21. Murphy, *Ecclesiastes*, lxviii.

22. Delitzsch called the phrase "fear God and keep his commandments" in Eccl 12:13 "the kernel and star of the whole book"; quoted in Murphy, *Ecclesiastes*, lxv.

23. Kaiser, "Qoheleth," 90–91. Kaiser distinguishes two epilogists who engage two levels of "fear of God"; the second epilogist (in Eccl 12:13–14) appears to be more legalistic, taking into consideration Qoheleth's call for obedience to God's commandment.

24. Barton, *Critical and Exegetical Commentary*, 48.

rhetoric of Qoheleth. Leland Ryken calls this rhetoric a "dialectical structure of contrasts."[25] Part of Qoheleth's rhetoric is to hold two existing phenomena that are in tension in juxtaposition, in order to search for satisfactory explanations in his pursuit of meaning. His search of course, is in vain. Here lies the heart of Qoheleth's signature sigh, *hebel* ("vanity"), which signifies a collapse of meaning. This collapse of meaning, according to Fox, unites all of Qoheleth's complaints.[26] The sigh of *hebel* however, is not the end. Qoheleth may not be addressing an "either-or" scenario.[27] The juxtaposition of the *hebel* complaint and the carpe-diem motif is indeed, as Craig Bartholomew suggests, "part of the very fabric of Ecclesiastes."[28] But against Bartholomew, Qoheleth has not seemed to even try to resolve the tensions between the alleged contradictory juxtapositions.[29] Qoheleth simply keeps in view two scenarios that are in tension. J. A. Loader names the tension as having "polar structure" thoughts.[30] And Edwin M. Good suggests the idea of irony in it.[31] The idea of contradictions or inconsistencies in Ecclesiastes should be ruled out notwithstanding. And the attempts to harmonize Qoheleth's "contradictions" would have dismissed his intended rhetoric.[32] Through the lens of exception, Qoheleth points out life's transitory nature and advocates against its absolute certainty. Qoheleth hence aims to depict a realistic view of human life. Wisdom, for example, is better than folly, but wisdom itself has limitations. For another example, enjoyment of life is good, but it is short-lived and unguaranteed. This "yes-but" scenario is critical and realistic, not contradictory nor inconsistent.[33] Qoheleth simply does not attempt to straighten out what God has made crooked (7:13). Life is full of ironies, but what is important is that God gives; for that, joy is

---

25. Ryken and Longman, *Complete Literary Guide*, 271.

26. Fox, "Inner Structure of Qoheleth's Thought," 225–26. Fox suggests the word *hebel* (vanity) as an organizing logic in Ecclesiastes.

27. Seow, *Ecclesiastes*, 40. Seow has pointed out that Qoheleth does not think of these contradictions in terms of "either-or" propositions.

28. Bartholomew, *Ecclesiastes*, 81. Bartholomew uses the idea of "gaps," which are opened up in the reading of the book when two contradictory juxtaposed perspectives are in view.

29. Bartholomew, *Ecclesiastes*, 81, states that "the book is precisely about how to resolve these tensions between the contradictory juxtapositions."

30. Loader, *Polar Structures*, 29–116.

31. Good, *Irony in the Old Testament*, 168–95.

32. Besides harmonizing the claimed "contradictory views," scholars also have tried to identify one of the suggestions as an unmarked quotation or to suggest a dialectic between Qoheleth and an opponent.

33. Seow, *Ecclesiastes*, 40.

sufficient; and the secret of the universe may remain hidden.[34] Therefore, unlike the ancient Near Eastern pessimistic texts, the underlying theme of Ecclesiastes is positive. Qoheleth presents an affirmative quest for meaningful survival. He communicates this quest through the recurring words *yôtēr* (6:8)[35] and *yitrôn*,[36] both meaning "surplus, advantage or profit." This quest results in Qoheleth's recommendations to embrace a certain attitude, which is a "reconstruction and recovering of meanings," according to Fox.[37] And this quest affects Qoheleth's political wisdom professed in Ecclesiastes.

Form criticism has identified wisdom literature as a broad corpus that displays particular characteristics. Qoheleth identifies himself as one among the wise who searches out wisdom (1:13, 16–17; 2:3, 9; 7:25; 8:16; 12:9). The frequent use of wisdom vocabularies, namely, *ḥokmâ* ("wisdom"),[38] *ḥākām* ("the wise one"), or *ḥākām* ("to make wise"),[39] *dā'at* ("knowledge"),[40] and verbs like *yāda'* ("to know"),[41] and *māṣā'* ("to find")[42] are characteristic of a wisdom text. As a biblical wisdom book, Qoheleth's wisdom relies upon the authority of human observation and experience rather than the assertion of divine revelation.[43]

Many parts of the book display Qoheleth's poetic skills with imagery, metaphor, and parallelism. Some are characteristic of typical wisdom essentials like short sayings (1:4–11; 3:2–8; 7:1–14; 10:1–3, 8–20; 11:7—12:7).[44] The book also exhibits evident prosaic features, prompting some scholars to

---

34. Good, *Irony in the Old Testament*, 194.

35. Ecclesiastes 2:15; 6:8,11; 7:11, 16.

36. Ecclesiastes 1:3; 2:11, 13 (twice); 3:9; 5:8, 15; 7:12; 10:10, 11.

37. Fox, "Inner Structure of Qoheleth's Thought," 225.

38. The word "*ḥokmâ*" (wisdom) occurs twenty-eight times as nouns in *Ecclesiastes*: 1:13, 16 (twice), 17,18; 2:3, 9, 12, 13, 21, 26; 7:10, 11, 12 (twice), 19, 23, 25; 8:1, 16; 9:10, 13, 15, 16 (twice), 18; 10:1, 10.

39. The word *ḥākām* occurs twenty-one times as a noun; in the singular—Eccl 2:14, 16 (twice), 19; 4:13; 6:8; 7:5, 7, 19; 8:1, 5, 17; 9:15; 10:2, 12; 12:9; in the plural—Eccl 7:4; 9:1, 11, 17; 12:11; and three times as a verb, *ḥākām* (2:15; 7:16, 23).

40. The noun *dā'at* (knowledge) appears seven times: Eccl 1:16, 18; 2:21, 26; 7:12; 9:10; 12:9.

41. The verb *yāda'* (to know) occurs thirty-six times: Eccl 1:17 (thrice); 2:14, 19; 3:12, 14, 21; 4:13, 17; 6:5, 8, 10, 12; 7:22, 25 (twice); 8:1, 5 (twice), 7, 12, 16, 17; 9:1, 5 (twice), 11, 12; 10:14, 15; 11:2, 5 (twice), 6, 9.

42. The verb "*māṣā'* appears twelve times: Eccl 3:11; 7:14, 24, 26, 27, 28, 29; 8:17; 9:10, 15; 11:1; 12:10.

43. Seow, *Ecclesiastes*, 66.

44. Nevertheless, its poetry displays an unusual metrical pattern and form, according to Loader, *Practical Commentary*, 4.

treat it as a mixture of both poetry and prose.[45] A mixed genre is likely at play in Ecclesiastes. This is due to the collective presence of biographies, personal reflections, quotations, rhetorical questions, and anecdotes, in addition to the standard "woe or blessing" proverbial sayings that are characteristic of wisdom literature. To typify Ecclesiastes as a whole a "royal autobiography" in light of 1:12—2:26, however, is inaccurate.[46] This is because the royal character of Qoheleth disappears after 2:16. Yee-Von Koh avers a pervasive royal voice throughout Ecclesiastes.[47] Yet the depictions of oppression in society (4:1; 5:8) and accumulations of wealth to a sad ending (5:13–17; 6:1–2) in Qoheleth's observation, seems to have derived from a non-royal perspective. Further, the political correctness Qoheleth exhibited in 8:2–6 and 10:16–20 also points to his facade as other than an imperial standing. In my opinion, Ecclesiastes is best regarded as a literary work with mixed genre; and Qoheleth, a literary persona.[48] There is also no need to differentiate the voice in the frame as the actual author of Qoheleth the persona, as it is a common feature to shift pronominal references in the wisdom writings of the ancient Near East.[49]

The ancient Near Eastern parallels of Job, rather than relating to issues of theodicy, has been suggested by Karel van der Toorn to be "literary dialogue" as a vehicle of critical reflection upon traditional values and beliefs.[50] The Joban literature and its parallels represent "a distinct literary genre characterized by a close correspondence between content, form and

45. Unlike the Hebrew version, which places Ecclesiastes among the *Mĕgilôt* under *Kĕthûbî*m (standing alongside the narratives of Ruth and Esther as well as the poetic Lamentations and Song of Songs), the Septuagint (LXX) includes Ecclesiastes among the poetic books. The latter listing was eventually adopted by the Christian tradition after Martin Luther.

46. Koh, *Royal Autobiography*, 25–37, 146–55.

47. Koh argues that the anti-royal passages purported by many (3:16–17; 4:1; 5:7–8 [Hebrew 5:8–9]; 10:5–7) and the texts about kingship (4:13–16; 8:1–5; 10:16–20) come with a pervasive kingly presence. However, Koh's criteria for such claim are less than convincing. See Koh, *Royal Autobiography*, 146–86.

48. Reminiscent of three Akkadian texts pointed out earlier: *The Cuthaean Legend of Naram-Sin*, the *Sin of Sargon Text* and *Adad-guppi Autobiography*. See Longman, *Book of Ecclesiastes*, 8 and 18–19. Longman has analyzed fifteen Akkadian texts that share common traits and suggests "fictional autobiographies" as Ecclesiastes has shared, where Ecclesiastes belongs further to its subgenre that ended with wisdom admonitions and instructions. All the fifteen texts Longman has examined appear to have been written a long time after the death of the first-person persona.

49. Longman, *Book of Ecclesiastes*, 9, opines that the voice in the frame is most likely the author of Ecclesiastes, perhaps a wisdom teacher who speaks as an insider when he critiques Qoheleth (12:8–12).

50. Van der Toorn, "Ancient Near Eastern Literary Dialogue," 59–75.

function."⁵¹ As such, these texts are seen as descriptive wisdom along with wisdom thought. In the case of Ecclesiastes, the "close correspondence between content, form and function" with other ancient Near Eastern parallels highlights Qoheleth's wisdom thought that inclines to be critical and descriptive. In many instances, Qoheleth appears to be challenging the traditional wisdom. It does not mean however, that Qoheleth dismisses wisdom. Wisdom is still relatively better in some instances. In fact, Qoheleth *yāda'* ("knows") that the good will be rewarded and the wicked punished. He presupposes that God will judge. Unfortunately, he *rā'â* ("sees") the realities that extricate his knowledge and presupposition.⁵² So Qoheleth questions the ultimate value of being wise and righteous (2:15–16; 7:15–16; 9:15–16). In seeking to be wise, Qoheleth finds wisdom itself elusive (7:23). Qoheleth's perspective is thus set on exceptions, even though he is in agreement with the common wisdom worldview (5:13–14; 7:15; 8:14–15; 9:11–12; 10:5–7). In van der Toorn's words, Ecclesiastes' literary genre is "a vehicle of critical reflection upon traditional values and beliefs."⁵³

The correspondence between Ecclesiastes and other ancient Near Eastern wisdom texts is compelling. Some, like the *Dialogue of Pessimism* correspond with Ecclesiastes in subject matters and theme. Others like the *Harper's Songs* share a close resemblance in their motif and observations of life. Yet some others, like the *Instructions of Any*, engage a similar attitude toward practical living. Those similarities generate scholars' recognition to specifically classify them as pessimistic texts.⁵⁴ This classification, however, is over-simplified. Qoheleth's seemingly pessimistic articulation is not the concluding position in the book. Further, a realistic attitude toward life may not necessarily be pessimistic. The texts are honest reflections of people who search for meaning and substance in living. Those reflections are realistic in counseling on how to gear oneself toward proper subsistence. After all, wisdom is about a way of steering in life. It is about skills for developing a true sense of humanity. Hence, Ecclesiastes, along with most other ancient Near Eastern parallels, represents a realistic text within wisdom literature.

---

51. Ibid., 75.

52. Fox, "Inner Structure of Qoheleth's Thought," 234–35.

53. Van der Toorn, "Ancient Near Eastern Literary Dialogue," 59.

54. The similarities discerned in various ancient Near Eastern wisdom texts, including Ecclesiastes, leads to the notion that wisdom authors may have shared common thoughts, epistemology, and even literary skill. Both biblical and ancient Near East authors in wisdom literature may have employed virtual quotations freely; their readers, who play an active role in ascertaining the meanings, could have recognized the allusions.

It is an honest personal reflection within a fictional autobiography.[55] This categorization is based on the most recurring first-person pronoun verb related to Qoheleth as the subject, *rā'â* ("to observe, to see").[56]

Ecclesiastes and Old Testament Wisdom

Unlike other Old Testament books, the wisdom literature depicts a literary paradigm that approaches the life of faith distinctively.[57] Within the wisdom literature itself, one can further notice the different approaches to wisdom. Rather than promoting instructions like that of Proverbs, Job questions their relevance and Ecclesiastes doubts their certainty. Ecclesiastes appears to further challenge the traditional wisdom, negating its confidence and absolute truth. Rather than aiming to foster a hard-and-fast rule like that of Proverbs, Ecclesiastes suggests moderation. Likewise, while Job records an encounter of Job with God, Ecclesiastes advocates the unfathomable mystery of God. Therefore, unlike Job and Proverbs, the goal of wisdom in Ecclesiastes becomes more ambiguous and challenging. It is ambiguous because the cosmos seems to have an order, but also appears to have disorder of certainty, for God hides aloof from life under the sun. The wisdom goal is challenging because, for Qoheleth, wisdom in the past seems to have placed enormous confidence in human intellect.

Scholars have various suggestions to account for the perceived tension of wisdom thought in Ecclesiastes. It is suggested that Qoheleth is engaged in a dialogue with the sages and their traditional wisdom, confronting wisdom's boast to solve every human problem.[58] Another opinion is that Qoheleth has entered a crisis situation with wisdom.[59] Fox maintains that Qoheleth does not attack wisdom or the wise but instead favors wisdom; he nevertheless examines the contradictions observed in human life rather

---

55. Crenshaw, *Ecclesiastes*, 28, has earlier classified the genre of Ecclesiastes as "personal reflection."

56. For example, "*rā'îtî*" appears throughout the book, in Eccl 1:14; 2:24; 3:10, 16; 4:15; 5:12, 17; 6:1; 7:15; 8:9,10; 9:13; 10:5, 7.

57. The most striking eccentricity of wisdom literature is the absence of familiar Old Testament themes describing Yahwism. The wisdom literature does not represent the actions of God in Israel's history nor does it depict religious activities among Israelites, but deals with daily human experience in the world created by God. As suggested by Murphy, *Tree of Life*, 1, there are "hidden connections" between wisdom and Yahwism. This is not to say that the wisdom literature is totally alien; rather, it should be regarded as a creative work of literature whose connection to the total covenantal faith is largely to be explored.

58. Clifford, *Wisdom Literature*, 111.

59. Murphy, *Tree of Life*, 55.

than explain them away.[60] There are many more scholars' opinions, and the issue concerns the interpretation of Qoheleth's wisdom compared to traditional wisdom. The teaching of traditional wisdom, for example, enables one to secure abundances in life. Yet Qoheleth is adamant that death cancels any advantage that wisdom brings about. Also, despite the fact wisdom is acclaimed in traditional wisdom, for Qoheleth, wisdom cannot achieve its goal every time. Qoheleth's language is nevertheless typical of Old Testament wisdom, for he recognizes wisdom's advantage. This explains the reason Qoheleth is regarded as one among the sages, even though he does not sing in tune with the others. Choon-Leong Seow avers that, since wisdom leaves more space for the explanations of events, Qoheleth's main concerns are with the plight of the larger humanity and with the quest for their benefit.[61] In Seow's word, "wisdom is regarded positively by Qoheleth, unlike folly, which is never commended. Yet, it is equally clear that wisdom has its limits and is subject to failure."[62] And at the point where such limits and failures are experienced, wisdom becomes communicative; this stretches far beyond the realm of didactic.[63]

Critical of the confidence in traditional wisdom, Qoheleth launches a search for truth. His search is expressed through a compound use of verbs for seeking, finding out, and scrutinizing: *dāraš, tûr* (1:13), *māṣā'* (7:24), *bāqāš* (7:25), *ḥēqer,* and *'āzen* (12:9).[64] In such pursuit, Qoheleth is aware of the challenges in the environment in which humanity has to live. This is "a critical encounter with the whole world of experience and its inherent laws."[65] After the search, when Qoheleth thinks he has discovered the truth, he also finds that the truth is illusive. This view is evident in 3:11, where Qoheleth states that humankind cannot find out what God has done. Again in 8:16–17, Qoheleth avows that, even though those who are wise claim to know, they cannot find out what is happening under the sun. In short, not

---

60. Fox, *Qoheleth and His Contradictions*, 10–12.

61. Seow, *Ecclesiastes*, 66–67.

62. Ibid., 68.

63. Von Rad, *Wisdom in Israel*, 97.

64. The rare verb *tûr* connotes an extraordinary measure for a firm resolve, more appropriate to spying. The verb is used in Job 39:8, referring to an animal's search for food and in Prov 12:26 to imply examining one's friend closely. See Crenshaw, *Old Testament Wisdom*, 116, 134.

65. Von Rad, *Wisdom in Israel*, 98. According to von Rad, the reality could no longer hide in the security of orders but instead was forced out into a worldly domain. He opines that it is a process of desacralization or "a secularization of the world."

only does Qoheleth draw on the wisdom tradition but also he brings the tradition to bear on human experience.[66]

Qoheleth has undeniably suggested a radical concept of God's guidance and of God's presence in the human world. By standing in the sapiential tradition, Qoheleth is ready to be critical when the evidence of reality warrants as such. Nevertheless, Qoheleth does not forsake the wisdom he once learned; he simply concludes that it sometimes provides no advantage in the grasping of one's destiny. Recognizing such human limitations is not depressing, but rather liberating.[67] Qoheleth nevertheless asserts God's timing (3:1–15), and that "God has done it so that all should stand in awe before him" (3:14). According to Seow, this fear-of-God motif in Ecclesiastes is the recognition of wisdom limitations.[68] Such emphasis on the fear of God makes Qoheleth stand with others in the wisdom tradition.

Traditional wisdom is largely effective for performing daily duties and succeeding at one's goals. But sometimes wisdom fails to accomplish what it should—when it does not provide sufficient knowledge, when it is determined by chance, and when it is restrained by death.[69] Thus, in Ecclesiastes, the scope of wisdom has extended to discerning the best means to survive meaningfully regardless of circumstances. To Qoheleth, life is momentary, and therefore one has to seize the moment by working diligently and enjoying life and, at the same time, observing the fear of God.

Social-Political Background

Persian Dating

The numerous occurrences of Aramaic and Persian words, *hapax legomena* and peculiar Hebrew grammatical usage in Ecclesiastes, point to a late period composition of Ecclesiastes. Antoon Schoors highlighted thirty-four features in Ecclesiastes typical of late biblical Hebrew.[70] Examples of the peculiarities include the demonstrative *zōh* taking place instead of *zōʾt*, *ʾănî* occurring (twenty-nine times) rather than *ʾănōkî*, and *ʾăšer* (eighty-nine times) alternating with *še* (sixty-eight times).[71] Besides, there are mixtures of

66. Seow, *Ecclesiastes*, 69.
67. Von Rad, *Wisdom in Israel*, 101, states that recognizing human limitations puts a stop to the false security in human wisdom and enables one to open to the activity of God.
68. Seow, *Ecclesiastes*, 69.
69. Fox, "Wisdom in Qoheleth," 123–26.
70. Schoors, *Preacher Sought to Find Pleasing Words*, 221–24.
71. Barton has pointed out a detailed list in Barton, *Critical and Exegetical Commentary*, 52–53. See also Seow, *Ecclesiastes*, 17–18.

Hebrew forms, the absence or infrequent use of characteristic construction such as the *waw* consecutive, and rare syntactical constructions.[72] Daniel C. Fredericks is an exception in suggesting an exilic and pre-exilic dating.[73] There is a general consensus that Ecclesiastes' language and spelling conventions indicate a post-exilic period.[74] Still, scholars' opinions vary from a Persian to a Ptolemaic period.[75] The Phoenician setting Mitchell Dahood suggested has not been generally accepted.[76] Some earlier scholars, like F. Zimmemann, H. L. Ginsberg, and C. C. Torrey, have taken a long shot to suggest an Aramaic origin for Ecclesiastes.[77] Charles F. Whitley argues for Aramaic influence in Ecclesiastes and locates the book within 152–145 BCE.[78] There also are scholars who mark the peculiarity of Qoheleth's language as a sign of transition between classical Hebrew and Mishnaic Hebrew.[79] They too suggest a Hellenistic period for the dating of the book, a position most scholars are in favor of, but it remains most contested.[80]

Qoheleth's catalogue of seasons (3:1–9) was suggested to reflect Heraclitus' influence and the Stoic theory of cycles.[81] Ecclesiastes 7:27 has been taken to reflect an Aristotelian inductive mode of thinking, and Eccl 2:3 as Aristotle's quest for the *summum bonum*, the highest good. In fact, virtually every school of Greek thought has been linked to Qoheleth's. The connection to a Hellenistic period, however, fails to explain the absence of Greek nuances, as Whybray has pointed out before.[82] Carol Newsom has

---

72. Barton, *Critical and Exegetical Commentary*, 52.

73. Fredericks, *Qoheleth's Language*, 262–66.

74. Seow, "Linguistic Evidence," 645–46.

75. Nevertheless, Longman in his *Book of Ecclesiastes*, 49, is one of the few who concludes that the language of Ecclesiastes is not a certain indicator of its dating.

76. Although there are possible Phoenician influences on late biblical Hebrew, Mitchell Dahood appears to have taken a long shot in suggesting that *Ecclesiastes* is written in the Phoenician setting. See Dahood, "Canaanite-Phoenician Influence," 191–221; and Dahood, "Phoenician Background," 264–82. See also Seow, *Ecclesiastes*, 15.

77. According to them, the Hebrew version of Ecclesiastes is therefore a translation from Aramaic text. See Zimmermann, "Aramaic Provenance of Qoheleth," 17–45; Ginsberg, *Studies in Koheleth*; Torrey, "Question of the Original Language of Qoheleth," 151–60.

78. Whitley, *Koheleth*, 119–21 and 148.

79. Crenshaw, *Ecclesiastes*, 31, for example, argues that Ecclesiastes employs an "Aramaizing" Hebrew with strong Mishnaic characteristics, placing it alongside other late canonical books like Daniel, Esther, Ezra, Nehemiah, and Song of Songs. See also Barton, *Critical and Exegetical Commentary*, 52.

80. For example, Gordis, *Koheleth–the Man and His Word*; Crenshaw, *Ecclesiastes*, 49–50; Murphy, *Ecclesiastes*, xxii.

81. Illustrated and refuted in Gordis, *Koheleth–the Man and His Word*, 51–53.

82. Whybray, *Ecclesiastes*, 15.

noted that many of the alleged Greek "influences" or Greek philosophical parallels do not survive close scrutiny.[83] Seow too points out that the affinities between Ecclesiastes and certain Greek philosophy is superficial at best.[84] Further, there also is lack of evidence to specifically identify "Greek thought," as James L. Kugel notes.[85] The Greek dating of Ecclesiastes is thus not compelling. The grammatical peculiarities of Ecclesiastes can mainly be explained in terms of the general development of the Hebrew language.[86] Since Aramaic was a kind of lingua franca in the Persian period, it is not surprising that Qoheleth may have been familiar with it. Franz Delitzsch seemed to be the first to place Ecclesiastes' origin in the Persian period.[87] There are indeed two Persian words in the book that are widely acknowledged, *pardēsîm* (2:5)[88] and *pitgām* (8:11).[89] Besides, a number of economic and legal terms that are familiar to the socioeconomic world of the Persian Empire are attested in the book.[90] The word pattern of masculine names *qōheleth* in Ecclesiastes, alongside *sōperet* (Ezra 2:55 and Neh 7:57) and *pōkeret* (Ezra 2:57 and Neh 7:59) from other biblical contemporaries, reflect Persianism in the Bible that occur only in post-exilic literature.[91] Therefore, the Persian period and its urban audience, as Kugel and Seow have suggested, thus seem most probable.[92] Kugel has further pointed out the lack of Israelite nationalism in Ecclesiastes that has escaped many interpreters. This lack of national consciousness precludes the very beginning and the very end of Persian rule, where "Judean self-awareness and national feeling

---

83. Newsom, "Job and Ecclesiastes," 185. See also Seow, *Ecclesiastes*, 16.

84. Seow, *Ecclesiastes*, 16, points out there are no Greek loan words or Greek constructions in Ecclesiastes.

85. Kugel, "Qoheleth and Money," 47.

86. Whybray, *Ecclesiastes*, 16.

87. Delitzsch, *Commentary on the Song of Songs and Ecclesiastes*, 190.

88. The word occurs also in Neh 2:8 and Song 4:13 and derives from Old Persian *paridaida*, attested to in Persepolis Fortification Tablets dated around 500 BCE. The Akkadian rendering of the word is *pardēsu*. Seow, "Linguistic Evidence," 649.

89. The word traces back to Old Persian *patigāma*, also attested in Persepolis Fortification Tablets dated around 500 BCE. Seow, "Linguistic Evidence," 650. Seow has listed twenty-two Hebrew words believed to be of Persian origin in other post-exilic biblical books, specifically, the Book of Ezra, Chronicles, Esther, and Nehemiah; in Seow, "Linguistic Evidence," 647–49. See also Barton, *Critical and Exegetical Commentary*, 52; Whybray, *Ecclesiastes*, 15; Seow, *Ecclesiastes*, 12.

90. Seow, *Ecclesiastes*, 20–23.

91. Ibid., 20.

92. Kugel, "Qoheleth and Money," 45–49. See also Seow, "Linguistic Evidence," 665–66.

might have been at an all-time low."[93] These observations make the fifth century BCE a most likely date of composition for Ecclesiastes.

Political Culture and Courtly Sitz im Leben

In brief, Ecclesiastes was written in the Jerusalemite setting (1:12) during the late Persian period, approximately from the mid-fifth century to the mid-fourth century. It was a period of centralized bureaucratic structures as well as stratified social and state administrations. A division of labor was reflected in the social hierarchy at the capital, as well as the rural-urban continuum that had been accentuated through the process of urbanization.[94] State political economies were centralized. Tribute and taxes were imposed upon subjects to intensify national surpluses.[95] There was a tolerance of local cultures and religious practices, organized under an overarching imperial ideology.[96] The Persian king stood at the centre of imperial rule. Around the king was a group of Persian nobles functioning as courtiers, advisors, and high-ranking officials.[97] The most important officials in the provincial administration were either Achaemenian family members or nobles from Persia who had personal ties to the imperial family.[98] It is documented that by the time Cambyses II (530–522 BCE) died in 522 BCE, the empire was divided into twenty-three lands or satrapies under the control of a governor.[99] The governors were appointed by the kings to administer city-states like Phoenicia and Jerusalem. They were of Persian nobility, mostly related to the royal family through political marriages. From the royal complex of these local governors, the kings expanded the parameters of rulership across the vast Persian empire—especially in administration, bureaucracy, and military.[100] These political organizations were reflected in Eccl 5:8–9

---

93. Kugel, "Qoheleth and Money," 47–49, here 48. The excavations of Persian coins and seal impressions that bear the word *Yehud* further reflect Qoheleth's possibility of being a "governor" who had Hebraized the designation "king" (Eccl 1:12; 2:12), ruling over "Israel" (the Jews) in Jerusalem.

94. Covey, "Political Complexity," 1850.

95. Ibid., 1850. The Persian court administration on the royal storehouse, food order and rations, taxation, monthly and annual accounts, were well documented and kept in the Persepolis archive then.

96. Ibid., 1852.

97. Brosius, *Persian Empire*, 62.

98. Garthwaite, *Persians*, 58.

99. A governor is alternately called a "satrap." See Boardman et al., *Cambridge Ancient History*, 41.

100. Garthwaite, *Persians*, 57.

[Hebrew 5:7–8]. They comprise layers of administrative functions and were effective in holding the vast empire together.

The Persian Empire consisted of a vast number of peoples with different cultures and a variety of languages. Given the size of the empire, non-Persians indeed shared secondary service. Their loyalty to the imperial court was paramount. Subjects from across the empire lived and worked in the capital centers of Susa, Ecbatana, and Persepolis, as well as in the provinces like Jerusalem.[101] The Persian Treasury Tablets clearly indicate that they were free people, not slaves, who were paid for their work and services.[102] Each satrap continued to use its own local language and functioned on a multilingual basis without facing the imposition of learning a dominant language like Persian.[103] The five hundred clay tablets found in Aramaic script in the Persepolis archive, still unpublished to date, show that the use of different languages and scripts did not pose a problem to the central government.[104] Aramaic was possibly one that was more prominent than the other languages. This background of language plurality sheds light on the writing of Ecclesiastes in Hebrew with notable Aramaisms.

The provincial systems that Darius I (521–486 BCE) inherited from Cambyses II, were in fact mainly the work of Cyrus the Great (559–530 BCE).[105] The policy of Cyrus was one of remarkable tolerance based on a respect for individual people, ethnic groups, other religions, and ancient kingdoms.[106] Cyrus's government gained him and his successors the trust to be seen as a legitimate king of Babylon rather than as a conquering foreigner.[107] This legitimacy ushered in stability and economic growth in the Persian period. It also explained the "linguistic chaos"[108] in Ecclesiastes that has occupied many scholarly debates. The vibrant economical activities explain Qoheleth's obsession with commercial terms. At least a dozen Persian terms found in post-exilic books are related to government terminology,

---

101. Ibid., 57–59.

102. Ibid., 59.

103. Brosius, *Persian Empire*, 63.

104. Ibid., 63.

105. Years after the fall of Babylon, Cambyses was preoccupied with the conquest against Egypt while his father, Cyrus II (Cyrus the Great) who occupied the Babylon, developed a system for organizing, controlling, and ruling the empire. See Boardman et al., *Cambridge Ancient History*, 41–42.

106. Boardman et al., *Cambridge Ancient History*, 42.

107. Ibid., 43.

108. Kugel, "Qoheleth and Money," 49. The "linguistic chaos" refers mainly to the peculiar Hebrew grammatical usage in Ecclesiastes that is recognized by most scholars.

two of which Qoheleth has rendered within a socio-political context.[109] This Persian government hierarchy complex, generally attested in extra-biblical texts, is reflected through Qoheleth's political articulation in the book.

The Persian royal court represented an intellectual center. Priestly sages and scribes were in charge of providing counsel to the kings. They too composed and kept important literature. There is evidence of the interaction between Persians and non-Persians, particularly in matters of offices, protocol, and philosophy in the royal court. Among this evidence, Persian languages written with a complex system of Aramaic allography were found.[110] This presupposed the presence of Mesopotamian scribes at Persian royal chancellery. In the Achaeminian period, when Aramaic became the lingua franca of the empire, there was a possibility that *dabīrs*, a word used primarily for scribe, translator, and lower-level bureaucrat, was non-Persian.[111] This background provides a proper *Sitz im Leben* for the work of Qoheleth, whose treatment of politics from a wisdom tradition aims to educate politicians and bureaucrats.[112] William Anderson places Ecclesiastes in the royal court.[113] But against Anderson who dates Ecclesiastes in a pre-exilic Israel royal court, this book seeks to propose a post-exilic Persian and its administrative province. Anderson's claim that post-exilic Jewish writers could not possibly "hold such a high view of political machinery and monarchy" is unfounded from a study of Persian ancient documents and its administrative system. The Persian governmental complex and its courtly sagacity, together with its related social issues, is directly linked to the political concerns this book strives to engage.

The dating of Ecclesiastes is significant to determine a historical setting. The period shaped Qoheleth's message and its subsequent interpretation. However, the meagre political data detected in the book, and the lack of direct historical allusion frustrates many attempts to suggest a historical background with certainty. Attempts have been made to relate Eccl 4:13–16; 9:13–16; and 10:16–17 to certain kings and political situations. Even so, there is no agreement among scholars about the identification. Sayings about kings are common in wisdom literature, as one can read from ancient Near Eastern texts. Hence, Whybray suggests that Qoheleth employs the proverbial sayings about kings or rulers in Eccl 1:12—2:26 and 5:13–17 as a

---

109. Whitley, *Koheleth*, 244.

110. Russell, "Sages and Scribes," 144–45. These interactions are evident since writing was a non-Persian invention, according to James Russell.

111. Ibid., 146.

112. Anderson, *Qoheleth and Its Pessimistic Theology*, 118.

113. Ibid., 81–82. Anderson sets the Israel royal court for Qoheleth's *Sitz im Leben*, rejecting its post-exilic dating.

pedagogical device.[114] Whybray's opinion about fictitious rendering of the passages is worth considering.[115] After all, Qoheleth is a literary persona. The articulation in the first two chapters also is a fictional autobiography. Fictitious rendering also evades speculation on identities involved in Eccl 4:13–16 and 9:13–16.

Political Ideas in Ecclesiastes

Duane Garrett examines eight passages in Ecclesiastes to assert Qoheleth's conception on the use and abuse of political power.[116] Garrett's eight passages are intended to form a statement on political authority woven into the fabric of Ecclesiastes to make up a significant part of Qoheleth's world view.[117] What is lacking from Garrett's paper, however, is a division that groups the passages under different categories. This book suggests that Qoheleth's approach to political wisdom can be grouped in two types of wisdom: instructions and admonitions on courtly behavior (Eccl 5:8–9 [Hebrew 5:7–8]; 8:2–9; 10:4–7; 10:16–20), and reflections on socio-political reality (Eccl 3:16–17; 4:1–3; 4:13–16; 9:13–16). As said earlier, the former type of political wisdom is prescriptive and is more direct, whereas the latter is descriptive and indirect. Given that both types of political wisdom are didactic in essence, such division is still important for discerning what constitutes Qoheleth's assertion on political instructions and admonitions. Likewise, what has caused Qoheleth to suggest certain wisdom pointers based on his observations? For Qoheleth, there is time for wise political actions as well as a time for knowing why a political incident occurs the way it does. Further, differentiating political wisdom in line with its type invites closer dialogues with that of the Analects.[118] Therefore, this chapter explores Qoheleth's political ideas according to these two types of political wisdom.

---

114. Whybray, *Ecclesiastes*, 9–10.

115. Yet, Eccl 5:13–17 does not speak of a ruler but a rich person who has lost everything in a failed business venture. Whybray believes the historical setting of Ecclesiastes points to the Ptolemaic period. See Whybray, *Ecclesiastes*, 10.

116. Garrett, "Qoheleth on the Use and Abuse of Political Power," 159–77. Garret's political passages are: Eccl 3:15c–17; 4:1–3; 4:13–16; 5:7–8; 7:6–9; 8:1–8; 8:9—9:6; 9:13—10:20.

117. Ibid., 159.

118. The Analects is more prescriptive and direct in its articulation of political wisdom. Yet the Analects also contains observations and reflections that make up the descriptive type of its political wisdom, albeit to a lesser degree. This book has consistently upheld that both types of political wisdom are didactic in nature. As such, political wisdom is not confined only to the prescriptive, instructive, and direct type.

The selection of the eight Ecclesiastes passages in this book is based on a combination of several criteria proper. First of all, a presence of the Hebrew word associated with those of power and authority: "kings," *melek*;[119] and "ruler or rulers," which includes two different words, *šallîṭ*[120] and *môšēl*.[121] Besides, some familiar words whose thoughts associate with political power or proper governance are considered. For instance, words like *kōaḥ* ("power") (4:1), *mĕdînah* ("province") and *gābōâ* ("high official") (5:8 [Hebrew 5:7]) are taken into consideration. These vocabularies also reflect a Persian coloring of Ecclesiastes' *Sitz im Leben*. Since the book contains observations of activities and people familiar to the royal court, Qoheleth's sentiment and attitude toward "foreign rulers" should not escape interpreters either. Further, words that relate to socio-political occurrences of the book—oppression, justice, and social wickedness—are included (3:16–17; 4:1–3). These social issues largely reflect the perspective of the commoner, rather than those who have power and authority. Qoheleth, in fact, engages more of his observation with this group of people. As a final note, the political passages usually belong to a larger literary unit. The discussion in this book focuses only on politically-specific verses and, hence, they comprise a smaller literary unit. For instance, not the entire 3:16–22 is engaged into translation and comments, but 3:16–17. Nevertheless, the interpretation of 3:16–17 naturally connects to the larger literary unit, and in some other instances, to the entire book.

As one can observe from the selection of these passages, the political passages are located almost evenly in the two halves of the main body of text. Four of them are situated within the first half of the book (especially 3:1—6:12). They largely comprise Qoheleth's observations. Another four passages are located within the second half of the book (7:15—12:7) and primarily comprise Qoheleth's instructions. This pattern suggests that political concepts do occupy a significant concern throughout the book. For each of these passages, this study presents its own translation, comments, and interpretation. Based on these passages, a reading of Qoheleth's political wisdom also is suggested.

There are two passages, 7:15–22 and 9:11–12, not included in the discussion of this study. In my judgment, they do not explicitly connect to the notion of politics. They do not contain words that associate with those of power and authority; neither do they address issues of social justice. They

---

119. Eccl 4:13,14; 5:8; 8:2, 4; 9:14; 10:20. The *melek* in Eccl 1:1, 12; 2:8 are left out, for they merely denote a kingly presentation of the Qoheleth or a noun per se unrelated to political intents.

120. Eccl 7:19; 8:8 (adjective, having mastery); 10:5.

121. Eccl 9:17; 10:4.

nevertheless embrace a sentiment that alludes to courtly experience, perhaps even Qoheleth's disappointment. Precisely that is why Qoheleth sees *hebel* ("vanity") in areas of righteousness besides wisdom, work, and pleasure. There is no surprise that Qoheleth's address in 7:15–22, with regard to righteousness, is perplexingly "lukewarm."[122] He instructs people not to be "too wicked" or "too righteous" (as if, a little wickedness is acceptable?), Perhaps Qoheleth is less convinced of the practical value of righteousness than of wisdom, as Fox suggests, therefore "he gives less effort to inspiring righteous behavior."[123] It seems that, it is wisdom, not righteousness, that will be more probable to assure survival in a foreign court in Qoheleth's thought. This idea connects with 9:11–12, where one's success in the royal court is possibly determined by time and chance, not by the swift, the strong, the skillful, the intelligent, not even by wisdom!

Instructions and Admonitions on Courtly Behavior

Ecclesiastes 5:8–9 [Hebrew 5:7–8]

> 8 If you see an oppression of the poor, and a violation of justice and righteousness in a province, do not be astounded over the matter. For a high official watches over high official, and high officials are above them.[124]
> 9 Yet in all, the advantage of the land is a king to a cultivated field.[125]

Ecclesiastes 5:8–9 [Hebrew 5:7–8] is notoriously difficult to interpret, not only in the philology and syntactical aspects but also in its meaning. The governing idea of 5:8–9 [Hebrew 5:7–8] is related closely to 5:8a, especially catchwords like *'ōšeq* ("oppression"), *mišpāṭ* righteousness, as well as its violation. The word *mĕdînâ* ("province") refers to a Persian governmental

---

122. Fox, "Inner Structure of Qoheleth's Thought," 234.

123. Fox has insightfully pointed out that, in any case, Qoheleth is not primarily a moralizer. See Fox, "Inner Structure of Qoheleth's Thought," 234.

124. Kittel et al., *BHS*, suggest a repointing in the critical apparatus to *wĕgābōah mē 'ălêhem* from *wûgĕbōhîm 'ălêhem*. But here a misdivision is more likely to be *šāmĕrû gĕbōhîm 'ălêhem*, as Seow, *Ecclesiastes*, 203 suggests.

125. Interpreters have to decide whether a *Ketib* reading *hy'*, or *Qere* reading *hw'* as a probable demonstrative pronoun referring to the advantage (ms), or the land (fs), or the king (ms). Eaton's reading is supported here. See Eaton, *Ecclesiastes*, 101, which reads, "But an advantage to a land for everyone is: a king over cultivated land." See also Kidner, *Time to Mourn and a Time to Dance*, 54. Fredericks, *Coping with Transience*, 50, who considers a wise king to account for the advantage meant in this passage.

division of satraps. Qoheleth elaborates on violations of justice and righteousness in a province, not in the centralized government. Seow is right to point out a possible word play between *mĕdînâ* ("province"; its etymological meaning "a place of jurisdiction") and *mišpāṭ* ("justice") in 5:8 [Hebrew 5:7].[126] The word play is a form of rhetoric used to convey an irony: there is injustice precisely where justice should be found. Qoheleth comments, "do not be astounded" over it. The corruption of power is real and common. The word *gābōâ*, translated as "high official" here, is contested before to be a substantive "arrogant one."[127] Yet the word that occurs here does contain a sense of higher socio-economic and political status notwithstanding.[128] Therefore *gābōâ*, as one with a high official standing, should be maintained (so NKJV and NRSV), and the bureaucracy is implied. Ecclesiastes 5:8 [Hebrew 5:7] is controversial and subject to scholars' emendation or repointing. The logical meaning appears to be "for a higher official watches over a high official, and even higher officials are above them."[129] This meaning reflects levels of government bureaucracy. It also implies layers of corruption. The highest level is not mentioned in the text but is implied through *melek* ("king") in 5:9 [Hebrew 5:8].

Ecclesiastes 5:9 [Hebrew 5:8] reads, "but the advantage of the land is, in all, a king for a cultivated field." Literally, the meaning of this line appears ambiguous. Some scholars either repoint[130] or emend[131] the text. Such endeavors are unnecessary. One should retain *mlk* ("king") and take a political interpretation to this passage. The ambiguity in the text is intended as part of Qoheleth's rhetoric. The verse speaks of the advantage a land possesses. The word *melek* ("king") in 5:9b [Hebrew 5:8b] is significant to drive home Qoheleth's point on this advantage. Reading from an agriculture background, "a cultivated field" is an imagery for a well-governed country. Ecclesiastes 5:9 simply means that having a political leader whose nation is well managed is an advantage to an *'erec*, a word that often means the whole earth or a country (Gen 10:10; 47:6; Isa 7:18; Ps 78:12; Jer 25:20). *The Instructions of*

---

126. Seow, *Ecclesiastes*, 202.

127. Attested elsewhere in Job 41:34 [Hebrew 41:26]; Ps 138:6; Isa 10:33; Ezek 21:26 [Hebrew 21:31]. See Kugel, "Qoheleth and Money," 35–38; and Seow, *Ecclesiastes*, 203.

128. The meaning is used by Barton, *Critical and Exegetical Commentary*, 127.

129. So Kidner, *Time to Mourn and a Time to Dance*, 54.

130. For example, Seow, *Ecclesiastes*, 204. Seow suggests a misdivision of phrase in 5:9b [Hebrew 5:8b]. Without changing the consonants of the Hebrew text and assuming Qere reading of *hw'*, Seow reads "the advantage of the land is in its yield, that is, if the field is cultivated for [its] yield."

131. For example, Fox, *Time to Tear Down and a Time to Build Up*, 234, eliminates *mem* for *beth*, reading *bklśdh* instead of *mlkśdh*, and hence "in every cultivated field."

Ankhsheshonqy communicates a similar idea, "The wealth of a town is a lord who does justice."[132] Qoheleth first warns about the reality of oppression of the poor, and a violation of justice and righteousness in a province. Then he suggests that a well-managed country comes from a political leader who performs his duty (5:9 [Hebrew 5:8]). Reading Eccl 5:8–9 [Hebrew 5:7–8] together, the passage means the oppression done by government officials in a province is a reality (in the local government), but on the whole an advantage is a king who governs well in a country (in the central government).

By this reading, Qoheleth does not engage in propaganda for the king. Rather, he brings in the concept of an ideal kingship. A king should exercise proper governance so that the people are well fed from the produce of his well-tilled field. A double entendre is at play here. Qoheleth uses a figure of speech in which his words are either to be understood in a literal sense, as above. Or, his message has an ironic meaning, implying a state of undermanaged government. Qoheleth targets at the pinnacle of the government structure in his time. The king should manage the nation properly by subjugating lower-level corruptions. The people then can benefit from it, and oppression can be reduced. The opposite could have been implied. Given a foreign imperial rule, Qoheleth uses this figure of speech to communicate a potentially offensive opinion without taking the risk of doing so. Longman's assertion—that this passage as a whole leaves little room for hope and, as such, the king should not be viewed as a savior of the land—is therefore subjective.[133] Also, by suggesting a mis-division and hence repointing the text, one eliminates the word *mlk* ("king") and misses the irony in the passage. Furthermore, this reading implies that political power vis-à-vis a government is necessary in regard to an ideal kingship.[134] The challenge lies in the capability of a king in managing his *'ereṣ*, a word used here to mean polity rather than a physical land.[135]

In sum, the hierarchical structure of any historical period can be the source of corruption and malpractice. The poor (*rāš*) often become the victim. Here, Qoheleth advises not to be astonished when facing the reality of such oppression. Yet a king in the ancient Near East is one who is responsible for the welfare of the people. A Babylonian proverb tersely illustrates the role of kingship in Mesopotamian society: "People without

---

132. Lichtheim, *AEL*, 3:166. Alternative translation: "Blessed is a city with a just ruler"; see Sparks, *Ancient Texts*, 72.

133. See Longman, *Book of Ecclesiastes*, 159. Longman's reading of Eccl 5:9 [Hebrew 5:8] is that the king represents part of the red-tape and corruption, "The profit of the land is taken by all; even the king benefits from the field."

134. Garrett, "Qoheleth on the Use and Abuse of Political Power," 167.

135. Fox, *Time to Tear Down and a Time to Build Up*, 234.

a king are (like) sheep without a shepherd."[136] The idea of the king being a shepherd is common in the Hebrew Bible. Likewise, the idea is common in ancient Near Eastern texts like *Sennacherib's Hexagonal Prism*, *Gilgamesh Epic*, and *the Code of Hammurabi*.[137] Mesopotamian legal documents, as well as the prophetic books of the Hebrew Bible, show royal officials and elders adjudicating civil cases at the city gates. However, the abuse of power and oppression of subjects did happen every now and then. One finds the most eloquent protests in the mouth of Hebrew prophets like Isaiah and Amos. Here, Qoheleth stipulates that one sees the reality of oppression and a violation of justice and righteousness in a province. He asserts an ideal concept of a kingship and points out the necessity of a government.

Ecclesiastes 8:2–9

> 2 I say,[138] keep the command of the king because of the oath to God.[139]
> 3 Do not be dismayed[140] before his presence and leave. Do not stand[141] in a harmful matter, for he will do whatever he delights.
> 4 As[142] which the word of the king is power[143], and who can say to him, "what are you doing?"

---

136. Lambert, *BWL*, 229, 232; lines 14–15.

137. In the prologue of the Code of Hammurabi for instance, Hammurabi self-depicts as one who "cause justice to prevail in the land, to destroy the wicked and the evil, and that the strong might not oppress the weak." In its epilogue, his shepherding role is depicted as coming from Marduk. See Pritchard, ed., *ANET*, 164–66 and 177–78. In the Code of Hammurabi, the king who deals fairly with the subjects should prescribe ordinances of the land and give justice to the oppressed, especially to the orphan and widow, through god-fearing wisdom and in peace.

138. There is a lack of verb after *'ănî* in MT; neither LXX and Peshita reflects the word. It could be a dramatic ellipsis, meaning "I say that . . ." See Gordis, *Koheleth-the Man and His Word*, 288, and Longman, *Book of Ecclesiastes*, 211. But it should not be emended to a direct object instead, as Murphy, *Ecclesiastes*, 80, does.

139. God is the subjective genitive, but it is interpreted here as God imposing an oath on the people that they should obey the king. Loader, *Polar Structures*, 70.

140. I follow Kittel et al., *BHS*; critical apparatus emends to *'al-tibbāhēl*, since it is attested in 5:2 [Hebrew 5:1] and 7:9.

141. "Do not stand in a harmful matter," in light of Ps 1:1; "Do stand in the path of sinners" does mean participating in wrongful activities. This understanding is hence probable and does not call for exchanging the word "stand" for another English verb.

142. Some manuscripts read *ka'ăšer* instead of *ba'ăšer*. So as LXX *kaqwj*.

143. The word *šilṭôn* occurs only here and in Eccl 8:8, elsewhere in Aramaic in Dan 3:2, 3 and Ben Sira 4:17; thus a late biblical Hebrew. See Whitley, *Koheleth*, 72, who also

5 The one who keeps a command will not experience harm. As for the time and judgment, a wise heart knows:[144]
6 that for every matter, there is time and judgment; that the evil of humankind is heavy upon them.
7 That no one knows what is going to happen, for who[145] can tell them what will happen?
8 No one has mastery over the life to retain the life,[146] and no one is a master in the day of death. There is no discharge[147] in the battle, and wickedness[148] will not deliver its practiser.
9 I have seen all these, and I gave my heart in every work which is done under the sun. There is time that one ruled over the other to his own harm.

The division of the literary unit in Eccl 8:2–9 differs among interpreters. Most treat 8:1–9 as a separate literary piece. Fox considers 8:1b–9 as a unit with different emphases.[149] Seow takes a larger unit, 8:1–17, to assert the theme of an arbitrary world.[150] J. A. Loader, who upholds polar structures in Ecclesiastes, also maintains the analysis of a polar structure in 8:2–9.[151] Garrett treats 8:1 as a transition from the preceding passage, also as a prologue to the entirety of 8:1–9.[152] Yet, at the same time, Garrett opines that Eccl 8:2 is the proper beginning. Garret's suggestion could be right, considering the

---

cites another Arabic cognate.

144. Seow, *Ecclesiastes*, 281 and 292, has pointed out that "no one knows what is going to happen" is repeated in 8:7. This will make the reading "a wise heart knows the time and judgment" here in 8:5 contradictory, hence improper. It should be, therefore, "a wise heart knows" about the following two observations in 8:6–7, both introduced by *kî*.

145. Horst in his *BHS* (Kittel et al.) critical apparatus points out *ăšer* instead of *ka'ăšer* is preferred; cf. Symmachus, Syriac and Vulgate.

146. The two occurrences of *rûaḥ* with definite articles in 8a are alternately "the wind" or "the spirit." The meaning of "the life" is adapted here as it anticipates *běyôm hammāwet* ("in the day of death") in 8b.

147. The *mišlaḥat* "discharge" is taken widely to mean exemption from war. Elsewhere, the word refers to the sending of an angel (Ps 78:49). When a king's subjects were sent to war, there is no reason for one to act otherwise. This is what Qoheleth probably has in mind when he says, "there is no discharge in a battle."

148. The critical apparatus of *BHS* (Kittel et al.) raises a question of emendation from *ršʻ* ("wickedness") to *ʻšr* ("wealth"). See Whitley, *Koheleth*, 74 and Longman, *Book of Ecclesiastes*, 210. There is also an effort to list the pattern of wisdom-related words, illustrate the negative notions in Qoheleth's conclusion in this literary unit, and critique the idea of emendation. See Beentjes, "Some Notes on Qoheleth 8, 1–15," 308–9.

149. Fox, *Time to Tear Down and a Time to Build Up*, 273.

150. Seow, *Ecclesiastes*, 276–77.

151. Loader, *Polar Structures*, 69–70. See also the polar structure of 7:23—8:1; ibid., 50.

152. Garrett, "Qoheleth on the Use and Abuse of Political Power," 168–69.

rhetorical question in 8:7b, "who can tell them?" forms an *inclusio* with that of 8:1a, "who is like the wise . . . who knows?" Nevertheless, 8:2–9 should be regarded as an entity.[153] Ecclesiastes 8:1 stands as a rhetorical question that concludes the preceding unit (7:26–8:1); it echoes the idea against foolishness. Also, it is typical of Qoheleth to usually recap *mî* ("who?") toward the end of his individual observations or statements (cf. 2:25; 3:21–22; 6:12; 7:13, 24; 8:7, 10:14). Further, Panc Beentjes advances a suggestion that *'ănî* ("I") in Eccl 8:2 recollects the *'ănî* in the royal persona in 1:12.[154] Accordingly, the vocabulary of Eccl 8:2–5 is an allusion to 1 Kgs 2:43, which is in part a narrative where king Solomon is given prominence. Beentjes has just pointed out, against his preference however, that *'ănî* begins a new section in Eccl 8:2 as of Eccl 1:12.[155]

One observes the presence of "keeping the command of the king" and "keeping one's oath to the LORD" in juxtaposition in Eccl 8:2, as well as 1 Kgs 2:43. Here, Qoheleth advances testimonials about God to the effect that God is the endorser of kings (Eccl 8:2). The idea of kingship in the ancient Near Eastern world relates closely with religion. Thus, "keep the command of the king as over the word of oath to God" is most probably the oath of allegiance taken at the king's coronation.[156] In consequence, a command given by a king is to be kept since one has made an oath before God to do so. Also, the "command" of the king, literally "mouth of the king," is of unquestionable authority recalling "mouth of YHWH" (cf. Num 14:41; 22:18; 1 Kgs 13:21).

Here in 8:2–5a, the caution that associates the king's command with the king's wrath parallels with *Proverbs of Ahiqar* from Elephantine during the Persian period.[157] Both texts teach on obedience to the king (Ahiqar 6:84, 93; cf. Eccl 8:2). They elaborate on kingly obedience in order to do no harm (Ahiqar 6:87–88; cf. Eccl 8:5).[158] Such obedience is indeed wise for survival in a royal court. Qoheleth utilizes familiar wisdom ideas common among people of that time to accentuate the supreme authority of the king and the powerlessness of his subjects. In so doing, Qoheleth gives counsel as to how to behave appropriately in the royal court. Therefore, Eccl 8:3 depicts that no one should resign from a position too hastily, even with a good

153. Longman, *Book of Ecclesiastes*, 209; Whybray, *Ecclesiastes*, 129.
154. Beentjes, "Some Notes on Qoheleth 8, 1–15," 306.
155. Ibid., 304.
156. See also Barton, *Critical and Exegetical Commentary*, 149.
157. Seow, *Ecclesiastes*, 290; Fox, *Time to Tear Down and a Time to Build Up*, 277, illustrates lines 101–104a of *the Proverbs of Ahiqar*.
158. This paralleling idea has been discussed in chapter 1. For the *Ahiqar* version, see Porten and Yardeni, *TAD*, 3: 36–37. See also Lindenberger, *Aramaic Proverbs of Ahiqar*, 81–86.

cause. The presence of the king designates a place near to political power, for one gets to see the king's face, *pānāyw*. The position near the king is instrumental in influencing political decisions, and it is unwise to renounce impulsively. "Standing in a harmful matter" refers to engaging an activity that may cause one hurt, such as a rebellion or a *coup d'état*.[159] It is dangerous to act tactlessly in the king's presence, especially when a king can do whatever he pleases. In light of Eccl 8:2, a king's word should not be questioned, let alone be challenged (8:4). It is precisely due to this absolute power that a king can easily abuse and corrupt. Thus, Qoheleth instructs readers in 8:5a that the king's power should be properly observed to avoid harmful political consequences, *dābār rā'*, such as incurring the king's displeasure (recalls *dābār rā'* in 8:3). Ecclesiastes 8:2–5a clearly shares the wisdom tradition that has shaped the *Proverbs of Ahiqar*, and it becomes Qoheleth's rhetoric to educate readers about observing political authority.

Facing autocracy, observing political authority is wise, and a wise person discerns that there is a time and judgment (8:5b–6). Qoheleth does not advocate slyness here. Rather, Qoheleth cautions against an immediate clash, which is inappropriate. When the political reality is very challenging, a wise person knows to act with diplomacy by concealing negative sentiments. Thus, Qoheleth warns against direct confrontation. He encourages instead the wise handling of courtly matters. One should know how to coexist with the political reality because the trouble of humankind is heavy upon them.[160] In view of the intimidating absolute power, a repetition of depicting the idea *rā'* ("evil") is certainly intentional in this passage (8:3, 5, 6, 9). Tyranny is indeed a serious political evil. William Anderson too asserts that part of Ecclesiastes' literary purpose is to expose the exploitative and oppressive nature of the aristocracy who have the power to do away with the problems.[161]

Qoheleth then continues to the crux of the matter, that "no one knows what is going to happen" (8:7). Here, Qoheleth's rhetorical question, "who can tell them what will happen?," is an oratory against the idea of absolute power in Eccl 8:4. No one knows what is going to happen, not even the one who has supreme authority that threatens everyone. Soon in 8:8, four counts of negative statements marked by *ĕn* and *lō*, underscore the powerlessness of the subjects. With this rhetoric, Qoheleth delivers his main twist of thought here, which stands as a direct challenge to absolute power he maintained earlier. "No one has mastery over the life to retain the life, and

---

159. Anderson, *Qoheleth and Its Pessimistic Theology*, 130.
160. Garrett, "Qoheleth on the Use and Abuse of Political Power," 170.
161. Anderson, *Qoheleth and Its Pessimistic Theology*, 130.

no one is a master in the day of death." Not even a master who possesses absolute power. This incapability of a master gives hope to people: a king's death liberates his subject from tyranny.[162] "There is no discharge in the battle" states one's compulsory service to the government; and it picks up the theme of control from 8:4 to remind the reader of the reality of people under the king's command. And "wickedness will not deliver its practiser" represents a statement that serves a dual purpose: to re-instate the avoidance of self-imposed trouble of the one being ruled, and to state the possible negative consequence of the one who rules. Abuse of political power is simply harmful to all people. Qoheleth continues and concludes in Eccl 8:9, with all the works that he has seen under the sun, "There is time that one ruled over the other to his own harm." Qoheleth hints that there is harm in an absolute political power. He repeatedly uses the cognate of rā' (translated as "harm," "evil," or "bad") in 8:3, 5, 6 and 9, except that the last usage ironically applies to the one who ruled over others. With the same thought from Eccl 8:6, Qoheleth advances an idea of hope: there will be a time and judgment whatever the present reality is.[163]

Political power is in the hands of the king, and powerlessness is the destiny of the subjects.[164] The passage here counsels wise subordination and diplomacy toward a ruler. This pointer is crucial given that the government of that time is of Persian rule. Persian policy allowed the colonized civilian to observe their own customs and native regulations. As long as they pay taxes, offer appropriate homage to the kings, and remain loyal subjects to the empire, they are generally safe from trouble. Under these circumstances, Qoheleth warns against unjustifiable rebellious actions. Qoheleth elucidates the political reality and the scale of problems in an oppressive power structure. The evil of such a power structure makes the job of a government officer even more responsible.[165] Wise government officials act prudently for the benefit of a larger society. Or else there will be more disastrous consequences (8:5, 10–14). Qoheleth's immediate concern is to minimize risk at the moment.[166] His political wisdom is therefore apparent in his following instructions. First, one is to keep the command of the king (8:2). Second, one does not leave one's position hastily due to an incident (8:3). Third, one should not plan harmful matter to avoid further hurt (8:3). It is wise to acknowledge that any occurrence of tyranny will expect judgment (8:6).

---

162. Fox, *Time to Tear Down and a Time to Build Up*, 280.
163. Jones, "Qoheleth's Courtly Wisdom," 226.
164. Loader, *Polar Structures*, 70.
165. Anderson, *Qoheleth and Its Pessimistic Theology*, 131.
166. Jones, "Qoheleth's Courtly Wisdom," 227.

Qoheleth's wisdom also is conveyed through his assertion that even an all-powerful king will have limitations (8:7–8). He points out that there is time when one rules over the other only to his own harm (8:9).

Ecclesiastes 10:4–7

> 4 If the anger[167] of the ruler[168] goes up against you, do not leave your place. For composure will calm many offences.
> 5 There is a misery I have seen under the sun, as an error which goes forth from the ruler.
> 6 The folly[169] is given in many high places, and the rich sit in low place.
> 7 I have seen servants on horses[170], and princes walking like servants on the ground.

Ecclesiastes 10:4–7 is another passage of Qoheleth's advice on proper behavior within a power structure. When one faces the anger of higher authority, self-control should be maintained. One should not leave the position after being intimidated by the wrath of those in power, for "composure will calm many offences." This advice makes one recall Eccl 8:3, where one is told not to be too dismayed and left one's position to engage in harmful behavior. Here again, one is advised to remain diplomatic in the event that the ruler's wrath is stirred. The use of the word *môšēl* ("ruler"), instead of *melek* ("king"; cf. 8:2), should be noted here. The "king" is concerned with the pinnacle of power structure in the central government. While the "ruler" here is local, provincial administration is in accordance to Persian satraps. Qoheleth targets the king in 8:2 (the central government) and here the ruler in 10:4 (the local government). He states here in 10:4–7 that defiance does no good to people who are being ruled in local administration (as in the central government in 8:2–9). Accordingly, staying in a position would amend situations. Otherwise, one may have caused offenses. Wisdom in the royal court asserts such composure not only for one's good but also for calming the situation. An angered ruler will be further offended by the

---

167. Literally, *rûaḥ* ("wind").

168. The difference between *melek* ("a king"; 8:2) and *môšēl* ("a ruler"; 10:4) is that the latter probably represents a local or provincial authority who also rules over others. See Fox, *Time to Tear Down and a Time to Build Up*, 304.

169. The *hapax legomena*, *hassekel*, is *ho afrōn* in LXX, Syriac, Targum and Vulgate, which is a noun *hussākāl* ("the fool"; 2:19; 7:17; 10:3). There is no difference in both meanings nevertheless.

170. There is a manuscript that adds *rokĕbîm* ("riding") before *'ăbādîm*. The meaning remains the same.

harsh reactions of a lower-ranking officer. The word *môšēl* ("ruler") appears again in Eccl 10:5. Hence the sayings in 10:5–7 should be treated as Qoheleth's illustration of the advice in 10:4. The misery that Qoheleth has seen in 10:5 (illustrated in 10:6–7) is a result if one has not stayed in position after a ruler's wrath (10:4). The text says that it is the error of the ruler, however, not of the counterpart who had decided to leave. Qoheleth seems to imply that the "misery" meant in 10:5 comes from the ruler's error in losing his temper, in light of the fact that "anger lodges in the bosom of fools" (cf. 7:9). Such rulers could have lost many good and competent subordinates. This yields to *rāʿâ*, human misery under the sun: the folly are given many high places, and the rich sit in a low place (10:6). And that servants are found on horses, while princes walk like servants on the ground (10:7). Qoheleth points out that "the folly" (the ones who lack sense; a thought that runs from Eccl 10:3) and "servants" (the ones who are not positioned at the decision-making platform) are incompetent people. Yet they occupy important offices in government bureaucracy. Such is the misery he has seen under the sun. The question of "unfairness" in society, due to the reverse treatment of "the folly–the rich" and "the servants–the princes," is secondary here. Qoheleth elaborates on human misery, not unfairness per se. The situation surely has to do with inappropriateness. And here Qoheleth indicates that the wrongs are not largely due to the ones in lower position. The wrongs often are due to the rulers. Fools are placed in positions of authority and power, resulting in a topsy-turvy society (cf. Prov 24:2; 30:22).[171] Qoheleth refocuses on the error of the ruler rather than on the offense of the one being ruled. He wants to make clear his point: composure is necessary in political survival. His admonition, "do not leave your place" when a ruler's anger is stirred (Eccl 10:4), is wise political counsel. Therefore, Qoheleth's political wisdom rests in this guidance on political survival of lower–ranking government officials. At the same time, he warns that decision makers could be wrong. Qoheleth affirms that competent people should be near to the power structure. They can then channel their ability toward the influential institution.

Ecclesiastes 10:16–20

> 16 Woe to you, O land, whose king is a boy, while your princes feast[172] in the morning!

---

171. Longman, *Book of Ecclesiastes*, 241–42.
172. Literally, *yōʾkēlû* ("they will eat").

17 Blessed are you, O land, whose king is a noble,[173] while your princes feast in the proper time, for strength and not for drunkenness![174]
18 By sluggishness[175] the beam-work collapses; by slackness of hands the house leaks.
19 One prepares a feast for laughter, while wine gladdens the living, and money occupies[176] everyone.
20 Even in your thought[177] do not curse the king, and in your bedroom do not curse the rich. For a bird in the sky will carry the voice, and a winged creature will make known the matter.

Ecclesiastes 10:16–17 denotes an obvious antithetical parallelism typical of proverbial wisdom. The *na'ar* ("a boy"), someone not of mature status to judge wisely, is set against *ben-ḥôrîm* ("a noble"). And the verb for feasting in the morning (an inappropriate time for a feast) juxtaposes feasting in the proper time. The literal meaning "they eat" should be understood as "they feast," as logically there is nothing wrong with eating in the morning. Besides, the presence of "drunkenness" in 10:17c supports the reading of feasting instead of eating. The word *leḥem* ("food") is for laughter, and the presence of *yayin* ("wine") in 10:19 further confirm this understanding. Ecclesiastes 10:17c, "for strength and not for drunkenness," is out of place in the parallelism. But it functions to point out the contrast further: feasting is set for the right purpose. There are two morals in the parallelism concerning feasting. One has to do with the proper timing of having a feast; the other has to do with its purpose in filling the stomach. Feasting in the morning certainly deters one from formal duty. It suggests the incapability of fulfilling one's responsibility. Drunkenness, on the other hand, suggests

173. Literally *ben-ḥôrîm* ("son of nobles").

174. The *hapax legomena*, *šĕtî* ("drunkenness") is verifiable in Esth 1:8 *šĕtîyyah* ("drinking"), another *hapax legomena*. In the critical apparatus of BHS (Kittel et al.), LXX reads *aischunthēsontai* as *(bĕ)bošet* ("shame") raising a question that some words might have dropped out. A feast is most probably meant in light of the idea of feasting that runs through the literary unit, where drinking is usually expected.

175. The feminine dual form of *'aṣaltayim* ("sluggishness") only occurs here in the Hebrew Bible (cf. its feminine singular form only occurs in Prov 19:15), and it connects "slackness of hand," which means "laziness."

176. Seow, who treats Eccl 10:16–20 as risks in the political realm, suggests taking *ya'ăneh* as a hiphil verb to consider Qoheleth's criticism of the elite: "money preoccupies everyone" rather than "money answers everything." Seow, *Ecclesiastes*, 332–33; 338–41.

177. The critical apparatus of BHS (Kittel et al.) notes a possible emendation from *maddā' 'ăkā* to *maṣṣĕ 'ăkā*, "your couch" in light of parallelism with "your bedroom." However, *bĕmaddā' 'ăkā*, "in your thought" or "in your mind," is a meaningful hyperbole, "do not even think about it!" Attested to in 1QS 7.3; 7.5 and 6.9 and Aramaic usage in *Targum* Psalms 34:1. See Fox, *Time to Tear Down and a Time to Build Up*, 310.

an excessiveness of drinking while feasting, thus self-indulgence. In sum, self-control and personal orderliness are crucial for political leaders. This conduct-related counsel is typical of Proverbs and is reminiscent of ancient Near Eastern wisdom texts like *Instruction of Amenemope* and the *Proverbs of Ahiqar*.

The reading also can be rendered satirically. Qoheleth hints at self-indulgence at a high level of political hierarchy. The self-indulgence is disastrous when a nation has a king who is yet a grown-up. For his reliance depends on competent leaders in the ruling class. Hence 10:16-17 can be read both ways, affirmatively and critically. The double entendre as to whether one should read it affirmatively or critically is intended. Such ambiguity is a rhetoric of Qoheleth.

With this parallelism, Qoheleth conveys the case in point in 10:18-19, where a political satire is clearly discernible. "By sluggishness the beam-work collapses//by slackness of hands the house leaks." Thus, 10:18 is a parallelism in itself. "Sluggishness" connects with "slackness of hand," which means laziness. By the same token, beam-work (or roof) parallels "house," and "collapses" parallels "leaks." Ecclesiastes 10:18 contains another double entendre. By taking its natural meaning, it is a proverb advising diligence for building a household. Yet by rendering a critical understanding, it is a parody against the power structure. The "house" also could mean a dynasty, and the "beam-work" implies the political framework of a government.[178] Qoheleth aims to warn against the laziness of those who hold political power. Such laziness potentially crumples a state.

Further, the triplets in 10:19 concern the subject matter of the rich and the powerful whose focuses are on feast, wine, and money. The feast (literally, "food") here recalls the feasts in 10:16-17, so thoughts on the subject of princes are connected.[179] "Money occupies everyone" implies the idea of greed, even corruption. In sum, 10:19 aims to deliver a political ridicule against the lifestyle of the powerful and the rich. They feast, drink, and are preoccupied with money. In retrospect, 10:16-17 too implies that they feast at the wrong time and drink too much. Qoheleth is indirectly pressing against the misbehavior of the ruling class, as well as the elite. He asserts the value of having a mature king and leaders who govern wisely rather than engage in feast, drunkenness, and greed. Therefore, the text of 10:18-19 does not dwell on the thought of wisdom and folly in regard to wisdom

---

178. See "house of David" in 1 Kgs 12:19; 2 Chr 10:19; 2 Kgs 17:21; Isa 7:2; 22:22; Jer 21:12. See also Seow, *Ecclesiastes*, 331 and 340.

179. Fox, *Time to Tear Down and a Time to Build Up*, 309, states the subjects here clearly refer back to 10:16, namely the princes and the nobility.

theology only, as Chin-Wen Chen suggests.[180] The text specifically concerns a political dimension in wisdom thought.

Ecclesiastes 10:20 does not seem to fit in with the thought that runs so far in 10:16–19. Qoheleth ends here with a warning not to criticize the powerful and the rich, yet Qoheleth himself has been criticizing them so far. But again, this is precisely why Qoheleth uses parody to make his point clear indirectly. Direct criticisms against the political establishment are unwise, even though they are done in a bedroom presumably with someone who can be trusted. Words may be spread out through "a bird" and "a winged creature," possibly referring to informants who carry messages. A passage in the *Proverbs of Ahiqar* from Elephantine that was circulated during the Persian period, echoes similar courtly advice:

> do not curse the day until you have seen the light,
> do not let it come upon your mind,
> since their eyes and their ears are everywhere.
> ... for a word is a bird and one who releases it is without sense.[181]

A brief look into the political background is useful for illuminating one's understanding of the text in Eccl 10:20. The ancient Persian royal family or the Achaemenid dealt with quite a number of rebellions during its conquest.[182] Until the years of Artaxerxes I (464–425 BCE) and Artaxerxes II (405–359 BCE), rebellions were frequent, not only from the conquered nations but also within the royal family.[183] Under these circumstances, words that reflect anti-government sentiments became highly sensitive in the royal court. The king functioned at the highest level of classified society. He remained centralized in the royal court and did not often interfere with local affairs.[184] Since the empire was organized into provinces (satrapies),

---

180. Chen, "Study of Ecclesiastes 10:18–19," 117, 125.

181. See Porten and Yardeni, *TAD*, 3:37 (column 6, lines 80–82); quoted and translated in Seow, *Ecclesiastes*, 63.

182. Young, "Persians," 297. Herodotus (3.67–88) and Darius' Bisitun inscription (I. 71–72) recorded an early rebellion concerning a Median priest, Gaumata, who impersonated Cambyses' royal brother, Bardiya. Widespread rebellions soon followed, especially in the first year of Darius' kingship, started in Elam and Babylon, and later in many parts of the empire. Darius, who was a competent general, succeeded in commanding the situation; his son, Xerxes (486–465 BCE) who assumed the task of Persian conquest, too had to put down rebellions in Babylon and Egypt. Numerous revolts recurred in the later part of Persian history.

183. There is Greek evidence in the form of inscriptions and documents regarding how Persian kings dealt with the revolts from Bactria and Egypt. See Brosius, *Persian Empire*, 57–60. Young, "Persians," 298.

184. Young, "Persians," 299.

each ruled by a governor (satrap), the governors were the king's trusted ones, functioning as the king's "eyes" or "ears."[185] These royal secret agents were members of Persian nobility. They are often relatives of the king or a noble Persian who had married into the royal family.[186] They had local grasp within their administration. They travelled and reported to the king about any possibility of revolt. Hence, the empire's control of the provinces was indirectly facilitated by the presence of royal informants.

Interestingly, West Semitic archival documents illustrate a similar depiction of the king's officials who functioned as royal spies. Among Ugaritic letters excavated at Ras Shamra in 1929, there were in-coming and outgoing letters of the royal courts. One of them, namely *Tiptiba'lu (Shibti-ba'lu) to the King* (RS 18.040) that was published by Virolleaud (1965:90, no. 63), depicts the author with the name *Tiptiba'lu*, who was the king's son-in-law, addressing the king of Ugarit saying:

> As for your servant, in Lawasanda I am keeping an eye (on the situation) along with the king. Now the king has just left in haste to SYR, where he is sacrificing MLG[GM]. The king, my master, must know (this).[187]

This ancient document points to a trusted official of the king of Ugarit who operated as the latter's eyes and ears in Cilicia.[188] Many other West Semitic archival documents display contents that identify the sending of words to the royal court, for example, to the queen.[189] Some documents mention someone's name to the king.[190] Some others sent messages to the king in order that the king could investigate an enquiry.[191] The historical information illumines Ecclesiastes. This background is helpful for interpreting Eccl 10:20. Thomas Krüger has maintained that Eccl 10:20 should not be taken at face value, for it is an advice to provoke readers to act in exactly the opposite way.[192] Non-Persians who are serving the foreign imperial court were aware of the supporting political coalitions in the local imperial

---

185. Ibid., 298.

186. Brosius, *Persian Empire*, 62.

187. Hallo and Younger, *COS*, 3:104.

188. Ibid.

189. Specifically, a correspondence between members of the royal family, *Talmiyanu to His Mother Tarriyelli* (RS 15.008); see Hallo and Younger, *COS*, 3:89.

190. For example, *Getting One's Name before the King* (RS [Varia 4]); see Hallo and Younger, *COS*, 3:114.

191. Namely, *From an Official in Alashia to the King* (RS 18.113A+B); see Hallo and Younger, *COS*, 3:104.

192. Krüger, "Meaningful Ambiguities," 71.

rule. They also were aware of the political culture within the royal court. Qoheleth's saying in 10:20 reflects such awareness. In this reading, Seow comments more eloquently about what one has in this passage:

> [It] is a parody of subversive political comments in Qoheleth's time. The perpetrators were apparently taking jabs at the political establishment, but they were doing so through what they thought were the safe havens of sapiential forms. They were criticizing the rulers and aristocrats but pretending that they were only proffering disinterested wisdom teachings.[193]

Reflections on Socio-Political Reality

Ecclesiastes 3:16–17[194]

> 16 Besides, I saw under the sun that in the place of justice,[195] there was wickedness; and in the place of righteousness, there was wickedness.
> 17 I said in my heart, "God will judge the righteous and the wicked, for there is a time for every matter and for every work there."[196]

The conjunction *wĕ 'ôd* before *rā'îtî* in 3:16 serves double functions of indicating a new unit and continuing the observation activity (*rā'îtî*; 3:10) from the preceding unit. As such, Garrett's judgment to tie in 3:15c (to make up 3:15c–17) has ignored this conjunction.[197] Qoheleth saw the

---

193. Seow, *Ecclesiastes*, 340.

194. Ecclesiastes 3:16–17 belongs to a larger literary piece which is loosely connected, namely Eccl 3:16–22. Ecclesiastes 3:16–17 states the problem (wickedness), elaborated in a different subject matter (death) in 3:18–21, before a conclusion in 3:22. This larger idea is in the thought and a brief discussion notwithstanding.

195. The two-fold particle adverb *šāmmâ* ("there") in Eccl 3:16 makes it unlikely that "the place of justice" is the object of the verb *rā'îtî* as the LXX and Vulgate suggest. Thus, "in the place of justice," (so NKJV and NRSV) is correct, and the object of the verb "*rā'îtî*" is *hārešaʿ* ("wickedness"), which occurs twice in 3:16.

196. The word *šām* ("there") leaves no clue as to what it refers. Seow, *Ecclesiastes*, 166–67 takes it to mean "there is a destiny" corresponding to Akkadian *šimtu*. I take the word as connecting the same particle adverb "*šāmmâ*" in 3:16. Meaning, a time for judgment "in the places of justice and righteousness"; "*šām*" ("there") thus refers to "the places of justice and righteousness."

197. Garrett, "Qoheleth on the Use and Abuse of Political Power," 160–62. Garrett reads, "God seeks the persecuted" in order to introduce the subject matter of oppression and injustice. Garrett reasons that the discussion in 3:11–15b was introduced with the concept of political injustice in 3:15c, "God seeks the persecuted," because "oppression

occupation of humankind in 3:10; now he sees also wickedness. Twice *rešaʿ* is used with definite article to stress what he saw in 3:16. The root *ršʿ* occurs for the third time as an adjective in 3:17, also with a definite article. The three-fold *ršʿ* conveys the very concern of Qoheleth: wickedness abounds in a numerous scale. The three-fold "there" (twice as *šāmmâ*, once as *šām*) likewise communicates that repeated wickedness occurs ironically in place of justice and righteousness. "Justice" and "righteousness" form a word-pair reflecting a social order. And Fox's opinion that this word pair is an equivalent to *mišpāṭ ṣedeq* ("righteous judgment")[198] is unlikely. The pair is here rendered to intensify Qoheleth's observation of repeated wickedness, where "justice and righteousness" should abide. The crowded city gates are the scene of the ancient court house, hence are probably what the places of "justice and righteousness" meant here. The city gates also are active economically. They are places near to where people work, conduct business, and meet people. But here in the city gates, wickedness occurs repeatedly. The pairing of "righteousness-wickedness" in Eccl 3:16 recurs as adjectives "righteous-wicked" in 3:17.[199] Ecclesiastes 3:16 seems to contrast righteousness against wickedness, but 3:17 ironically places them on par, suggesting that God will judge both in due time.

Ecclesiastes 3:16 depicts a reversal of social order embedded in wisdom's creation theology. It is thus no surprise that "God will judge" comes as a comforting outlook in 3:17. Judgment is in the hands of God. "For there is a time for every matter and for every work," recalling the catalogue of time and event in 3:1–8. The timing *ʿēt*, in light of 3:1–8, refers to a potential occurrence at *a* time in human life. Contrary to what Franz Delitzsch believes, the time need not refer to an eschatological judgment.[200] A right social order can be re-instated in due time in human history. The word *šām* ("there") in 3:17 is silent in most English translations. Yet, in my opinion, it alludes to "the place of justice" and "the place of righteousness" in 3:16. Having God in the picture now, *šām* refers to the divine place of justice and righteousness. Since there is wickedness abounding in human places of *mišpāṭ*, God will

---

and injustice, more than anything else, fill a man's heart with bitterness and sorrow and make it impossible to live according to the philosophy recommended in verses 11–14, of accepting one's lot in life with contentment."

198. Fox, *Time to Tear Down and a Time to Build Up*, 214.

199. Unlike the LXX and Targum, which read "the righteous//the wicked" in 3:16, anticipating the same pairing in 3:17. See Seow, *Ecclesiastes*, 166.

200. Delitzsch, *Commentary on the Song of Songs and Ecclesiastes*, 266. Seow, *Ecclesiastes*, 166, declines the idea of eschatological judgment as the meaning of "time" here.

šāpāṭ ("judge") "there."²⁰¹ So the fact that "God will judge" is comforting, as it can happen at any time in God's hands.

There is a blow to the wicked in 3:18–19 that suggests their being "is" that of the animal, not "like" the animal. And that "God will judge the righteous and the wicked" in 17b is consistent with "for every work" *maʿăśeh* in 17c, where *maʿăśeh* can be human work (cf. 2:17; 4:4; 5:5; 8:9), evil work (cf. 4:3; 8:11), or God's work (cf. 3:11; 7:13; 8:17; 11:5; 12:14). Indeed, God will judge not only the wicked but also the righteous, the bad deed and also the good deed. The judgment of God hence carries a positive meaning: not only the evil work will be adjudicated but also the righteous work will be made known. Here Qoheleth's political wisdom is articulated through his observation of numerous wickedness occurring in society. He envisages God's judgment in this reality. Qoheleth describes the socio-political reality rather than giving instruction for proactive measure. Despite the lack of justice and righteousness, Qoheleth draws in the reality of timing and divine judgment. Therefore, Qoheleth recommends rejoicing for the moment in one's own work (3:22), in spite of wickedness that is in sight.

In sum, Qoheleth looks to the royal court, the judicial systems, and the city gates—the place of justice and righteousness—expecting to see justice and righteousness. But he saw *repeated* wickedness. A prophet would surely cry out in furious protest, calling for the day of the Lord. Qoheleth is no less moved by what he saw either, affirming that God will judge in due time.²⁰² Ecclesiastes 3:16–17 acknowledges that wickedness in judicial administration is present, real, and recurrent. Only God can set right the evil in due time of human history. The how and when God is going to do that is concealed to human comprehension. Qoheleth simply points to God to vindicate the situation. The time of this judgment is spontaneous. It is as spontaneous as the occurrences of life and death, planting and plucking, weeping and laughing, silence and speaking, and the like.

---

201. Underlined in my translation.
202. Garrett, "Qoheleth on the Use and Abuse of Political Power," 162.

Ecclesiastes 4:1–3[203]

> 1 Again, I turned and saw all the oppressions which are done under the sun. And look![204] Tears of the oppressed![205] But they have no comforter; while from the hand[206] of their oppressors, is power. Yet, they have no comforter![207]
> 2 So I commend[208] the dead who[209] have already died, more than the living who are still alive.
> 3 Still, better than the two of them is the one who has never been, who has not seen the evil work which is done under the sun.

Ecclesiastes 4:1–3 marks the beginning of a literary unit (4:1–16) as Qoheleth "turned" to a new observation. Here stands a literary unit that illustrates a series of *tôb-spruch* ("better-than") sayings. The *waw*-consecutive imperfect of *rā'â* in Eccl 4:1 follows a series of Qoheleth's "seeing" activities in Eccl 3:10, 16, and 22. Qoheleth kept observing and reflecting. Now he turned and saw again. His eyes set on oppressions in human society, the life "under the sun." This phrase "under the sun" is a this-worldliness expression

---

203. Ecclesiastes 4:1–3 belongs to a larger 4:1–16, where series of *tôb-spruch* ("better-than") sayings are located. Ecclesiastes 4:1–3 and 4:13–16 will be discussed in this chapter with different subject matters respectively.

204. "*Wĕhinneh*" ("And look!") indicates a common perception or recognition from both Qoheleth and his readers. It is an exclamation to depict the immediate scene of events such as oppression.

205. The same qal passive participle *hā 'ăšûqîm* occurs twice in 4:1 but should be translated differently. The first occurrence should be "oppressions," in light of the niphal participle *'śh* ("done"); while the second occurrence should be "oppressed" in light of the construct noun *dim'at* ("tear"). The singular "tear" is taken as a plurality here.

206. *Miyyad* is "from the hand" as it stands in the text and presumes the action of going forth; it is not necessary to emend it to *bĕyad* ("in the hand") to indicate possession of power, as Fox, *Time to Tear Down and a Time to Build Up*, 219, as well as others, suggests.

207. The critical apparatus in Kittel et al., *BHS*, points out the word *mĕnahēm* ("comfort") has been proposed to be *mĕnaqqēm* ("avenger"); but cf. 3:16 where there is a repetition of "wickedness"; hence, here a repetition of "comfort" should be expected.

208. Qoheleth's usage of an infinitive absolute *šabbēah* ("to commend") instead of a finite verb, is peculiar in Hebrew. Schoors, *Preacher Sought to Find Pleasing Words*, I: 178, points out its wide acceptance nonetheless by Rashbam, Barton, Gordis, Hertberg, Whitley, and more. Some take it as a verbal adjective, as a perfect tense, as an abbreviated form of the perfect, or as an emendation to *šbḥty*. Elsewhere, Fox, *Time to Tear Down and a Time to Build Up*, 219, comments that it cannot be explained as consequential, epexegetical, nor as a gerund; and asserts that the piel infinitive *šabbēah* is declarative, hence "I declare."

209. *Še* ("who") is a late biblical Hebrew typical of Ecclesiastes, and is taken as *'ăšer*, as in 4:3.

attested to in ancient Near Eastern texts. It denotes a universality of human experience reminiscent of a less frequently rendered phrase, "under the heaven" (1:13; 2:3; 3:1). It means simply the realm of living.[210] In this realm of living, Qoheleth saw "all the oppression," a phrase not likely to mean literally, but to convey the extent and kinds of oppression in human society.[211] Further, the root for the verb ʿšq ("oppress") occurs thrice in Eccl 4:1. This recalls the three-fold occurrence of the root ršʿ ("wicked") in Eccl 3:16–17, again indicating repeated occurrences of oppression here.

The word *kōaḥ* in Eccl 4:1 refers to human "strength" or "power," including political power (Josh 17:17; Dan 8:22), human ability (to get wealth, Deut 8:18) and efficiency (in battle, 2 Chr 14:10).[212] The word is elsewhere applicable to that of God (Jer 10:12 in creation; Ps 29:4 in governing the world; Exod 15:6 in deliverance and judgment). The power "from" the hand of the oppressors in Eccl 4:1 presumes the action of going forth. It means here an oppressive use of power.[213] And in light of Eccl 4:3, Qoheleth refers to the ability of humans to exercise evil unto others when they are capable of it. This power may come from a social status like that of aristocrats, from an economic privilege as with the rich, or from a bureaucratic jurisdiction as with, for instance, government officials. Naturally, from here one can ruminate who represents the oppressed ones in a human society. They were the poor, the commoners, or the civilians.

Qoheleth does not spell out explicitly from whose hand has the power here in Eccl 4:1, perhaps for an unspeakable reason. Yet the text does specify that they have power: the power to protect the people and the authority to govern a society. It is possible that Qoheleth implies the officials of authority. Qoheleth's eyes are set on the oppressed. He thus invites his reader to look at their own tears. Twice Qoheleth points out that the oppressed ones have no one to comfort them. Each time, it begins with the conjunction *wĕ*, meaning not "and" but "yet," taken to mean that comfort is expected to be otherwise shown to them. Qoheleth finds the lack of comfort for the oppressed as offensive. His disappointment brings him to commend the dead as better than the living. Even better is the one who has never existed (4:2–3). It is because the dead and the non-existent do not have to endure seeing this evil in human society, the life "under the sun." Qoheleth is not being pessimistic here, nor does he hint at the prospect of suicide. Rather, he is reflecting a common thought among the powerless. Their hands are too short to right

---

210. Seow, *Ecclesiastes*, 104–5.
211. Ibid., 186.
212. Brown et al., *BDB*, 470.
213. Barton, *Critical and Exegetical Commentary*, 114.

wrongs, and they have no one to comfort them. Also, Qoheleth's words are analogous to an ancient Near Eastern text, *The Admonition of Ipuwer* from Egypt, whose persona is recorded by saying, "I wish I were dead," and little children echoing, "He should not have made me live!"[214] More importantly, this "better-than" assertion comes after Qoheleth's conclusion in Eccl 3:22, that "nothing is better" than for one to rejoice in his work.[215] "Nothing is better" than to enjoy oneself should stay in view when reading Qoheleth's "better is the one who has never been" in Eccl 4:1–3. Reading Eccl 4:1–3 in light of Eccl 3:22 brings the idea of one's *ḥēleq* ("lot"). This idea of "lot" always entails a constructive value in Ecclesiastes (Eccl 3:22; 5:17, 18).

The repetition of the related terms "oppressions," "oppressed," and "oppressors," and the dramatic "look!," as well as the use of emotive words like "tears" and "comfort," combine to produce an effect of emotional intensity.[216] Such emotional intensity is rare for Qoheleth. That oppressions happened in human society clearly troubles Qoheleth. Social values and power structures no longer function meaningfully. Qoheleth makes it clear that the ones who are oppressed are those without power, because those who have power are the oppressors. The oppressions that occur in human society will likely recur as long as there is the existence of a power structure. In this regard, Qoheleth commends those who had died and those who are non-existent, for they do not have to endure seeing the oppression in human society. Qoheleth's thought is burdened by the ideas of death and the unborn in a moment of grief.[217] Those who have died and those who have never been are better off than the living. Qoheleth asserts that as long as a mortals live to see daylight, surely one sees the reality of social oppression and pain. Therefore, Qoheleth's wisdom lies in his honest reflections on the painful reality of living within a human social structure. Surely a reading in light of the previous literary unit, Eccl 3:22, is necessary: "there is nothing better than a human to enjoy their work, for that is their lot. Who can bring them to see what will be after them?" Oppressions occur every now and then. No one who is living can elude this painful reality. As long as one lives within an oppressive power structure, one still needs to move on. Qoheleth's political wisdom here rests in his honest reflection of this reality and his pointer to enjoy one's work as one's lot.

---

214. Lichtheim, *AEL*, 1:153; see also Seow, *Ecclesiastes*, 178.
215. Seow, *Ecclesiastes*, 186.
216. Whybray, *Ecclesiastes*, 81.
217. Fox, *Time to Tear Down and a Time to Build Up*, 220.

Ecclesiastes 4:13–16

> 13 Better is a youth who is a commoner[218] but wise, than a king who is old but foolish, who no longer knows to be admonished.[219]
> 14 For *one* went forth from prison[220] to rule, but *the other* was born into his kingdom, is poor.[221]
> 15 I saw that all the living who are walking under the sun are with the second youth who will raise instead of him.
> 16 There is no end to all the people, to all who are before him, even who are after him. They do not rejoice in him. Surely, this is vanity and a pursuit of wind.

Ecclesiastes 4:13–16 is the last of the *Tôb-Spruch* "better-than" sayings series in 4:1–16. Many treat 4:13–16 as an anecdote.[222] Some argue for its historical references.[223] The historicity of this literary piece is nevertheless subjective. None of the suggested historical characters fits this depiction completely. Thus, 4:13–16 should be read as an anecdote. It is typical of wisdom literature to draw on anecdotes to make a point. Therefore, one has here an anecdote that is set in two parts: wisdom sayings (4:13–14) and reflections (4:15–16), typical of Qoheleth's style.

---

218. The word *miskēn* ("commoner") (4:13) is often taken as "poor," but a social status rather than an economic one is probably meant here; it is attested from Old Akkadian and Old Babylonian for people of ordinary status. See Seow, *Ecclesiastes*, 183.

219. Textual variants point to multiple meanings of "*lĕhizzāhēr*," which itself has at least two meanings: "admonish" and "take care of." Most commentators favor "admonish," but LXX has *tou prosecein* ("take heed"), Targum has *arhdza*, suggesting the king's inability to grasp the consequences of divine action rather than refusal to take advice. Vulgate has *praevidere in posterum* ("to foresee the future"), suggesting a lack of foresight. Rudman, "Contextual Reading of Ecclesiastes 4:13–16," 60.

220. Masoretic text here, *hāsûrîm* may stand for *hā'ăsûrîm*; it is supported by LXX, Peshita, and Vulgate. Gordis, *Koheleth-the Man and His Word*, 244 points out similar occurrences of *hărammîm* in 2 Chr 22:5 and *'ărammîm* in 2 Kgs 8:28.

221. The pronouns and subjects of the verbs here, in fact the whole 4:13–16, are ambiguous. Here literally, "For *he* went forth from prison to rule, while also *he* was born into his kingdom but poor." Two characters, namely the commoner and the king, are involved. The presence of two *kî* clauses in Eccl 4:14 gives the rationale for the "better-than" saying in 4:13, with the first *kî* referring to the destiny of the youth, and the second *kî* to the fate of the old king. See Seow, *Ecclesiastes*, 183–84. The personal pronouns are refined in my translation following Seow's to make better sense.

222. For example, Weisman, "Elements of Political Satire," 547–60; Fox, "What Happens in Qoheleth 4:13–16," 1; Longman, *Book of Ecclesiastes*, 144.

223. Notably, Ogden, "Historical Allusion in Qoheleth IV 13–16?" 309–15; and Rudman, "Contextual Reading of Ecclesiastes 4:13–16," 57.

A young but wise commoner is set in contrast to and in favor of an old but foolish king. The comparisons here are typical of wisdom literature. The ideas of young and old, wise and foolish, a commoner and a king are set in comparison. The association of being "old" to the idea of being "foolish" is subtle, for an old king is not necessarily foolish. That is why the conjunction *wĕ* in *wûkĕšîl* should be "but" instead of "and" (4:13). The text further indicates the reason for this judgment. The old king will no longer be admonished or taking counsels. When a king does not listen to advice anymore, he acts solely on his political authority, amounting to foolishness. The "poorness" of the youth in 4:13 only comes in 4:14 when he was depicted as going forth from a "prison."[224] Qoheleth may be depicting a wisdom tale familiar to the readers or may be alluding to political events that were well known. Yet placing historical references aside, Qoheleth does not disclose any identity here. Qoheleth is more interested in asserting a point rather than an identity in this anecdote.

There is ambiguity in 4:14–15 about how many characters are involved. This is due to the obscure subjects in 4:14 and the third masculine singular (3ms) suffix at the end of 4:15.[225] Also, it is not clear whether the third masculine singular (3ms) subject in 4:14 depicts only one but the same youth mentioned earlier. These difficulties have caused considerable interpretive debates. There is also a lack of immediate historical reference to illuminate its *Sitz im Leben*. There are most probably two characters involved in 4:14, namely the young but wise commoner and the old but foolish king who are depicted in the preceding verse. The same youth from 4:13 has now become a ruler in 4:14, it seems. At the same time, the king from 4:13, though born into royalty, has now become *rāš* ("poor"). He was deprived of his dynasty.[226] Hence the parallelism between the young but wise commoner and an old but foolish king is still in view.[227] The young but wise commoner is meant in the third masculine singular (3ms) of *taḥtāyw* ("instead of him") in 4:15. A second youth now rises to take the place of the earlier "young but wise commoner," who had earlier gone forth to take the place of the "old but foolish king" in 4:14. The dynamic of taking over one's political power is at play in the passage. The people surely follow a new leader in the beginning. Yet

---

224. A "prison" is a place of imprisonment for political and economic reasons in the ancient Near Eastern world, probably to pay off a family debt. See Seow, *Ecclesiastes*, 184 and 190.

225. Most interpreters understand from one youth (the old king's immediate successor), to two youths (the wise youth and his successor). Fox, "What Happens in Qoheleth 4:13–16," 2, suggests a third youth: the youth called "*hayyled haššēnî*" in 4:15.

226. Seow, *Ecclesiastes*, 184–85.

227. Pinker, "Qoheleth 4, 13–16," 182.

soon they will not rejoice in the leader anymore, and the cycle goes on. The point is not only the recurrent take-overs, but also how soon one's political power comes to an end. And Qoheleth sees there is no end (4:16) to these political takeovers. There is short-lived popularity of a new ruler. And there is an ephemeral glory of power. Political power cannot stand the historical test. Hence, he judges it as a *hebel* ("vanity")[228] and a pursuit of wind. The word *hebel* ("vanity") contains a meaning of "ephemeral and short-lived realities" as of vapor or breath (for instance 4:16; 6:12). The word here is an expression of a futile political pursuit. The popularity associated with political leadership is unpredictable and uninformed. From this anecdote, Qoheleth illustrates that political power is short-lived. This reading is logical in the present position of 4:13–16. And Charles Torrey's effort to import 10:16–17 immediately after 4:13 for an alleged "lacuna" in the Hebrew text, has made this difficult text even more obscure and confused.[229]

Wisdom is prized in the political realm, but it has no lasting value. When people hold power in their hands but fail to be counseled, they fail to discern the sentiment and the needs of their subjects. Qoheleth sets ridicule against wisdom in this passage. He begins with a "better-than" judgment: the young but wise commoner is better than the old but foolish king. Yet he ends with no existential difference between the youth and the old king in the political arena. Despite the superiority of the wise over the fool, their fates are alike.[230]

Irony is one of the literary characteristics in Ecclesiastes, especially here. Ze'ev Weisman suggests three satirical barbs in this passage.[231] The first satire is directed against the old but foolish king who was no longer

---

228. The word *hebel* ("vanity") carries a semantic that includes: 1) of ephemeral and short-lived realities, as of vapor or breath (Eccl 4:16; 6:12); 2) insubstantial (Eccl 1:17; 2:17); 3) worthless (Jer 10:15; 51:18); 4) fruitlessness (Eccl 1:2; 2:14–15); and 5) uselessness (Jer 2:5, 2 Kgs 17:15; Prov 13:11). Cf. Brown et al., *BDB*, 210. The list goes on as scholars have suggested more of its meanings: "enigmatic and mysterious" (Ogden), "futility" (Fox), "ephemerality and absurdity" (Crenshaw), "beyond human comprehension" (Seow). See Ingram, *Ambiguity in Ecclesiastes*, 91–129, for a full chapter searching for the precise meaning of *hebel* by surveying scholars' working definitions and concluding that "the use of *hebel* in *Ecclesiastes* is ambiguous, . . . it is unclear precisely what it refers to and because it often open to more than one interpretation" (129). In view of the many possible meanings to the word "*hebel*," Seow is accurate to point out it being an "imagery of a futile pursuit" for matters beyond the grasp of mortals, both physically and intellectually. Things that are associated with *hebel* are hence unpredictable, arbitrary, and incomprehensible. Seow, *Ecclesiastes*, 102.

229. Torrey, "Problem of Ecclesiastes 4:13–16," 176; see also Pinker, "Qoheleth 4,13–16," 181.

230. Weisman, "Elements of Political Satire in Kohelet," 551.

231. Ibid., 552.

capable of taking advice and lost his kingdom. The second one is aimed at the poor but wise youth who met with the very same fate after obtaining power by deposing his predecessor. The third satire is directed at the masses. They are fickle and alter their opinions with the change of rulership. Weisman's suggestion seems probable, except that he concludes, "Koheleth can do nothing other than despair when presenting the concluding moral" in 4:16b.[232] If the irony is Qoheleth's rhetoric, he intends to convey something other than despair. The political world is indeed highly unstable, ever changing, and dangerous.[233] Wisdom, despite being a better choice, cannot guarantee one's success in the royal court. Surely there will be one taking over another. Indeed, there is a time to rule and a time to lose one's rule (a reading with 3:1–8 in mind). Here, Qoheleth's sarcasm is pointing at the recurrent takeovers by political superpowers, first by Assyria, then Babylon, and now Persia. Thus, Qoheleth is not being despairing or pessimistic, as Weisman suggests.[234] Rather, he points out a possibility that soon there will be a time for the king to be deprived of his power. Qoheleth's political satire rests in his indication of Persians soon passing dominion. They will have short-lived popularity. Qoheleth raises attention to the present reality: an existing king will be replaced by others soon. His political wisdom conveyed through this anecdote is that popularity associated with political leadership is short-lived. Rather than despair, Qoheleth prepares his readers for a possible new turn in political arena. The new turn, however, is also elusive for mortals to grasp. On the role of wisdom in this passage, wisdom's practical value is limited and transient.[235] But it is important to note that wisdom still has relative *advantage* notwithstanding.

Ecclesiastes 9:13–16

>13 This also I have seen under the sun, wisdom,[236] and it seems great to me.

---

232. Ibid.
233. Garrett, "Qoheleth on the Use and Abuse of Political Power," 165.
234. Weisman, "Elements of Political Satire in Koheleth," 549 and 552.
235. Fox, "What Happens in Qoheleth 4:13–16," 1.
236. The word *ḥokmâ* ("wisdom") is deleted by some since a question was pointed out in Kittel et al., *BHS*' critical apparatus. Fox, *A Time to Tear Down and a Time to Build Up*, 297–98, omits the whole word for the reason that *ḥokmâ*, by being an opposite predicative complement, does not fit the whole passage where wisdom is wronged. But the word is the direct object of "*rā'îtî*" ("I have seen"), the object that *zōh* ("this") refers to.

14 There was a small city with few people in it. And a great king came against it, besieged it, and built great siege-works[237] against it.

15 He found[238] in it a wise commoner[239], that he delivered the city by his wisdom. But, no one remembered the very commoner!

16 So I said, "Wisdom is better than might; but the wisdom of the commoner is despised, and his words are not heeded."

Weisman regards 9:13–16 as the second anecdote of political satire in the book after 4:13–16.[240] Weisman opines that the anecdote is a reflection of different events united into a single formation, not a report of a particular historical occurrence.[241] He further points out that the satirical elements in the anecdote rest on historical allusions.[242] However, attempts to locate the story in history have not satisfied most interpreters. The ambiguities with regard to historicity are perhaps intended to serve universal phenomena. Hence the attempts to locate the story in history are not necessary, considering Qoheleth's point is an ironic one.

There are three counts of comparisons in 9:13–16: great against small; a king against a commoner; and wisdom against might. First, the comparison of the idea of greatness (thrice in 9:13–14) against smallness operates in a larger thought spreading across 9:13–10:3. The anecdote begins with the siege of a "small city" by a "great king" who built a "great siege-work" surrounding it. The doubling of the root *gdl* ("great") in 9:14 is intended to anticipate the efficacy of wisdom against them in 9:15. The invading king found a wise commoner who thwarted his invasion and delivered the city by

---

237. Two manuscripts, alongside the LXX, Syriac, Symmachus and Vulgate read *měṣôrîm* instead of *měṣôdîm*. The word *měṣôdîm* is attested elsewhere as "net" (cf. Eccl 7:26; 9:12; Prov 12:12; Ps 66:11; Ezek 12:13), and "stronghold" (1 Sam 22:4; 2 Sam 5:9; Isa 29:7). The literal meaning of "net" should be understood as "prey" or "hunted" in Eccl 9:14 (cf. Ezek 13:21; 19:9), and since the verb *bānāh* ("build") is used, "siege-work" is a proper substitute for "prey" or "hunted." The translation of "stronghold" is disregarded as it makes less sense in the invasion motif of this verse.

238. The subject of the third masculine singular (3ms) verb *wûmāṣā'* ("he found") is ambiguous, but the king (ms) in 9:14 is possible, not the city (fs) though. The king found "in the city" a situation that thwarted his invasion.

239. Many Hebrew manuscripts and Targum read *wěḥākām* instead of *ḥākām*, taking the meaning of "a poor but wise man." But the Masoretic text is preferred and *ḥākām* ("wise") is the adjective that qualifies *miskēn* ("commoner"), keeping in view the comparison between a king and a commoner (not a noun, "poor," as many interpreters maintain).

240. Weisman, "Elements of Political Satire in Koheleth," 554.

241. Ibid., 557.

242. Ibid.

his wisdom. Second, the comparison of a king against a commoner recalls 4:13–16. This recurrence perhaps alludes to a similar wisdom tale. The understanding of *miskēn* being "a commoner" instead of "poor" makes better sense, as in 4:13–16. A socio-political but not economic status is in direct contrast with the king. Here 9:13–16 depicts a commoner who delivered a city in the time of a political crisis. There is no mention of the relationship of the wise commoner with anyone in legitimate political power. He is definitely not a ruler, nor an elite, but is a *miskēn* (9:15), a term that fits a less-than noble class in society. This common status has caused his contribution to be ignored. Recognition and glory are not usually attributed to the one who deserves it, but to the one who has the power and authority in society. And this socio-political disadvantage is what Qoheleth acknowledges and observes.

Third, the comparison between wisdom against might is at play. In 7:19, wisdom is said to give strength to the wise more than ten rulers that are in a city. And in 9:18, wisdom is depicted to be better than weapons of war. It is remarkable that there is no mention here of how the deliverance from invasion was done, except by wisdom. It is possible that the deliverance is done through wise diplomacy or efficient defense, yet it escapes the main issue. The case in point is the reverse outcome of what he has done. No one remembers the wise commoner. His wisdom is despised. And no one pays attention to what he has to say. As Seow suggests, Qoheleth uses the story to illustrate a point about the effectiveness of wisdom, which is also subject to chance.[243] "Wisdom is better than might," Qoheleth concludes in 9:16. The word *gĕbûrâ* ("might") refers to the greatness of the king and the great siege-work in 9:14. Wisdom is certainly better than the military greatness displayed by the invading king. The city is after all delivered by the wisdom of the commoner. But, ironically, as a wise person he met an unworthy fate. So, wisdom has its limitations. As such, this anecdote is used by Qoheleth to illustrate wisdom's limitations. And the *'ēt wāpega‘* ("time and occurrences") in the preceding 9:11 is probably effectual to illumine the reading here. Time and occurrence befalls all people. Even for the wise person who has contributed to the nation, since time and occurrences are beyond human control, his wisdom is despised. The political satire herein is that people are more impressed by social status and commanding authority. People are not impressed by genuine ability like wisdom. The wise commoner "was deemed worthy of no memorial trophy or similar high honor because he did not possess political power. Rewards are given only to those

---

243. Seow, *Ecclesiastes*, 321.

who are in a position to demand them."²⁴⁴ This depiction recalls the young but wise commoner whose political power was taken over by another young upstart in 4:13–16. So here 9:13–16 too concludes similarly. Wisdom, despite being better than might (wisdom is better than foolishness in 4:13–16), clearly has not gained an upper hand.²⁴⁵ It is again Qoheleth's "yes-but" rhetoric in both literary units: wisdom is better than foolishness but the popularity associated with the wise is short-lived (4:13–16). Wisdom is better than might but the wise are forgotten (9:13–16). Qoheleth by no means devalues wisdom, as he always states that "wisdom is better." But Qoheleth consistently counters wisdom's absolute efficacy. And twice Qoheleth makes this point applicable to the political powers through anecdotes in 4:13–16 and 9:13–16. Qoheleth's political wisdom rests in his honest reflection of political reality. One's wisdom is needed when crisis is in view. The very wisdom, however, is despised later. There is a caution to wisdom's absolute advantage in both anecdotes. In 4:13–16, the wisdom of a political leader is elusive, due to short-lived popularity. And in 9:13–16, the wisdom of a commoner is forgotten, despite earlier contributions. Qoheleth's reflection here is thus consistent with his assertion of *hebel* ("vanity") throughout the book. Political reality is ephemeral. On one hand, Qoheleth advises not to place an absolute value on wisdom. On the other hand, he warns against placing too much confidence in political experience.

A Reading of Ecclesiastes as Political Wisdom

The sages of Israel often were connected to the royal court.²⁴⁶ This *Sitz im Leben* necessitates Qoheleth's articulations about politics. And here Qoheleth advances on political counsels in the Persian court. He seeks "an orderliness that is experienced in terms of limits of power, the contours of responsibility, and the shapes of freedom."²⁴⁷ Politics by nature involves social and economic spheres. Critical of the wisdom thought itself, Qoheleth is concerned with the occurrences of social oppression in the power structure (3:16–17; 4:1–3; 5:8–9 [Hebrew 5:7–8]). While traditional wisdom instructs

---

244. Garrett, "Qoheleth on the Use and Abuse of Political Power," 173.

245. The comparison of wisdom against might represents part of "better-than" sayings, which continues until Eccl 9:17–18.

246. Such association is elucidated through biblical characters like the wise Joseph and Daniel, who counsel the foreign kings. Solomon too, as a king in his own right, was wiser than all others while having composed three thousand proverbs and a thousand and five songs (1 Kgs 4: 29–32 [Hebrew 5:9–12]).

247. Brueggemann, "Social Significance of Solomon," 129.

on the use of political power, Ecclesiastes is vividly packed with illustrations of power corruption. Under a critical scrutiny of Ecclesiastes, wickedness appears to abound in places of justice and righteousness (3:16–17). Qoheleth speaks of oppressions (4:1–3; 5:8–9 [Hebrew 5:7–8]), the self-indulgence of the elites (10:16–20), and the danger of absolute power (8:2–9; 10:4–7). Words like *rāʿ* ("evil"; 4:3; 8:3, 5, 6, 9) and *rešaʿ* ("wickedness"; 3:16 [twice]; 3:17; 8:8) are used recurrently to communicate Qoheleth's perception of political realities.[248] The words *kĕsîl* ("fool"; 4:13) and *hassekel* ("folly"; 10:6) depict sad pictures of those in power. Thus Qoheleth elaborates on "a foolish king" (4:13–16) and "the folly is given in many high places" (10:4–7)—humanity is generally affected by the consequences that come with inappropriate political activities. The wisdom once acclaimed in the wisdom tradition does not deliver its promise. Thus, Qoheleth's evaluation of human activities is one that is critical. His observations on socio-political life under the sun are done through lenses of irony (10:4–7). His comments on socio-political happenings are satirical (10:16–20). But it does not appear that Qoheleth is "utterly pessimistic"[249] about the political realm. As this study will seek to demonstrate below, Qoheleth is depicting a realistic picture of living in a corrupt power system. In such reality he gives pragmatic counsel accordingly, reflecting profound theology.

Qoheheth asserts the value of having mature leaders who govern wisely (5:8–9 [5:7–8]; 10:16–20). Yet corruption of power and oppression are painful realities (3:16–17; 4:1–3; 5:8 [Hebrew 5:7]). Nevertheless, Qoheleth does not advocate revolution to overthrow the unjust government and cautions those who would (8:2–5).[250] Rather, he educates through anecdotes (4:13–16; 9:3–16) and proverbial sayings (10:16–20). He also points out that no one, not even the wise, can resolve the problem of socio-political disorder.[251] He nevertheless advocates that there is time and judgment for every human work (3:16–17; 8:6–8), even though he questions how it all works.

The remedy Qoheleth appears to suggest is twofold. First, while wickedness and social oppression are realities, it is important for them to acknowledge God's time and judgment in these socio-political realities. Second, addressing an audience who had access to the higher authorities, Qoheleth advocates a prudent attitude toward authority. A right behavior

---

248. The cognate of *rāʿ* ("evil") is used elsewhere in Eccl 1:13; 2:17, 21; 4:8, 17; 5:12, 13, 15; 6:1, 2; 7:3, 14; 8: 9,11 (twice), 12; 9:3 (twice), 12 (twice); 10;5, 13; 11:2, 10; 12:1, 14; while *rešaʿ* ("wickedness") is used elsewhere in Eccl 7:15, 17, 25; 8:10, 13,14 (twice); 9:2.

249. Words of Anderson, *Qoheleth and Its Pessimistic Theology*, 139.

250. Miller, *Ecclesiastes*, 233.

251. Ibid.

eludes trouble, for political power can be devastating (8:5; 10:4). Qoheleth hints that mature leaders, proper management, and leadership skill will be beneficial (10:16–20). Political establishment is necessary; if the government functions properly, it will bring advantage to the people (5:9 [Hebrew 5:8]).

On account of wisdom, it is axiomatic of course that folly is never an option to choose in political maneuvers. Wisdom has advantage. One's wisdom may thwart the invasion of a great army to deliver a small city. While the advantage of wisdom over political power is affirmed, Qoheleth points out its vulnerability (4:13–16; 9:13–16). Thus, wisdom has its limitations. Even leaders who possess wisdom do not survive lasting popularity (4:13–16). A commoner who has wisdom is much less to be remembered (9:13–16). Therefore, Qoheleth is keeping wisdom honest.[252] On one hand, Qoheleth affirms the advantage of wisdom; on the other, he cautions about the absolutism of wisdom. Hence, Qoheleth certainly pushes wisdom beyond the conventional understanding, which assumes that wisdom always works.[253]

On the whole, Qoheleth offers pragmatic political wisdom. Qoheleth employs irony and political parody as his rhetoric. Edwin Good suggests that Qoheleth uses the term *hebel* to mean something very close to "irony" and "ironic" in his pursuit of value and purpose (4:13–16).[254] By the term "*hebel*," Qoheleth does not choose one reality from the other, nor does he reject both realities. Rather Qoheleth points out the incomprehensibility whenever an irony is felt or perceived.[255] Such persistent observation of tensions is noticeable in the book. These tensions are articulated through Qoheleth's speeches throughout. As maintained before, Qoheleth directs attention to the limitation of one's wisdom if compared to one's mortality. In my reading of these political passages, Qoheleth's irony also occurs at the king's role as an overseer of justice in the realities of social injustice (in the

252. Murphy, "Sage in Ecclesiastes and Qoheleth the Sage," 271.

253. Ibid.

254. Good, *Irony in the Old Testament*, 182. In Good's view, irony begins in conflict, marked by "the perception of the distance between pretense and reality" (p.14). Good provides the Greek origin of the word "irony," *eirōnia*, and the designation of a character in the earliest Greek comedy, *eirōn* ("ironical man"), against another character, *alazōn* ("the pretentious fool"). The comedy holds both characters in conflict and ends with the triumph of *eirōn*. Examples of the conflict according to Good are Eccl 7:4, keeping in view of 8:15, 3:19–21 in light of 12:7, and 7:16–17 in light of 12:13; ibid.,169–70.

255. To Sharp, *Irony and Meaning*, 196–220, there is a consistent and rhetorically purposeful irony that shapes the entire book of Ecclesiastes. Commenting that Ecclesiastes is saturated in irony thoroughly like no other biblical work, it is not surprising that Sharp reads the book, the entire Bible in fact, through the lens of irony. Even the persona of Qoheleth is itself ironic, according to Sharp.

cases of 3:16–22; 4:1–3; 5:8–9). Yet at the same time, the king is the possible source of injustice himself (in the case of 8:2–9). Likewise, irony is perceived when the achievement of a ruler does not assure lasting popularity (in the cases of 4:13–16). Furthermore, Ecclesiastes' irony lies in the peculiar master-slave reversal of social living, where incapable people are placed in high political status (10:4–7). In Ecclesiastes' larger picture, central to Qoheleth's irony is his repeated description of the epistemology "wisdom," where Qoheleth progresses with a nagging doubt in the book.[256] This irony, of course, is finally resolved when the readers reach 11:7–12:14.[257]

Irony in Ecclesiastes carries an element of helpful self-critique within it. From one perspective, the Israelite kingdom and her kings have no one to remember them in post-exilic Persian imperialism. For another, the present oppression and injustice reminds Qoheleth's readers of the oppression and injustice in Israel in the past. Qoheleth's readers were aware that the powerful and the rich among Israelites were once oppressive to others. The Israelite officials and rulers also were sources of social injustice. The scenarios were depicted vividly and confronted furiously by the words of Israel prophets. Now the political landscape in Ecclesiastes is post-exilic, Persian rule. By perceiving oppression and injustice from the lens of the oppressed in a foreign political structure, they witness their own deeds in the past. At the same time, they have to look to the future, with the knowledge that no king, despite a competent one like Cyrus the Great, Darius the Great, or Darius II, will live and be popular forever. No kingdom indeed will stand the test of time. Ecclesiastes invites readers to a risk-taking hermeneutics, especially in dealing with foreign rulers in pagan imperialism.[258] Qoheleth speaks indirectly through word play, calling attention to the self-indulgence, laziness, and greed among the powerful. And his critique is enveloped within wisdom teaching.

The association between Qoheleth and the position of the king only lasts for the first two chapters in Ecclesiastes. Longman has correctly pointed out that, when kingship is mentioned later in the book, there appears to be a large gap between the speaker and the political institution.[259] This is due to Qoheleth's identification of the ones who are being ruled after the second chapter in Ecclesiastes. The royal persona in chapter one to two is a fictional autobiography, as noted previously. Thus, there is no internal inconsistency

---

256. Bartholomew, *Ecclesiastes*, 79.

257. Ibid.

258. The idea of "risk-taking hermeneutics" comes from Sharp, *Irony and Meaning in the Hebrew Bible*, 61, although Sharp depicts another biblical book, Daniel, as illustrating foreign rulers and the fear of God, 61–65.

259. Longman, *Book of Ecclesiastes*, 5.

in Ecclesiastes. Further, Bartholomew points out that "my son" designation in 12:12, the "youth" in 11:9, and "the people" in 12:9 allude to a younger and wider readership.[260] They are people learned in the wisdom tradition and perhaps "advanced students" who were familiar with the struggles Qoheleth communicates.[261] They identify more with Qoheleth's questions and perspectives on life. The post-exilic context of Israel with the demise of past kingdoms and kingship might have lead Qoheleth and his learned people to examine the reality of political life. Qoheleth as a wisdom teacher (12:9) juxtaposes the tension between a living reality and violation of power. He reflects on "justice, righteousness, and equity, on the kinds of behavior (and policies) that are politically permissible and that are tolerable to the non-negotiable perimeters of created order."[262] In Fox's words:

> Qoheleth's counsels are not solutions; they are only *accommodations*. These came down to embracing the very activities that elsewhere he judges senseless: work and pleasure, wisdom, and righteousness. These are allowed value for the moment only, but the moment is all we have. These accommodations allow humans to create little meanings, local meanings, within the great absurd.[263]

Conclusion

It has been long recognized that Ecclesiastes gives noteworthy attention to the realities of economical realms—concepts about money and possessions, wealth and property, investment and profit.[264] This chapter has sought to demonstrate that Qoheleth's attention is on the political domain as well, as Qoheleth illustrates critical perspectives of political survival. Power is dangerous and potentially corrupt, but the necessity of political institutions and the proper use of power are affirmed. Political oppression, corruption, and the abuse of power are socio-political depravities that Qoheleth scrutinizes in the book. Accordingly, Qoheleth discerns the proper conduct in a given

260. Bartholomew, *Ecclesiastes*, 54.
261. Ibid.
262. Brueggemann, "Social Significance of Solomon," 130.
263. Fox, "Inner Structure of Qoheleth's Thought," 232.
264. See Kugel, "Qoheleth and Money," 32–49; Seow, *Ecclesiastes*, 21–36; and Dahood, "Canaanite–Phoenician Influence," 30–52. The commercial terms include *yitrôn* ("advantage or profit"), *'āmāl* ("toil"), *'inyān* ("occupation or business"), *keseph* ("money"), *ḥeleq* ("portion"), *kishrôn* ("success"), *'ôsher* ("riches"), and *ḥesrôn* ("lack or deficit").

political situation and advises his readers to dwell efficaciously in their political environment. Qoheleth affirms repeatedly that time and God's judgment are the sustaining factors that offer hope. Thus, people are advised to live wisely, especially when facing oppression, injustice, and abuse of political power. Wisdom fundamentally concerns the ability to guide behavior for basic survival. In Ecclesiastes, such ability defines Qoheleth's political wisdom.

3

The Analects and Political Wisdom

POLITICAL WISDOM CONSTITUTES A significant place in the philosophy of Confucian thought.[1] The Analects is arguably the earliest book on politics in the world, preceding any works of ancient Greece on politics, including Plato's *Republic*.[2] It is the intention of this chapter to examine the Analects' practical wisdom on politics. The central idea of Confucius'[3] political thought is commonly summed up into two inter-related concepts: moral management, *dezhi* (德治) and virtuous governance, *renzheng* (仁政). These familiar concepts are traceable to the Confucian classics, the *Four Books*,[4] among which the Analects, one of the most important of the Confucian classics, is notable in reflecting Confucius' political ideals. Most scholars uphold the centrality of virtuous quality as Confucius' sole political rhetoric. Yet, it appears that Confucius' political ideas deliberate on both virtuous quality *and* management competence. Confucius' political ideas reflect the ancient wisdom tradition in which administrative capacity is

---

1. "Confucian" refers to the plurality of intellects who commit to the study and praxis of Confucius' teaching. The term "Confucian thought" entails its school of thought. Whenever the words and ideas of the person of Confucius, rather than the school of thought, are intended in discussion, this book uses "Confucius." "Confucian thought" (*rujiasixiang*儒家思想) is preferred in this book rather than "Confucianism" (*rujiazhuyi*儒家主义). The origin of "Confucianism" can be traced to the writings of the sixteenth century, when the Jesuits used "Confucius" as a Latin transliteration of *Kong Fu Zi*. An "-ism" was added to Confucius in the nineteenth century in order to be regarded as a distinctive philosophical entity different from Buddhism and Daoism. Yao, *REC*, 1. See also Huang, "Confucius and Confucianism," 540.

2. Yuezhi, *Kongzi de Zhengzhixue* [Political Philosophy of Confucius], 3–5. The author explores the Greek word for "politics," *polis*, to mean city-state, and he suggests that Analects is the first book on the study of city-states in the world, a century before Plato and Aristotle.

3. Confucius is the Latin version of his Chinese name Kong Qiu (孔丘), with an alternate name Zhongni (仲尼). He was called Kongzi or Kongfuzi, literally, and Master Kong as an address of respect. The Latin name Confucius was made popular ever since the encounter between Chinese and Western cultures in the sixteenth century.

4. *The Four Books* are the Analects or *Lunyu*《论语》, *the Great Learning* or *Daxue*《大学》, *the Doctrine of Mean* or *Zhongyong*《中庸》, and *Mengzi*《孟子》.

accentuated as much as moral standard. Consequently, Confucius' politics is instrumental for evoking effectual ways of political organization in the wisdom tradition of ancient China.[5]

The Analects at a Glance

Structure and Theme

The Analects has a Chinese title, *Lunyu* 《论语》, which means "selected sayings," and is a post-Confucius compilation of short texts concerning Confucius (551–479 BCE) and his disciples.[6] The compilation includes a variety of sayings, brief discussions, observations done mostly, although not exclusively, by Confucius. There are some other conversations between Confucius and his disciples not included in the Analects yet they appear in the *Classic of Rites,* or *Liji* 《礼记》. This phenomenon has raised debate on its source and authenticity. There are also passages in the Analects repeated elsewhere among other Chinese Classics.[7] The exact date of completion of the Analects cannot be ascertained, yet it is believed that writing started around the early Warring States Period (around 400 BCE)[8] by Confucius' first and second generation's disciples.[9] Some scholars believe that the disciples of Zeng Shen (曾参), Confucius' student, were responsible for most of the writings in the anthology of the Analects, because Zeng Shen is mostly addressed as Zengzi (曾子) in the Analects (1:4, 9; 8:3–7; 19:16–18), a title used as a sign of respect to the teacher. Meanwhile, it is suggested based on recent archeological findings, that Confucius' grandson, Kong Ji (483–402 BCE), seemed to have played a crucial role on the transmission of Confucius' teachings.[10]

---

5. Yao, *Confucianism*, 34 points out that as an intellectual tradition, Confucian thought is characterized by its deep involvement in politics, which aspired to bring order and peace to the world.

6. "The Analects" is a term coined by James Legge (1815–97).

7. For example: *Doctrine of the Mean* (chapter 3, cf. the Analects 6:27; chapter 28:5, cf. the Analects 3:9, 14), *Great Learning* (chapter 4, cf. the Analects 12:13), and *Mengzi* (II A 2:19, cf. the Analects 7:33). See Legge, *Chinese Classics*, 17.

8. Legge, *Chinese* Classics, 17.

9. Having decided to recollect what their teacher had taught them, Confucius' disciples wrote and gathered some early chapters of the Analects. Other earlier writings might have been gathered shortly after Confucius' death. Ames and Rosemont, *Analects of Confucius*, 8–9.

10. Shaughnessy, *Rewriting Early Chinese Texts*, 10–11. In 1993, an excavated tomb in Guodian (郭店) had led to the discovery of 804 bamboo strips, which contained Confucian texts, among other ancient manuscripts such as Laozi. The transmission of

The present the Analects of twenty books[11] have gone through a lengthy process of development. The Analects has recorded a variant of other versions in the Han dynasty (206 BCE—220 CE), spanning even up to twenty-two books: the State of Lu version, *Lulunyu* (鲁《论语》) has twenty books, the ancient version, *Gulunyu* (古《论语》) has twenty-one books, while the State of Qi version, *Qilunyu* (齐《论语》) has twenty-two books.[12] Attempts to harmonize these versions had been made as early as 55 BCE. Yet its final form of twenty books was established only 200 years later in the Han dynasty by Zheng Xuan (郑玄, 127-200 CE).[13] It is therefore understandable that a long line of debate, as well as interpretive controversies, have been involved over the text and the authenticity of the Analects.[14] In short, most agree that the Analects is a composite record of Confucius' teaching in forms of sayings and dialogues.[15] In the past, most readers have taken all twenty books of the Analects as an accurate record of what Confucius and his disciples have said. Yet recent scholarship has highlighted several objections based on investigations regarding the composition, pointing

---

Confucius' teachings from the time of Confucius himself to Mencius had been suggested; for example, see Li, "Jingmen Guodian Jian" [Master Zisi in the Bamboo Strips], 28–30, or *Zhongguo Zhexue*, 75–80. See also Pang, "KongMeng Zhijian" [Between Confucius and Mencius], 88–95.

11. The "books" in the Analects are roughly the size of "chapters" according to more common classifications. Each book is further classified into verses (commonly depicted as "chapters" in the scholarship of the Analects) of different lengths. This book follows common terminologies, describing the Analects as having twenty "books" and within each book, many "chapters."

12. Xu, *Kongzizhidao* [Way of Confucius], 100–105. See also Zhang and Li, *Ruxue Yuanliu* [Origins and Development of Confucianism], 180. The Ancient Version, *Gulunyu* (古《论语》) was written in ancient script and has 21 books. A new book is created from the middle of the last book, *Yaoyue* 《尧曰》, of the twenty-book version, and is entitled *Zizhang* 《子张》. Therefore, it has the same content as the State of Lu Version, *Lulunyu* (鲁《论语》), which has 20 books. But the State of Qi version, *Qilunyu* (齐《论语》) contains two additional books entitled *Wenwang* 《问王》 and *Zhidao* 《知道》 respectively.

13. Legge, *Chinese Classics*, 14. The existing text of the Analects is believed to have combined features of three versions. Furthermore, Dingzhou fragments (定州竹简), recovered in 1973 in He Bei (河北), are believed to have incorporated features of the three the Analects versions mentioned earlier, yielding multiple scholarly debates. See Xu, *Kongzizhidao* [Way of Confucius], 104–5.

14. Pertaining to the title, origin, and authorship of the Analects, numerous theories were also suggested. For details, see Li and Yang, *Lunyu Zhimi* [Mystery of the Analects], 3–5.

15. Some passages do not record Confucius' involvement but his disciples', especially Book 19.

to possibilities of multiple authorship and redaction.[16] This has not deterred the purpose of this study, nevertheless. Aiming to compare political wisdom in Ecclesiastes and the Analects, this study emphasizes the literary works without trying to reconstruct original authorship.

The collection of twenty books in the present form of the Analects are titled by the first noun or name (apart from the name of Confucius himself) that begins each book. The Analects was written in classical Chinese language, which is poetic in nature.[17] The contents of the Analects are wide-ranging—conveying multiple thoughts that comprise themes on ethics, politics, social living, cultures, and religion—and mostly in the form of conversations.[18] Yet their common theme can be distilled in a nutshell: wisdom on how to be human.[19] This common theme thus makes the Analects a wisdom text about how to be a responsible and sensible person, with the ultimate goal of becoming an exemplary person, *junzi* (君子). The text is classified as sapiential, for it communicates the wisdom pursuit of order in human subsistence. The arrangement of the twenty books within the Analects have been considered to be arranged in a deliberate stream of thought,[20] although similar verses recur in different books (Analects 1:3 cf. 17:17; 8:14 cf. 14:26).[21] Many adjacent verses are believed to be related, though not thoroughly, to each other. From the perspective of literary criticism, this suggests multiple authorship and redaction.

---

16. Van Norden, *Confucius and the Analects*, 3–9. This position has been pointed out as early as 1895 by James Legge; see Legge, *Chinese Classics*, 15–17.

17. The classical Chinese language, *Wenyanwen* (文言文) is an official language of ancient China. Most ancient Chinese classics are written as such. The language encapsulates characteristics of parallelism, imagery, and phonetic features that are evident of poetic genre.

18. The themes of the Analects contain aspects of philosophical and ethical ideas, daily activities, living concerns, socio-political observations, cultural matters, and even personal temperaments and preferences.

19. Zhang, *Lunyu Pingxi*, 401.

20. Some maintain that the Analects embodies a deliberate structure, especially in Book 10 and Book 19. The contents in Books 1, 3, 5, 6, 7, 10, 11, 18 and 19 are often said to have evidence of deliberate structures as a result of Zhu Xi's compilation during the Song dynasty. The recurrences of several passages in various books within the Analects are also suggested to be intentional to suit wider literary contexts. Ding, *Lunyu Duquan* [Interpreting the Analects], 15. See also Chen, "Zuowei Zhengzhi Xingdong de Xiushen" [Self Cultivation as a Political Activity], 82. According to Chen (陈赟), the literary context of chapters 1 to chapter 4 in Book Two, *Weizheng* 《为政》is on political ethics with an educational purpose underlying the subsequent passages; chapter 4 is strategic in outlining the learning process for the whole unit of Books 1 to 4.

21. Other instances: the Analects 1:11, cf. 4:20; the Analects 3:15, cf. 10:21.

Books 3–10 are arguably the oldest texts traceable to Confucius and his immediate disciples. They also are treated as a unit, in that they share some common features and editing style, and seem to belong together in a way that Books 1–2 do not. Books 1–2 seem to lack an overall unifying feature, encompassing a number of sayings by Confucius' disciples rather than Confucius himself.[22] As for Books 11–20, most scholars divide them into two sections: 11–15 and 16–20,[23] where the latter is highly possible to have been composed much later, based on linguistic evidence.[24] Book 20 also appears distinctive from the rest of the books, for it contains much longer discourses. It is, in my opinion, difficult to construct with certainty the structure of the Analects. The reading of the Analects in this book therefore does not follow its literary sequence, consistent with most interpreters. The Analects is referred to as an entirety—according to its final form, and its author as Confucius.[25]

The Analects, regarded as *Rujia Jingdian* (儒家经典), "Confucian Classics," since the Early Han dynasty, was grouped into *the Four Books* or *Sishu* (四书) by Zhu Xi (朱熹) during the Song Dynasty, and is commonly

---

22. Van Norden, *Confucius and the Analects*, 14–15.

23. Littlejohn, *Confucianism*, 19. See also the classification by Brooks and Brooks, *Original Analects*.

24. Van Norden, *Confucius and the Analects*, 13.

25. Nevertheless, the classification within the Analects by Littlejohn based on its chronological formation is acknowledged. See Littlejohn, *Confucianism*, 19–24. Stratum one dates back to Confucius; they are Books 3–10, the oldest materials traceable to Confucius himself with an exception of the Analects 8:3–8:7, where Zeng Shen (曾参), is addressed as Zengzi (曾子) evidently as a sign of respect from Zeng Shen's disciples. Stratum two dates from Confucius' disciples and the second generation of disciples; they are Books 1–2 and Book 11–15 along with 8:3–8:7. The rest of Confucius' disciples are being addressed by name, except Zeng Shen (1:4, 9; 8:3–7) and You Ruo (Analects 1:2). Their title of respect indicates that Confucius' disciples had their own disciples who later formed different groups and varied in their interpretation of Confucius' teaching (Cf. Analects 19:3, 12, 18–19). In Books 11 and 12 especially, Confucius' assessments of his disciples are recorded, where comparisons and preferences between disciples are indicated. The Analects 11:3 for instance, is evidently a compiler's note cataloguing ten of Confucius' main disciples according to their talents. It is more probable that it was written by their disciples after they died. See also the Analects 19:3, 12, 18–19 for their depiction of conversations among Confucius' main disciples. These depictions suggest the possibility of competition among these groups for leadership after Confucius' death. As pointed out also in Legge, *Chinese Classics*, 15. Stratum three dates from the third generation and beyond; they are Books 16–20. Confucius is largely addressed by name rather than "the Master," especially in Books 16–17, indicating a later period. Also, as a sign of later writing, literary features in these books, such as numerical listings of attributes (Analects 16:4–8; 19:9; 20:2), are employed for easy memorization. Book 20 is a very late addition with the last verse serving as an ending to the collection.

considered the main and most reliable source of Confucius' teachings.[26] The main section in this chapter concentrates on exploring political ideas from the Analects. Due to differences of etymology between Chinese and English words and their hermeneutical meanings respectively, many familiar terms in the Analects are translated into different English words by various commentators. For example, *ren* (仁) is taken differently as "humanness," "humaneness," "virtue," "morality,"[27] and "benevolence." *Li* (礼) is translated otherwise as "propriety," "decency," "ritual" or "rite." Likewise, *junzi* (君子) is undertaken as "exemplary person," "noble," "excellent man," "superior man," "benevolent" and the like. For each of these familiar terms, I typically use italicized original terms, *junzi*. At other times when necessary, I employ consistent translations throughout based on recent usage. Furthermore, Confucius' thoughts in the Analects undertook various expansions and diversions due to wide-ranging appearances of Confucian scholars throughout history. Though within the same Confucian lineage, their views varied and often disagreed. The existence of different thought-streams within Confucian tradition is a result of the history of interpretation from a long historical development". This chapter attempts to be sensitive to these distinctive interpretations but will avoid investigation of the evolution of Confucian political ideas. Therefore, as a sensible yardstick, I position Confucian political thought more on Confucius' sayings from his socio-political background. Considerable amount of discussion among different interpretations is nevertheless inevitable.[28]

Social and Political Background

The *Commentary of the Thirteen Classics*, or *Shisanjing Zhushu*《十三经注疏》, depicts Confucius' encounter with a grieving widow. It yields his comments on a tyrannical government. Confucius was passing along a hilly way with his disciples, when they saw a woman crying in front of a grave. He was touched by the deep sense of grief in that woman, and had one of his disciples, Zi Gong, enquire about the reason for her sorrow. She replied that she was deeply sorrowful because her brother-in-law, husband, and her son were all dead, one by one having been attacked by a tiger. Confucius then

---

26. Tang, *Lunyuxue dao Xingcheng* [Studies of the Analects], 5. See also Cua, "Confucian Philosophy, Chinese," 538–39.

27. The translation of *"ren"* (仁) into "morality" should be avoided, for it can be easily confused with another word, *"de"* (德), which is closer in meaning to "morality."

28. Those discussions also reflect various socio-political backdrops at different historical stages in the development of the Confucian tradition.

asked why they had not left that place when it first occurred. And she replied, "There is no tyrant government here." Then the disciples heard Confucius comment that, "A tyrant government is more ferocious than a tiger." Confucius' perception of the political institutions of his day came from the collapse of power structure.[29] He ascribed this collapse to those in power, for their moral capacity did not measure up to their assigned titles. In those days, official titles were easily obtained through noble family lineage, internal connection, or some kind of relationship. This entailed a hierarchy of power that consisted of many morally questionable people, resulting in internal struggles and social tensions. To Confucius, a wicked government is too oppressive to live with, much less to work with. A virtuous government, therefore, represents the political wisdom he asserts throughout his life to confront this socio-political reality.[30]

The social and political background of Confucius shed light on his ideas expounded in the Analects.[31] Confucius (551–479 BCE) was born at the end of the Spring and Autumn period (722–481 BCE) and the early Warring States period (480–221 BCE) in the history of ancient China. The Zhou dynasty (1122–221 BCE) was already on the decline from the beginning of the Spring and Autumn period. The nobles of several states had in fact gathered their own military force competing against the Zhou emperor, "the Son of Heaven," *Tianzi* (天子).[32] This happened when foreign invasions from the North and the West had taken a toll on the dynasty, in addition to a number of natural disasters.[33] During the later Spring and Autumn period, larger states emerged with increasing military strength and unrestrained warfare.[34] The long-standing feudal society had gradually fallen, giving way

---

29. Kong, *Kongzi Yanjiu* [Studies of Confucius], 455.

30. Confucius' lifelong activities can be summarized in three areas: service in the government, teaching, and the compilation of texts. His life in the service of government was of the shortest duration, given the fact that the Duke of Lu was not really interested in his policies. Confucius then began to travel from one state to another with his disciples for years, hoping to advance his political ideas in a desperate attempt at socio-political reform. He was disappointed most of the time, until he finally devoted his time to concentrating on teaching and the compilation of texts. He imparted valuable insights on political organization gathered from observations, reflections, and travel experiences.

31. Confucius' political thoughts later undertook various expansions due to wide-ranging interpretations within the Confucian school. Nevertheless, as a sensible yardstick, Confucius' political sayings in the Analects should be positioned in his socio-political background.

32. Loewe and Shaughnessy, *Cambridge History of Ancient China*, 546.

33. Ibid.

34. Black, *World History of Ancient Political Thought*, 93.

to rivalries for political power among dozens of smaller kingdoms. A new branch of government officials, *shi* (仕), translated as "scholars" or "intellectuals," emerged. Selected for their skill and intelligence, these men of service were experts in politics, management, warfare, and even cosmology.³⁵ The Analects 13:20 depicts a *shi* as having the gravity of being responsible, filial, respectable, trustworthy, and consistent in word and deed. A *shi* could become a legitimate member of the ruling elite by being appointed to government offices.³⁶ Confucius was taught and nurtured as a *shi*, this placing him in line for employment in civil and military roles. Nevertheless, he did not equate having government posts, *dangguan* (当官), with the idea of "political involvement," *weizheng* (为政) (e.g. Analects 2:21). Julia Ching even states that Confucius identified himself with the cause of the ruling dynasty of his day, but he was never clearly a man of the establishment.³⁷ Inasmuch as politics concerned everyday living, one can exert influence by living as a good person. Under these circumstances, Confucius inspired his disciples to strive to achieve the disposition of *junzi* (君子) besides acquiring the rank of *shi*.

At the time of Confucius, common living was marked by the disintegration of the feudal empire, recurrent social unrests, political tyranny, and wars. Political instability and economic exploitation made the livelihood of the people perilous. Political power was in the hands of some noble families, who at times combined strength to manipulate the state-lord or the duke, and influenced policy. Power struggles and the removal of political rivals persisted and resulted in the breakdown of social order.³⁸ Against such a chaotic political backdrop, Confucius observed in the Analects 16:2:

> When the Way prevails in the empire, the rites and music and punitive expeditions are initiated by the emperor. When the Way does not prevail in the empire, they are initiated by the feudal lords . . . When the Way prevails in the empire, policy does not rest with the counsellors. When the Way prevails in the empire, the commoners do not express critical views.³⁹

---

35. Ibid, 93–94.

36. Ibid, 94.

37. Although Confucius served a brief term as minister of justice in his native Lu State. See Ching, *Confucianism and Christianity*, 184.

38. Strife among warring states later ended when the kingdom of Qin (221–206 BCE) finally conquered and united all others into a single military and imperial empire. See Blocker, "Chinese Philosophy," 231.

39. The English translation here is translated by Lau, see [Confucius], the Analects; nevertheless, I am responsible for all other English translations of the Analects in this book, unless otherwise stated.

In short, Confucius looked from the turmoil of his own era and sought for a model society.⁴⁰ The early Zhou dynasty reflected such an ideal of a good society: a learned elite culture, a period of relative tranquility, a common and persistent goodwill.⁴¹ On the contrary, there was no order in the world under the heaven when political power was held by the noble class rather than by Zhou emperor, the real ruler. As such, Confucius endeavored to improve the former customs of hereditary nobility into an inwardly directed moral imperative for everyone.⁴² Confucius' political ideas thus are communicated with an intention to transform the disordered society through proper political organization, making possible "an order in the world under the Heaven." In Julia Ching's words, this political move aims toward "the restoration of a lost order—based on moral leadership and persuasion."⁴³ The political court and its expected behavior therefore represent Confucius' main concern in the Analects.⁴⁴

On Defining Politics in the Analects

There are two recurring Chinese words appearing in the Analects on political organization: *zheng* (政) and *zhi* (治). These words always appear separately in the Analects, but are commonly used today in a pair to signify the word "politics," *zhengzhi* (政治). The Chinese concept of *zhengzhi* is a later construct, but *zheng* (政) and *zhi* (治), if used independently, are cognate; they both mean "governance."⁴⁵ Since *zheng* or *zhi* always occur in the Analects by themselves and always denote the same meaning, either one of the

40. Schwartz, *World of Thought in Ancient China*, 40. The happenings that Confucius witnessed in his own era was mediated through written records that are still available to us.

41. Schwartz, *World of Thought in Ancient China*, 41. There is skepticism about whether the Zhou system had actually achieved a degree of pacification. Many Western scholars have described major features of the system as "feudal." The word implies disintegration of power rather than stability and order. At base, there were yet three battles recorded during the reign of Western Zhou. See Schwartz, *World of Thought in Ancient China*, 41–42.

42. Blocker, "Chinese Philosophy," 231.

43. Ching, *Confucianism and Christianity*, 183.

44. Hsü, *Political Philosophy of Confucianism*, 27. The dynamic in political involvement, *weizheng* (为政), in the Analects encompasses three layers of relationships: between the ruler (the duke of a state) and the minister, between the superior and the subordinates, and between the officials and the people. This dynamic of ruler-minister-official-people represents Confucius' focus of political restructuring and social reform, bearing in mind that there was another higher level in the hierarchy, namely the Zhou emperor, who was figure head and Confucius' ideal ruler.

45. Jiang, "Lunyu de Zhengzhi Gainian" [Political Ideas in the Analects], 195 and 216.

words is representative enough of what one understands as *zhengzhi*. This term is analogous to the Greek notion of "politics," a term derived from the Greek word *polis*, to mean "city." Its root suggests an entity grounded in the governance of a city, as well as the ruling mechanism, public affairs, citizenship, and political experiences that come along with its meaning.[46] The conception of *polis* therefore actually differs from the kinship community where Confucian tradition originated sociologically.[47] In this sense, the word "politics," used commonly in the Western world referring to the affairs of *polis*, differs from the understanding of the Chinese term *zhengzhi*. In spite of this, in the exchange of ideas between the Eastern and Western worlds, *zhengzhi* and "politics" today are equivalent.

This chapter does not attempt to obtain political ideas depicted in the Analects from the Western perception of politics, for the political history of China does not relate precisely to the experiences of the Greek *polis* or the Greek understanding of "politics."[48] In general, "politics" refers to activities of administration and governance of public affairs in a country.[49] From the perspective of wisdom, one should engage in a broad understanding of "politics," which includes coping with the socio-political reality. The articulation of politics in the Analects deals mainly with a kind of political attitude rather than policies and systems. Therefore "politics" in the Analects is a practical skill referring to the ability and experience in the governance of a state and its public affairs, rather than a science involving systematic studies of the state, the government, and its functional roles.[50] The practical skills meant here reflect the wisdom of the ancient Near East, whose essence is "the ability to cope," "the art of steering," and "the quest for self-understanding and for mastery of the world."[51] Wisdom involves the practical pursuit and management of daily subsistence to attain well-being. Political wisdom, therefore, is practical wisdom concerned with the management of political activities and survival in times of uncertainty. Since the governance of states and public affairs involves execution of power, politics inevitably entails competition, leadership, delegation, and management.[52] As a result, society

---

46. Ibid., 195.

47. Chen, "Modernity and Confucian Political Philosophy," 95, outlines "kinship community" as a political and sociological domination based on blood lineage, as opposed to the idea of *polis*, which is based on a human-made contractual agreement.

48. Jiang, "Lunyu de Zhengzhi Gainian," 197.

49. Soanes and Stevensons, "Politics" and "Political," 1362.

50. See Jiang, "Lunyu de Zhengzhi Gainian," 193.

51. Crenshaw, *Old Testament Wisdom*, 9.

52. Jiang, "Lunyu de Zhengzhi Gainian," 195.

as the community of people in any given state is an entity directly connected to politics.

Political Ideas in the Analects

The political ideas in the Analects encapsulate mostly direct instruction on political organization and, to a lesser degree, reflections on socio-political reality. This chapter illustrates the Analects' political wisdom according to the division between direct, prescriptive instructions *and* indirect, descriptive reflection, consistent with that of Ecclesiastes in chapter 2.[53] Political ideas may be grouped by certain catch-words and themes rather than by literary order. First, the occurrence of the words *zheng* (政), *zhi* (治), and *bang* (邦), all meaning "governance" in the Analects, are markers for the selection of passages. Second, the thoughts on governing a nation and bureaucratic organization, despite the absence of the words *zheng* (政), *zhi* (治), and *bang* (邦), also are considered. The selected verses are then categorized into various subject matters, each with a specific focus. Third, the qualities that are believed to have constituted the content of Confucian political wisdom—*ren* (仁), *li* (礼), *yi* (义), and *de* (德)—are engaged for discussions, albeit only selectively due to their copious occurrences in the Analects.[54]

---

53. Although Book 2 of the Analects is entitled "On Government," *Weizheng* (为政), political ideas are in fact scattered throughout the Analects.

54. My suggestion on this selection of passages based on the third criteria will be subjective and not exhaustive. Some passages which, in the opinion of other interpreters, are significant may be excluded in my exegetical employment. Further related Analects passages can only be included in brief discussions.

Instructions and Admonitions on Virtuous Governance[55]

Moral Guidance—Analects 2:3 and Analects 2:19

> **Analects 2:3**—The Master said, "If those in power[56] guide[57] the people by regulations[58] and keep them in line with punishments, the people will stay out of trouble but will lose their sense of shame. *If those in power* guide them by morality and keep them in line with propriety, then they will rectify[59] themselves besides having a sense of shame."

In the Analects 2:3, two different ways of governing a state are drawn out: one by law-punishment, *fazhi* (法治), and another by morality-propriety, *dezhi-lizhi* (德治-礼治). These approaches to governance have different emphases. One concerns coercion and the other persuasion. The former makes clear regulations and prohibitions, and punishment awaits anyone who violates them. This way of governing, namely, by law (*zheng* 政) and punishment (*xing* 刑), have their advantages in keeping the civilian from committing offenses. They are negative reinforcements making people fully aware of, and prepared for, the consequences of wrongdoings. However, governance by law and punishment do not inculcate a sense of shame when one commits wrongdoings. Guo Xiang (郭象) notes that governmental regulations may correct people's outer behavior, but they may not convince people's hearts.[60] People may comply due to practicality and avoidance, but still behave shamelessly. Zhu Xi (朱熹) adds, "Although they will probably not dare to do anything bad, the tendency to do bad will never

---

55. "Virtuous governance," *renzheng* (仁政) is related to "moral management," *dezhi* (德治). Some differentiate the two concepts when articulating Confucian political thought. But making a sharp distinction between both concepts is difficult and not necessary. This section about "virtuous governance" takes in both concepts by acknowledging them but without differentiating them.

56. The subject of the series of verbs here is unknown, yet in light of "the people" *min* (民) as the object in the text, the subject is understandably "those in power" and is italicized as my own insertion. The same applies to the second occurrence here. The immediate context of the verse is obscure, hence the stipulation "if" is interpretive. The verse should be regarded as a general statement on moral government.

57. The word *dao* (道) is to be understood as *dao* (导); both are cognate meaning "guide."

58. Though the word *zheng* (政) is consistently taken as "governance" elsewhere, and here it should be interpreted as "regulations," "law" or "decree" to suit the context.

59. *Ge* "格" is *duanzheng* (端正), hence it is "to rectify" or "to straighten."

60. Guo Xiang (郭象; AD 252–312), according to Huang Kan's (皇侃; 488–545) *Lunyu Yishu* 《论语义疏》, quoted in Slingerland, *Confucius Analects*, 258–59.

leave them."⁶¹ Instead, the political ethics that Confucius advocates in the Analects 2:3 is virtuous governance: management guided by morality and an administration straightened by propriety. It means that virtues guide behavior, and social refinements straighten conduct. Scholars point out the idea of "effortless action," or *Wuwei* (无为), in this passage. Roger Ames and Henry Rosemont, for example, assert *Wuwei* here and define it as "non-coercive" governing.⁶² To Edward Slingerland too, the morality-propriety way of governance is *Wuwei*, "spontaneous, unselfconscious, and perfectly efficacious."⁶³ This *Wuwei* approach to governance is preferable to force. It does not mean "no action" or "no effort at all," because practices of morality-propriety are emphasized. Morality and propriety inculcate subtle influence that is unknowingly transformational to a person's character.⁶⁴ Therefore, governance by morality-propriety is instinctive and effective.

It is important to note that Confucius does not dismiss regulations. Rather, he emphasizes an ethical renewal from within. Gradual self-cultivation is a way to rectify human behavior in the quest for political stability. Besides, even though Confucius himself presided over lawsuits, his own preference was that lawsuits do not occur at all (Analects 12:13). The cultivation of morality-propriety will yield a norm that is gradually transformative.⁶⁵ The way of law and punishment is effective in the short run, but the way of morality and propriety way will endure and is more effective in the long run. In my opinion, the Analects 2:3 articulates a preference for management by moral influence and propriety, without the elimination of law and punishment. Neither should morality-propriety and law-punishment be regarded as "entirely mutual," as Zhu Xi has suggested.⁶⁶ Confucius simply opposes the way of governance that depends exclusively upon strict law and severe punishment, without making prior effort to use reformatory

---

61. Slingerland, *Confucius Analects*, 8. Zhu Xi (朱熹; AD 1130–1200), who combined the ideas of several previous thinkers and his own into a comprehensive philosophy, was the primary Confucian exemplar of the Song dynasty who canonized *the Four Books* of the Confucian School. Later the Yuan dynasty (AD 1279–1368) decreed Zhu Xi's commentaries on *the Four Books*, or *Sishu Jizhu*《四书集注》to be brought together to form mandatory texts for the imperial examination system. During the Qing Dynasty (AD 1644–1911), there was a revival of interests in Zhu Xi's commentary to Confucian classics. See Perkins, *Encyclopedia of China*, 101.

62. Ames and Rosemont, *Analects of Confucius*, 232.

63. Slingerland, *Confucius Analects*, xix and 8.

64. Ya Se, *Lunyu Daquanji*, 19.

65. Zhang, *Lunyu Yizhu*, 26.

66. Gardner, *Zhu Xi's Reading of the Analects*, 111.

measures through education.⁶⁷ In Confucian political thought, there is no total rejection of the practice of law and punishment.

> **Analects 2:19**—Duke Ai asked, saying, "What should be done in order to secure the submission of the people?" Confucius replied, "Elevate⁶⁸ the upright and set them over the crooked ones,⁶⁹ then the people will submit. Elevates the crooked and set them over the upright, then the people will not submit."

Duke Ai of the State of Lu asked about the way to acquire submission from the people whom he ruled. Confucius emphasized delegating duties to people who were upright, *zhi* (直). Confucius endorses upright ones to be political leaders, so that civilians would submit to their authority. The idea is reiterated in the Analects 12:22 with a different motif: the upright people will straighten the morally crooked ones. The Analects 2:19 communicates that entrusting authority and responsibility should be grounded on character rather than social alliance, favoritism, or nepotism. Elevating the upright people, *juzhi* (举直), is important in Confucius' management wisdom. It is essential to Confucius' general emphasis on moral standards. It also implies Confucius' rhetoric that crooked people often occupy high posts in the government. Morally questionable people, who often have close relations with higher authority, were often promoted. Subsequently corruption, mismanagement, and abuse of authority ensued. The civilian was then inevitably oppressed, society was in chaos, resulting in public noncompliance. Confucius' solution was to elevate upright people instead. Together with the preference of morality-propriety in the Analects 2:3, here once again the importance of morality is stressed. Leaders should have commendable moral aptitude to guide the people at large.

Leadership by Example—The Analects 12:17 and 12:19

> **Analects 12:17**—Ji Kangzi asked Confucius about the way of governance. Confucius answered, "To govern is to correct.⁷⁰ Should you lead correctly, who would dare to be incorrect?"

67. Hsü: *Political Philosophy of Confucianism*, 125.
68. "*Ju*" (举) meaning "to employ" is understood as *yong* (用), "to use." See Chen, *Sishu Duben* [Texts of the Four Books], 76.
69. The word "*cuo*" (错) should be understood as *cuo* (措), meaning "to place." Thus, "*cuozhu*" (错诸) means "to place over some others." The term "*wang*" (枉), meaning "crooked," is the opposite of "*zhi*" (直) "upright." See Zhang, *Lunyu Pingxi*, 26.
70. The two words "*zheng*" (政) and "*zheng*" (正) are cognates as well as homophones; *zheng* "政" (government) comes from the root *zheng* "正" (correct, straighten

Analects 12:19—Ji Kangzi consulted Confucius about the way of governance, saying, "What would you think if I were to execute those who do not follow proper path in order to ensure order?"[71] Confucius answered, "In your governance, what need is there for execution? If you do good, the people will do good as well. The morality of the exemplar person is like wind; the morality of the inferior person is like grass. When the wind blows over, the grass will bend."

Confucius emphasizes top-down management where the ruling class play an archetypal role. The leader should be the one who sets an example.[72] In the Analects 12:17, Confucius evokes a simple but significant idea for political involvement: to govern effectively is to do what is right. The root *zheng* (正) suggests that one ought to be an upright person in order to be able to govern, *zheng* "政." Both words are cognate and homophonous, and the word play is no doubt intended. In this text, Confucius was speaking to Ji Kangzi (季康子), who held *de facto* political power in the Lu state (instead of the duke) and who also headed three illegitimately powerful noble families of Lu.[73] Political leadership is stated in this text, as *shuai* (帅) is a verb to mean "heading" or "commanding," *shuailing* (率领). Confucius necessitates political leadership, *zheng* (政), with correctness or uprightness, *zheng* (正). Uprightness is expected from the apex of political institutions to the lower levels of its hierarchy.[74] Confucius' similar rhetoric is also found in the Analects 13:13; if a ruler self-governs, governing others will entail. Also, in the Analects 13:6, "If a ruler is morally correct, one can command obedience without even giving orders; on the contrary, if a ruler is not morally correct, one cannot command obedience even after orders are decreed." People who lack uprightness cannot govern, for they are not capable of correcting others.

---

or being upright). See Lau, *Analects*, 172; and Leys, *Analects of Confucius*, 179, who suggests the idea of the phrase "politics is rectitude."

71. Meaning, killing people who do not follow the proper path; *wudao* (无道) so that the proper path is being followed; thus, there is order, *youdao* (有道). Alternately, the whole phrase can be "killing the disorderly people for the benefit of the orderly." See translation of Pound, [Confucius], Analects, 57, who takes it as "killing the wayward for the benefit of the well behaved."

72. The leader sets an example of morality to gain the trust of the people, then the people will work diligently. See Chen, *Sishu Duben*, 211.

73. Slingerland, *Confucius Analects*, 14. Ji Kangzi, whose family name was Jisun and is named Fei (季孙肥) was the prime minister, *shangqin* (上卿) or *xiangguo* (相国) of Lu state, which came to power in 492 BCE, during the time of Duke Ai.

74. In line with the interpretations of Dong Zhong-Shu (董仲舒; 179–104 BCE) and Zhang Ju-Zheng (张居正). See Ya Se, *Lunyu Daquanji*, 256.

Confucius saw violence as the breakdown of political structure. A good model of political leadership spurns violence and removes the need for coercion.[75] As such, Confucius objects to the idea of execution as the basis of government measures, even the execution of those who do not conform to proper social behavior. The Analects 12:19 depicts Confucius confronting Ji Kangzi about the necessity of execution, insisting that if a ruler does good, the people will do good as well. Killing has nothing to do with governing. And in the Analects, persuasion is always better than coercion.[76] Thus, brute force should not be rationalized under any political excuse.[77] The subsequent lines in the Analects 12:19 mention *de* (德), where morality is evoked as a requirement of a ruler. A ruler educates the people simply by being a moral example. If the ruler imposes moral requirements on subjects without personally fulfilling them, a political organization would not have any effect.[78]

Appointment Based on Competence—The Analects 13:2

> **Analects 13:2**—While Zhong Gong was a steward to Ji, he asked about the way of governance. The Master said, "Set an example for your officials,[79] show leniency towards minor offenses, and promote talented people."

Confucius laid out to his disciple, Zhong Gong (仲弓),[80] an important principle on governance: promoting talented people. He contends that when a political leader acknowledges talents and elevates them, more talents will be brought to notice. This passage tells of one's political involvement based on ability. It heightens the importance of appointing capable people to government offices. It was, at that time, a challenge to the normal practice of lineage and nepotism. In a separate passage in the Analects 6:8, neither morality nor virtue is mentioned in the text, rather competence is. Zhong You (仲由), Duanmu Ci (端木賜), and Ran Qiu (冉求) are Confucius' disciples who displayed distinctive qualities. Zhong You is resolute, *guo* (果), that

---

75. Black, *World History of Ancient Political Thought*, 106.
76. Ibid.
77. Zhao, "Axiological Rules," 163.
78. Ibid., 162.
79. Slingerland, *Confucius Analects*, 138 points out the possibility of "*xian*" (先) being a verb rather than an adverb, meaning "to do first." "*Xian yousi*" (先有司) thus literally is "to do first before your officials do." See also Zhang, *Lunyu Pingxi*, 242.
80. Zhong Gong (仲弓), a disciple of Confucius, had an alternate name, Ran Yong (冉雍).

is, one who was firm in decision making. Duanmu Ci is a learned man, *da* (达) who is well informed by knowledge and experience. And Ran Qiu is versatile in various official duties, *yi* (艺). All of them have abilities that suit political appointment. Confucius affirms their proficiency in the appointment to government offices. Here, political involvement does not solely rely on one's moral strength, but one's capability and know-how as well.

At its most basic, a *ru* (儒), at the time of Confucius, generally was known as a learned person well versed in *the Six Classics* and the six skills: ceremonies, music, archery, driving carriages, calligraphy, and calculation.[81] A scholar, *shi* (仕), like a *ru,* is not only knowledgeable but also skillful, combining intellectual aptitude as well as physical handiness. To the understanding of *ru* and *shi,* Confucius further intensifies moral cultivation, in addition to the basic nurturing of knowledge and skill.[82] One's knowledge and skills, besides inner and personal cultivation, will eventually certify one's political functioning. Thus, Confucian of a later period fosters "inner saintliness and outer kingliness," *neishenwaiwang* (内圣外王),[83] where "saintliness" refers to personal cultivation and "kingliness" refers to management skills.[84] In short, equipping people to be managerially competent is equally important in the Analects' rhetoric. Confucius and his disciples were nurtured to be both proficient and knowledgeable. In the Analects' political organization, skills and managerial competence all are crucial.

Trustworthiness—The Analects 1:5

> **Analects 1:5**—The Master said, "In guiding a state of a thousand chariots,[85] approach your duties with reverence and

81. He, "Hewei Ruzhe" [What Does *Ruzhe* Mean?], 172 and 179.

82. In the modern sense, *ru* (儒) too is a learned person who possesses knowledge and skills and, at the same time, also has moral character, *pingxue jianyou* (品学兼优). See also Huang, "Confucius and Confucianism," 536, 540.

83. The word "saintliness" to translate "*sheng*" (圣) is better than a more common translation in the terminologies of Confucian writings, "sageliness." The "sage" as in the word "sageliness" is a Confucian construct actually denoting sainthood. Even if the word is used, it is not to be understood as "the sage" in the sense of "the wise"; cf. the ANE understanding.

84. Zhang and Li, *Ruxue Yuanliu,* 7. It is said in chapter 5 of *The Great Learning* that a self-conquered person is decisive in conquering a nation. *The Great Learning* serves as a Confucian guide on Analects' political ethics, stressing the training process from acquiring knowledge, *qiongli* (穷理), to the rectifying of the heart, *zhengxin* (正心), then cultivation of the person, *xiushen* (修己) and then the governing of people, *zhiren* (治人).

85. A chariot, *sheng* (乘) is a two-wheeled vehicle pulled by four horses. The number

trustworthiness; keep expenditure under control and love your fellow people; employ the labor of the people[86] at the right seasons."

In the Analects 1:5, reverent attention to one's duty is imperative in the administration of a state. At the same time, trustworthiness from the people also should be secured. Confucius further teaches economical wisdom, in addition to proper handling of duties; that is, by keeping expenditures under control. Nonetheless, loving one's fellow people should be maintained along with budget consciousness. Thus, the "bottom line," as it were, in guarding national expenses, should be the welfare of the people. One should not preserve national funds at the expense of the people. In addition, the administration of a state also involves the wise management of people and timing: the right season for employment. The right season, given an agricultural background, is the season that is slack in farming. Employment of the people in public work in a slack season will not interfere with agricultural production.[87] Consequently, a government that gives priority to the well-being of the people will be trusted.

The people, *min* (民), are important as they constitute a nation.[88] Their trust in political leaders is significant. Their concerns, which should be treated with seriousness, are likened to officiating a sacrifice as in the Analects 12:2. In the Analects 12:7, Confucius also has outlined three crucial elements about governance in increasing priority: sufficient military strength, sufficient food supply, and trustworthiness. Again, trustworthiness of the political leaders is highlighted as of the utmost significance on governance.

---

of chariots is an ancient measurement of the military strength of a state. Some believe that a state of a thousand chariots is a sizable state; see for example, Legge, *Chinese Classics*, 118; Dong-Fang Qiao, *Fangfaxue* [The Methodology], 217. Others think that it is a rather small state; see Huang, *Analects of Confucius (Lun Yu)*, 48. Leys, *Analects of Confucius*, 108–9 points to the historical factor: before Confucius, a state of a thousand chariots was large; by the time of Confucius, it was a medium-sized one. This understanding is more probable considering the textual evidence of Analects 11:26, where a state of a thousand chariots was compared to a great state.

86. "*Min*" (民) is literally "commoner." The phrase takes literally "to love people," *airen* (爱人) and "to employ commoner," *shimin* (使民). Ames and Rosemont, *Analects of Confucius*, 72, therefore differentiate the two groups of people by translating "love your peers" and "put the common people to work."

87. A majority view on employing people "at the right season" is during non-harvest season, when intensive labor is needed on the field. See for example, Khu et al., *Confucian Bible*, 32. See also Ya Se, *Lunyu Daquanji*, 5–6.

88. The size of a nation could more probably be a middle-sized land of approximately one hundred miles, which was usually ruled by a noble (诸侯). Li and Ma, *Lunyu* [Analects], 5.

Yangming Wang (王阳明) comments in this passage, that one who wishes to govern skillfully should secure "the hearts of people."[89]

The cognate of the term *xin* (信 "trust") depicts a person (人) standing by his or her word (言). The term essentially conveys a person who keeps his or her word and is thus trustworthy. Good governance requires trust (信). Faith in the governing body entails productivity and general well-being. The Analects 13:4 avers that when the ruler is trustworthy, the people will be sincere in return. Corruption, maladministration, abuse of power, tyranny, misappropriation of national fund, and other misconducts will consequently bring about distrust in the government. Confucius' primary emphasis on *xin* (信 "trust"), indicates his perception of a basic governing concern: trust in the ruler is more important than the food supply and military advantage (Analects 12:7).[90] Precisely on what ground the trust of the people should be secured is implied: the virtue of their ruler.

There is another related term worth mentioning, *cheng* (誠 "honesty"). In the Analects, the term is mentioned less frequently (for example, in the Analects 12:10), but its idea is repeatedly communicated from Confucius' lifestyle and his teaching. Its traditional writing, *cheng* (誠 "honesty") depicts also the term *yan* (言 "word"). The word construction of both "trust" and "honesty" are therefore connected by the same term. This means that the words of a person do display honesty and can secure people's trust. Hence, one of the political concerns also lies in being honest in government policies. Dishonesty creates distance between the ruler and the people: the civilian simply does not trust leaders who are not honest to people.

On Humanness[91]—*The Analects 12:22*

> **Analects 12:22**—Fan Chi asked about virtue. The Master said, "Love your fellow people." He asked about knowledge. The

---

89. Words of Wang Yangming (王阳明; 1472–1529) quoted in Slingerland, *Confucius Analects*, 128. Wang Yangming was a famous neo-Confucian thinker and a vocal critic of Zhu Xi, due to Zhu Xi's overly theoretical grasp of Confucian philosophy.

90. The whole passage is suggested with a different interpretations as flexibility in political handling. This understanding is likely, but it will not be discussed here due to brevity and focus. See Chen, *Sishu Duben*, 202.

91. The term "*ren*" (仁) is frequently translated by scholars as "humanness," "humaneness," "virtue" or "benevolence." I prefer "humanness" as its etymology suggests; nevertheless, the use of another translation, "virtue," for *ren* is inevitable in the text of Analects. Perhaps none of the suggested translations suits all the occurrences of *ren* in Analects. Hence "humanness" and "virtue" are used interchangeably. Further, the passages that involve *ren* are too numerous to have listed here for examination. The

Master said, "Know your fellow people." Fan Chi has not understood yet. The Master said, "Elevate the upright and set them over the crooked, it will straighten the crooked ones."

A substantial number of key concepts are developed from Confucius' discussions of ethics, out of which *ren* (仁 "humanness") stands out as the most recurring theme, appearing about 109 times in the Analects.[92] The etymology of the word shows a pictographical division of two separate words: *ren* (人 "human") and *ren* (二 "two"), illustrating two persons in parallel.[93] *Ren* therefore essentially denotes the reciprocity in human relationship, where one's self-cultivation is related with others in a community of people.[94] *Ren* is intrinsically the basis that connects all of Confucian ethics. Confucius gives a short definition of humanness: "love your fellow people." Consequently, a political leader who has *ren* will love subjects impartially (Analects 12:22). Following the logic of a larger literary context of the Analects 12:22, this impartiality leads one to select upright people, rather than allied people, for government offices.

In the Analects 6:30 also, Confucius asserts the idea of humanness to Zi Gong (子贡) by a kind of "Golden Rule"—establishing others as one wishes to be established. He qualifies humanness as saintliness that surpasses Yao's and Shun's models of virtuous governance; that is, succession of rulership to capable people rather than to their own sons. Most Confucian scholars agree that the central idea of Confucius' moral teachings is *ren*.

---

passages in this section are thus subjectively selected; in my judgment, they necessarily relate to political wisdom.

92. Zhang and Li, *Ruxue Yuanliu*, 192.

93. *Ren* (仁) and *ren* (人) are not only cognates but also homophonous.

94. Confucius undertakes wide-ranging answers to the question of what constitutes humanness. To Fan Chi (樊迟), who consulted him about humanness on three occasions, he replied differently: "Love your fellow people" (Analects 12:22); "Encounter difficulties first, then reap the benefit" (Analects 6:20); and "Be respectful even at home, be reverent in your work, be sincere in dealing with people" (Analects 13:19). Whereas to Yan Yuan (颜渊), he says, "to return to the observance of propriety through overcoming the self, is humanness" (Analects 12:1). In reply to the enquiry by Zhong Gong (仲弓), he stated, "Behave as though you are receiving an important guest when you are abroad, and behave as though you officiate an important sacrifice when you employ the service of the people. Do not impose on others what you yourself do not desire" (Analects 12:2). To Sima Niu (司马牛), he said, "The mark of humanness is one who is loathe to speak" (Analects 12:3). And to Zizhang (子张), he listed five attributes that constitute humanness: gravity (*gong*恭), bigheartedness (*kuan*宽), trustworthiness (*xin* 信), earnestness (*min*敏), and charity (*hui*惠) (Analects 17:6). These many descriptions of *ren* in Analects are intended for specific political requirements and ethics. The various answers Confucius has provided suggest that he responds to the inquiry of humanness according to the aptitude of various disciples.

Confucius explicates *ren* as a quality that is worth the sacrifice when one's existence and moral value clash (Analects 15:9). Given a choice between one or the other, Confucius upholds humanness. For Confucius, the duty of obedience to the ruler was relative, but fidelity to humanness was absolute.[95]

Ren encompasses all other virtues as well. Love, honesty, courage, and so forth are organically related to *ren*; these qualities are different manifestations of *ren*.[96] Lin Yu-Sheng points out that the "humanliness" in the word *ren* (仁) essentially encloses a distinctive quality of a person (人).[97] As its etymology suggests, humanness concerns mostly the reciprocal relationship with people. Confucius illustrates in detail how humanness is to be lived out among people, namely, by affirming acts of generosity and mutuality among one another. In short, people of *ren* live contented lives inasmuch as they fulfill their interpersonal obligations and pursue common good in their conduct.[98] Though the concept of *ren* is not Confucius' creation, he has heightened its significance to a new level.[99] There are many more passages that discuss *ren* widely, yet there is one striking commonality that can be observed: *ren* represents the basic guideline for building an enriching interpersonal relationship as well as the basic requirement for governing people. In short, *ren* represents the core of Confucius' political thoughts and the foundation of his philosophy of ethics, *renxue* (仁学).[100]

On Righteousness[101]—*The Analects 13:4 (3), 15:18, and 17:23*

> **Analects 13:4 (3)**—If those of higher authority are fond of propriety, the people will not dare to be disrespectful. If those of higher authority are fond of righteousness, the people will not dare to disobey their authority. If those of higher authority are fond of trustworthiness, the people will not dare to be insincere.

---

95. Leys, *Analects of Confucius*, 193.

96. Lin, "Evolution of the Pre-Confucian Meaning of *Jen*," 184; see also Liu, *Confucianism in the Eyes of a Confucian Liberal*, 63.

97. Lin, "Evolution of the Pre-Confucian Meaning of *Jen*," 181.

98. Thompson, "Archery of 'Wisdom,'" 337.

99. Kong, *Kongzi Yanjiu* [Studies of Confucius], 454.

100. Zhang and Li, *Ruxue Yuanliu*, 192.

101. The term "*yi*" (义) is translated as "rightness" or "justice" by other interpreters. The idea of *yi* relates to the quality or the state of being just or proper, a meaning where "righteousness" appears to be closer and comparable to "rightness" (which means correctness, accuracy, fitness or even moral integrity).

The ancient orthography of the term *yi*, (義 "righteousness") consists of two roots: *yang* (羊 "sheep") and *wo* (我 "me").[102] The etymology derives from ancient tending of flocks in the plain, where people should attend to their own sheep and not steal from their neighbors.[103] It is translated here as "righteousness." The term is related to another Chinese word, *yi* (宜 "appropriate"). This particular *yi*, according to the *Doctrine of the Mean*, is an action which is appropriate.[104] A person of *yi* is one with creative insights, who is able to make ethical judgments in particular situations.[105] Its meaning also can be understood in light of *he li* (合理 "just"). *Yi* signifies what is ethically correct and at the same time what is reasonable.

In the Analects 13:4, *yi* relates to political leadership specifically. A person of higher authority, literally *shang* (上 "those from above") in the text, is expected to carry out what is right in order to command submissiveness. In the three-fold parallelism of the Analects 13:4, righteousness is set alongside *li* (礼 "propriety") and *xin* (信 "trustworthiness"), all of which qualify people of higher authority. The logic of the text is that if a political leader intends to exercise propriety, righteousness, and trustworthiness to the people, one will expect respect, submissiveness, and sincerity in return. Confucius' advice points out two ideas in political leadership. First, it is crucial to command respect from the public. Second, submissiveness of the people is gained through decent influence rather than through coercion. In the larger context of the Analects 13:4, Confucius' disciple Fan Chi (樊迟) was remarked as being *xiaoren* (小人), literally, "a minor person," as he was concerned more with farming and plantations, which are the aspirations of a commoner.[106] Confucius points out here that a leader should focus on the cultivation of propriety, righteousness, and trustworthiness rather than the cultivation of land. This notion also suggests that Confucius' fundamental thought for scholars is that they be the leaders while the working class should be followers.[107]

> **Analects 15:18**—The Master said, "The exemplary person considers righteousness to be essential: one performs it according to

---

102. *Yi* (義) is the original writing of the term *yi*, used here to illustrate the etymology. A simplified writing of *yi*, " 义, " is used throughout this book, consistently for all other Chinese fonts.

103. Jennings, *Confucian Analects*, 37.

104. "Righteousness, is appropriateness." *The Mean* 20:5, Chen, *Zhongyong Quanji* [Complete Collections on the Doctrine of the Mean].

105. Yu, "Yi: Practical Wisdom," 336; see also Cheng, "On Yi as a Universal principle," 272.

106. Huang, *Analects of Confucius (Lun Yu)*, 133.

107. Zhang, *Lunyu Pingxi*, 245.

the rules of propriety, brings it forth in humility, and completes it with trustworthiness. This is indeed an exemplary person!"

Analects 17:23—Zi Lu said, "Does the exemplary person esteem courage?" The Master said, "The exemplar person considers righteousness to be supreme. An exemplar person who has courage but lack of righteousness will create disorder; an inferior person who has courage but lack of righteousness will commit robbery."

In the passages above, righteousness is associated with the character of a political leader, as opposed to the character of the commoners. As in the case of the Analects 15:18, righteousness represents the principle of a *junzi*. It should be practiced with propriety as well as with an attitude of humility and trustworthiness. The *yi* in a person constitutes one's inner ethical consciousness and outer ethical action. A *junzi* possesses the intellectual quality of both judging and doing what is appropriate. Seeing righteousness but leaving it undone is a lack of courage (Analects 2:24). So, righteousness goes along with the courage to act. Yet courage by itself is potentially dangerous. Courage does not stand as the ultimate measure of action. As the Analects 17:23 suggests, righteousness determines the value of one's courage. Perhaps in light of the Analects 5:7, 7:11, and 11:22 that suggest Zi Lu's impudence, he is singled out for this teaching on *yi*.[108] The point on *yi* is hence two-fold. First, righteousness cannot be a true quality without the courage to act. It is thus not necessary to distinguish whether *yi* has an inner or outer locus, as if both loci can stand by themselves. Jiyuan Yu comments that righteousness as "an attribute of ethical action" and as "an intellectual quality" is inseparable, albeit the distinctiveness of both loci became an issue of interpretive dispute based explicitly on *Mengzi*.[109] Second, righteousness is preferred to courage. The Analects 17:23 points out that having courage despite the lack of righteousness will lead to chaos: political leaders will create disorder, and the subjects will resort to crime. Consequently, *yi* is the motive that determines the value of one's actions.

Elsewhere in the the Analects 4:16, "An exemplary person is conversant with what is right; whereas the inferior person is acquainted with what is profitable." The rhetoric of the Analects seems to place righteousness before profit, *li* (利), advancing the motive of the exemplary person to seek righteousness. Confucius' emphasis on righteousness relative to

---

108. Slingerland, *Confucius Analects*, 211.

109. Yu, "*Yi*: Practical Wisdom," 337. Mencius 4B.11 conveys, "A great person needs not keep his word nor see his action through to the end but aims only at what is appropriate."

profit has left a pedagogic legacy in Confucian thoughts, yielding Mencius' conception of humanness-righteousness philosophy, *renyiguan* (仁义观). This grouping idea of humanness-righteousness represents a contrast to the motif of profit-seeking, *li* (利).

In the Analects 16:1, Ran Qiu and Zi Lu were assigned by Ji Kangzi to war against Zhuan Yu (颛臾), a vassal state located within the borders of Lu.[110] Confucius disagreed with Ran Qiu and Zi Lu attacking their kindred, and he faulted them for preparing to do so. Zhuan Yu was appointed by a Zhou emperor to serve the altar of Lu and thus posed no threat to the state. Ran Qiu reasoned that both of them did not concur to the duty, but their commanding leader insisted on it. Confucius insisted instead that both of them should have resigned from their offices rather than advanced to war if they were unable to perform their duties according to what they believed was right.[111] To Confucius, a government officer has lost his function by not being able to uphold what is required of him. His students should know what constitutes righteousness in a crusade: warring against Lu's own kinfolk without a valid reason is fundamentally wrong. Thus, Confucius used the analogy of not being able to help a blind person who was stumbling insofar as it was the right thing to do. Confucius was actually rebuking them for knowing the right thing to do, yet failing to do it. The idea of *yi* is implied, though not stated, in the text of the Analects 16:1. It is again associated with right motive here, which Confucius points out explicitly. Ran Qiu claimed that the battle was justifiable since Zhuan Yu could be a future threat. Yet Confucius exposed Ji's motive of warring against Zhuan Yu, that it was the rule of Lu that Ji intended to acquire by strengthening his power through this supposed conquest.[112]

Furthermore, the Analects 11:24 depicts Confucius' comment: "A great minister is one who serves his ruler according to the proper way.

---

110. Zhuan Yu is located northeast of now Bi County, Shandong Province. Presently it is still the name of a village in that area. Huang, *Analects of Confucius*, 160.

111. This interpretation is reflected in most commentaries. See for example, Chen, *Sishu Duben*, 264; Li and Ma, *Lunyu*, 126; Zhang, *Lunyu Pingxi*, 325; Ya Se, *Lunyu Daquanji*, 360; Fu, *Wo Du Lunyu* [*The* Analects I Read], 345; Slingerland, *Confucius Analects*, 191, "He who can display his power should step into the ranks, he who is unable to do so should retire." Lau suggests an alternative reading, "Displaying your strength you join the ranks, but, finding yourself wanting, you give up," see Yang and Lau, *Lunyu*, 239–240. However, Cui, *Sishu Wujing* [Four Books and the Five Classics], 83, suggests yet another reading that is contrary to that of most interpreters. The majority view is reflected here in this passage.

112. Slingerland, *Confucius Analects*, 191–92, suggests instead the phrase means "Ji's wrong decision lies within his own home (getting bad advice from their ministers) rather than external threat." There is no record of an attack on Zhuan Yu in the *Annals*, indicating that the attack had never occurred.

When this is no longer possible, he should retire."¹¹³ The idea of resigning if one is unable to execute duty rightly is consistent with that of the Analects 16:1 above. Furthermore, the Analects 15:40 gives an imperative that people who follow different ways cannot lay plans together. The several depictions in the Analects above communicate several points about *yi*. First, the people who are in politics know the right thing to do. Their motive justifies their action. Second, political leaders should by all means act upon the matters that are perceived to be right. Third, when a political leader can no longer have the capacity to assert what one thinks is right and instead is compelled to do otherwise, one should resign from office.

Reflections on Socio-Political Reality and Political Involvement

Moral Requirement of a Person—The Analects 2:1 and 12:19 (3)

> **Analects 2:1**—The Master said, "One who governs with morality is like the Pole Star, which commands the homage¹¹⁴ of the multitude of stars simply by remaining in its place."
>
> **Analects 12:19 (3)**—The morality of the exemplary person is like wind; the morality of the inferior person is like grass. When the wind blows over, the grass will bend.¹¹⁵

"Morality," *de* (德), occurs thirty-one times in the Analects, mostly describing its importance but not its specific definition.¹¹⁶ Yet, the text makes clear that *de* is the mark of legitimacy to dominate. Also, when *de* is mentioned in the Analects, it is mostly connected to the idea of political behavior. In the case of the Analects 2:1, an image of how the universe runs its course centering on the Pole Star is employed to depict the significance of a moral leader. The people will encircle a ruler of morality as naturally as the order of the universe in which a myriad of stars surround the Pole Star. In light of the Analects 15:5, therefore, Zhu Xi, Cheng Yi (程颐), and Cheng Hao (程颢) assert that the morality of a ruler is an influential force

---

113. It is uncertain if dao (道) "the way" here refers to the mandate of heaven, social order, or the collective attributes of *ren*, *li* and *yi*. Yet, in Confucius' rhetoric, the composite qualities of *ren*, *li* and *yi* seem most appropriate.

114. "Commanding the homage" is from the word *gong* (共), which should be understood as *gong* (拱), an action of cupping one's hand on the other in front of the chest, as sign of respect. See Ya Se, *Lunyu Daquanji*, 18.

115. The saying has been discussed earlier, and is also quoted in *Mencius*, 3A.2.

116. Jiang, "Lunyu de Zhengzhi Gainian," 204.

even without making an effort, *Wuwei* (无为).[117] A Confucian political idea is thus formulated to convey this power to rule: "governance based on non-action, *wuwei erzhi* (无为而治)."[118] As maintained before, this "non-action" way of governance does not mean "no action" or "no effort at all." Rather, *Wuwei* is "effortless action," which is "spontaneous, unselfconscious, and perfectly efficacious."[119] It refers to the *manner* in which something is done, not to an action that is not done.[120] Therefore, *Wuwei* should not be misinterpreted as not doing anything at all. Instead, it is having moral significance to bear on others. As reflected in Zhu Xi's reading, "governance with morality" is "governance based on non-action," whereby all people pay homage to it.[121] In brief, the imagery in the Analects 2:1 illustrates three points. First, the ruler's moral strength is his power to rule.[122] Second, the moral strength of a ruler commands respect. Third, the moral strength of a ruler represents the centrality of influence. The reflection of political involvement, according to the Analects 2:1, is that the government should be established in accordance with moral requirements. And the Analects often distinguishes one who has moral quality as an exemplary person, *junzi* (君子).

In the case of the Analects 12:19, another imagery of nature, namely wind and grass, is used to draw the contrast between the exemplary person and the inferior person. There are two understandings of the meaning of the term *junzi* (君子), "exemplary person," in contrast to *xiaoren* (小人), "inferior person," in the Analects. First, the "exemplary person" is the one who governs as opposed to the "inferior," the one who is being governed.[123] Second, the "exemplary person" is the one who holds a high moral standard as opposed to the "inferior person" who is morally questionable. Both of these meanings sometimes overlap, given that Confucius' ideal of a political leader it that he meet a high moral requirement. Also, in Confucius' ideal, the commoner should be governed by one who embraces high moral principles. Yet there are times both meanings should be distinguished, as in the case of the Analects 16:6, 17:4, and here, 12:19, where morality is not

---

117. This idea of *wuwei* (无为), "nonassertive effort," has perhaps incorporated Daoist's thought; see Ames and Rosemont, *Analects of Confucius*, 231–32; see also Legge, *Chinese Classics*, 121.

118. See Ames, *Art of Rulership*, 28–64, for its diverse interpretations according to Confucian, Daoist, and Legalist perspectives.

119. Chen, *Sishu Duben*, 68; Slingerland, *Confucius Analects*, xix.

120. Slingerland, *Confucius Analects*, xix.

121. See Ya Se, *Lunyu Daquanji*, 18.

122. Zhao, "Axiological Rules," 162. Such power recalls ancient rulers who have ensured harmony under the heaven. See also Ya Se, *Lunyu Daquanji*, 18.

123. "Inferior" as a noun also means "subordinate."

intended but rather the social hierarchical status between leaders (*junzi*) and commoners (*xiaoren*). Since Confucius' ideal of an "exemplary person" well-suits the office of government, both the moral meaning and the political meaning of the *junzi*, as opposed to *xiaoren*, have to be kept in view.

In the Analects 12:19, the imagery of the grass bending over with the wind blowing indicates that the morality of a political leader commands the morality of the commoners. The moral quality of a ruler signifies one's strength to assert influence. And the term *feng* (风), "wind," here is indicative of ethos, *fengqi* (风气), suggesting that the morality of political leaders will create a moral social norm. Therefore, the morality of political leaders is not Confucius' only goal; rather, it is the morality of the people as a whole in order that a moral society can be attained. This moral requirement for political involvement recalls the belief of "matching nature with morality," *yide peitian* (以德配天),[124] from the Zhou period.[125] During the Zhou dynasty, morality was upheld as the ultimate prerequisite in succession to rule a kingdom; whereas the lineage was secondary. The emperor bore responsibility for governing the people on one hand and, on the other, for educating the people toward morality.[126] Therefore, in another passage, Confucius is saying, "guide the people by morality" (Analects 2:3). The emphasis of morality from the Zhou is very much prototypical of Confucius' political ideal.[127]

---

124. The word "*tian*" (天) has a wide semantic field; it may mean "sky," "day" (as opposed to night), "a period of time in a day" (early of the day), "season" (as in summer day or rainy day), "weather" (for example, wet day), "nature" (as opposed to humankind), "God/god" (as opposed to humankind), and "Heaven/heaven" (the dwelling place of the saints after death). Among these meanings, "nature" appears to be a closer meaning as *tian* here refers to the course of nature or the predestined order of universe.

125. Yu, "Rujia Zhengzhi Sixiang" [On Moral Governance], 148.

126. Ibid.

127. The emphasis on the government as an overarching authority to promote moral development of the people is later figured predominantly in *the Four Books*. *The Great Learning*, for example, spells out clearly at the onset, "The way of *the Great Learning* involves manifesting pure morality;" and it entails cultivating the self, then regulating the family, which will eventually lead to governing the state and to pacifying the world. See Gardner, *The Four Books*, 143. See also preface by Yao in [Confucius], *Ta Hsueh and Chung Yung*, vii. In short, "cultivating the self" has to do with attaining moral standards. Like the Analects, the *Great Learning* is socio-politically inclined, articulating the importance of moral cultivation to deliver peace and harmony in society as well as good governance of people.

Propriety as a Way to Maintain Order—The Analects 4:13, 13:4 (3), 14:41, and 3:5

> **Analects 4:13**—The Master said, "Can *a ruler*[128] govern one's kingdom with propriety and deference? How difficult would that be?[129] If *a ruler* cannot govern one's kingdom with propriety and deference, what has one got to do with propriety?"

In general, propriety (礼 *li*) has religious, social, and psychological dimensions, and its meaning hence extends into rituals, customs, expectations of behavior, and civil laws.[130] On politics, Confucius upholds the governance of the state by observation of proper *li*. Propriety is alternately translated as decency or rite, and it appears seventy-five times in the Analects. Etymologically, *li* in its fullest orthography (禮) signifies a type of ritual display on an altar, probably representing a religious sacrifice.[131] In the Analects, *li* comprises proper costumes, correct arrangements and usage of ritual tools, engagement of ceremonies, the right kind of music, suitable titles in a family, proper human relationship, social etiquette, and political protocols. In the Analects 4:13, a ruler is to govern the kingdom with propriety and deference. The idea of rang (让), "deference," here is reminiscent of the practices of Yao, Shun, and Yu in terms of succession of leadership to capable people. Its original and complex writing (讓) pictures two people extending hands in respect to each other with a word (言) on the left. Deference thus conveys the idea of people in mutual respect or speaking on good terms. Rivalries, conflicts, and competition for political power are ruled out. It is associated with the idea of propriety in a pair in the Analects 4:13 (礼让), communicating respect in addition to propriety. By way of propriety-deference, the society will be in order and stable, making possible the Way under the heaven.

When the Zhou dynasty was established, a sense of normative tradition emerged. Under the regency of Duke Zhou (周公), the status quo was maintained and further expanded to a full-scale observance. The political stability and its cultural heritage was a model particularly worthy of conservation. Confucius, who states, "I am for the Zhou" (Analects 3:14), therefore

---

128. The subject, which is absent in the text, should be "a ruler" in light of the presence of the word "kingdom" in the text.

129. Waley, *Analects of Confucius*, 243; Khu, *Confucian Bible*, 72; Zhang, *Lunyu Pingxi*, 60.

130. Yao, *Introduction to Confucianism*, 192.

131. Ibid., 191 points out the original meaning of *li* (禮) is "to arrange ritual vessels" for the purpose of serving gods and praying. The understanding of this character was later extended and developed to become more complex in encompassing the laws, codes, and rules of the natural and human world.

emulates their cultural richness in terms of observance of seasons, public facilities, social ceremonies, and musical choices. This prominence contributes significantly to the formation of Confucian ideals, elucidated conceptually in the Analects under the general rubric of the dao, or "the Way" (道).[132] For Confucius, *li* is central to the flourishing of the dao.[133]

> **Analects 13:4 (3)**—If those of higher authority are fond of propriety, the people will not dare to be disrespectful.
>
> **Analects 14:41**—The Master said, "If those of higher authority are fond of propriety, the people will be easy to command."[134]

The Analects 13:4 and 14:41 depict a political leadership by way of *li*. Observance of propriety secures respect (Analects 13:4) and compliance (Analects 14:41) from subjects. The people will be respectful and easy to command. Functionally, *li* is visible; it is an outer form of inner attitude about the proper order of things. In a passage discussed earlier, effective political leadership involves an act of keeping orderliness among the people by means of propriety (Analects 2:3). In Confucius' political thought, *li* is in fact the tool to govern a state.

The sayings of Confucius in the Analects 3:19 also uphold the relationship between a ruler and a subordinate administered through proper manner: the ruler treats the subordinate with *li*, and the subordinate returns to the ruler loyalty, *zhong* (忠). The practice of *li*, according to the Analects 3:19, is thus also reciprocal.[135] Further, the idea of *li* is implied in the Analects 12:11.[136] Confucius told Duke Jing of the State of Qi that the ruler should function as a commanding leader, and the minister, a submissive minister. The lack of *li* in social protocols creates misplacement of positions and results in disorder.[137] Functions and obligations are attached to specific

---

132. Chan, "Confucian Ethics and the Critique of Ideology," 246.

133. Ibid., 249.

134. The word "*shi*" "使" (translated as "command" here) can be alternately understood as "employ" or "direct."

135. Huang points to the historical reality in Analects 3:19 where the nobles of Duke Ding of Lu state had ignored protocols while serving him, so he was concerned and forwarded this query to Confucius. See Huang, *Analects of Confucius*, 64. Duke Ding trusted Confucius' political insights and elevated him to be Minister of Justice, *sikou* (司寇) in the Lu state, where Confucius has recorded remarkable political achievement. Jennings, *Confucian Analects*, 58.

136. The whole phrase can alternately be translated as "The ruler, rules; the minister, serves; the father, instructs; and the son, obey," when all of the second recurring words in the phrase are taken as verbs rather than nouns.

137. The historical backdrop in this passage is a chaotic political affair in the State of Qi. Duke Jing was facing the challenge of his increasingly powerful minister, Chen Qi,

roles in society. In the State of Lu itself, Confucius had objected to the practice of ministers engaging the *modus operandi* of a ruler. Officials of various levels in the government had distinctive roles and authorities, and separate responsibilities were required of them.[138] There were also distinctive protocols for officials of different levels to host official gatherings. Thus, in the Analects 3:1, Confucius comments critically on Ji Kangzi who employed eight rows of eight dancers to perform in his courtyard. A dancing rite of 64 performers was in fact a prerogative of an emperor at that time, but Ji, who was a middle-level official, *qingdaifu* (卿大夫), was third in status and with authority after the noble, *zhuhou* (诸侯), who was second after the ruler, *jun* (君).[139] Ji had misused the privilege of a ruler in his favor. To Confucius, such misappropriation was intolerable (Analects 3:1). Similarly, a political leader should not perform inappropriate socio-political protocols, such as the choice of music (Analects 3:2) and religious rituals (Analects 3:10)—the prerogatives of those with higher authority. In addition, one who does not have the authority simply should not bear the responsibility of others (Analects 8:14).

A concept closely related to the idea of *li* is role definitions coined by Confucius as "the rectification of name," *zhengming* (正名).[140] This concept is worth attention here since it points to the office and function proper of political organizations. In the Analects 13:3, role definition represents the first thing that Confucius would do should he be given a state to administer. To Confucius, if names are not being rectified, one's speech will not be in accordance with a true picture of one's position, and management tasks cannot be carried out properly. This situation will eventually affect how the people function generally. Confucius' *Sitz im Leben* indicates the need to stress the rectification of name. The noble class of Confucius' contemporaries in the State of Lu had become very influential inasmuch as the Duke of Lu was easily manipulated. The noble class had in fact exercised dominant power, in violation of *li*, a mishandling of political roles. This misadministration was recurrent across various states in history. Official

---

who aimed to usurp his authority. Confucius advised Duke Jing on how to correct the state of affairs in Qi state by proper execution of duty. Slingerland, *Confucius Analects*, 131.

138. Dong-Fang Qiao, *Fangfaxue*, 7.

139. A middle official as Ji, according to social propriety, should only engage a dancing rite of 32 performers, *siyi* (四佾); whereas a noble or *zhuhou* (诸侯) requires 48 performers, *liuyi* (六佾); and a ruler, *jun* (君) 64 performers, *bayi* (八佾).

140. The word *zheng* (正) is a verb, meaning "to correct" or "to rectify." Cf. Analects 12:17, "To govern is to correct."

titles were then misappropriated, and functional roles became ambiguous. Without the rectification of name, social disorder entails and people will suffer eventually.[141]

> **Analects 3:5**—The Master said, "Yi and Di who have rulers, are inferior to the states of Xia that have none[142] at all."

The practice of propriety yields a way of order in any state. In the Analects 3:5, in his reflection of social chaos, Confucius mentioned barbarian tribes, Yi (夷) and Di (狄), who had had rulers (but had not known propriety in their cultural formation) and were inferior to states who had not had rulers (but had practiced propriety).[143] Yi and Di were tribes living to the East and North respectively in Confucius' time.[144] They had their own tribal organization but did not follow Zhou's propriety. As such, they were considered uncivilized. It would be preferable to remain correct in propriety as Xia (夏; generally taken as "Chinese" by all commentators) did, even if this meant going without any ruler at all. Huang Kan (皇侃)[145] understands this passage as a critique of the three families of Lu. They wield political power as do the barbarian rulers, and their breaches of propriety make them like Yi and Di.[146] As reflected in history, noble families were numerous. They held pivotal political power even though they had a duke above them. In so doing, the nobles had violated the social order by being disobedient to the dukes, the real rulers of a state. Whereas barbarian tribes had only tribal leaders, their people had obeyed their leaders. The actual social disorder of Xia was not only likened to Yi and Di, but was made inferior to them (not superior). Hence, an irony is probably meant in this passage: when the social order is violated, one finds a reversal of political status.[147] Thus

---

141. Liu, "Lun Kongzi de Zhengzhi Sixiang" [On Confucius' Political Ideas], 253.

142. *Wang* (亡) is pronounced as *wú*, meaning the same as "无," the absence of something, attested in ancient usage and consistent in the understanding of most interpreters. See Ya Se, *Lunyu Daquanji*, 43.

143. Li and Ma, *Lunyu*, 18–19.

144. The ancient China depicts those under-civilized nations from the East as Yi (夷), from the South as Man (蛮), from the West as Rong (戎), and from the North as Di (狄). Here only two of those nations are named, yet in fact Confucian meant to include all four, see Chen, *Sishu Duben*, 80–81.

145. Huang Kan was a Confucian scholar specialized in the early ritual texts esp. Analects, who created a variety of intellectual and practical links between Confucian thought with Buddhism and Daoism. See Slingerland, *Confucius Analects*, 259.

146. Slingerland, *Confucius Analects*, 18.

147. While the element of irony of this passage is suggested, this book nevertheless follows Xing Bing's (邢昺；931–1010) reading in his *Lunyu Shu* 《论语疏》, which takes it to mean superiority of Yi and Di over Xia because Yi and Di had leaders

Analects 3:5 is an irony, which literally reads the inferiority of Yi and Di but actually meant otherwise. The whole phrase therefore can be taken as, "Even under-civilized people like Yi and Di have rulers, unlike Xia who has no ruler in practice."[148] Confucius was scornful of the reality of hierarchical chaos at his time. To Confucius, propriety is a preferable way of order for the administration of a state.

The Middle Path as Method—The Analects 1:12

> **Analects 1:12**—Master You said, "In practicing the rules of propriety, harmony is to be prized. The ways of ancient kings had shown that this is the most excellent quality both in things small and great they had done. In the event that this does not work, aim at harmony without forcing it, instead regulating[149] it with propriety. Otherwise, this will not work as well."

Confucius places a premium on caution in exercising the collective attributes that he consistently has taught. In the Analects 1:12 above, for example, propriety is good in executing duty and serving rulers. Yet insisting too much of it will see a reversal of its goodness: harmony will be a fake. Elsewhere in the Analects 3:18, the skewed practice of propriety will be flattery.[150] Sensible rulers do well in deciding what measure of propriety will work in a given circumstance. In a related passage from the Analects 4:10, Confucius states that an exemplary person is not unvaryingly for or against anything in the world; appropriateness, or *yi*, will rather be the consideration.[151] Edward Slingerland notes here an indication of situational

---

although they did not practice propriety. See also Li and Ma, *Lunyu*, 18–19. Cf. different interpretations that liken Xia's breach of propriety to Yi and Di (nor superior), by Slingerland, *Confucius Analects*, 18, and by Chen, *Sishu Duben*, 80–81.

148. See Ya Se, *Lunyu Daquanji*, 43.

149. Li and Ma, *Lunyu*, 6–7. "Harmony" should be a measurement of how propriety should be practiced. But "harmony" is the means, not the end, for achieving propriety. Things will not work effectually when "harmony" becomes the end rather than the means. See translation of Lau in Yang and Lau, *Lunyu*, 7–8.

150. Scholars yield a different but well accepted interpretation of Analects 3:18, suggesting instead that Confucius was actually defending his insistence of propriety. That insistent was taken as a flattery by some people. It showed that propriety had degenerated at that time, so that people viewed it with suspicion and cynicism. See Chen, *Sishu Duben*, 87 and Slingerland, *Confucius Analects*, 24.

151. *Shi* (适) is "certain," pronounced as *di* (敌). Its binary opposition here is *mo* (莫), "certainly not." *Yi* (义) is best understood here as *yi* (宜). See Ya Se, *Lunyu Daquanji*, 66; Chen, *Sishu Duben*, 95.

responsiveness, which requires one to rely upon "internal moral sense, rather than conventional social prejudice, when judging people or affairs."[152] The passage teaches one to be flexible in deciding what to do: never should one be rigid as to insist on certain things nor should one be adamant to repudiate on other things. Such flexibility should be considered according to its appropriateness. Elsewhere, in serving a ruler, asserting too much of one's opinion or being unrelenting in one's attitude will eventually meet with humiliation (Analects 4:26). One should stop giving counsel if the ruler does not pay notice anymore.[153] If the ruler can be annoyed with repeated details, advice rendered to the ruler should be in reasonable occurrence. These teachings of reasonability and flexibility in the Analects suggest the idea of *zhongyong* (中庸), the middle path, which has long been scarce in the practice of people at that time.[154]

There are scholars who believe that the middle path, or mostly rendered as the Mean, is the most valuable thought in Confucius' standard of human conduct. The Analects communicates the idea of attaining wisdom through the thinking method of *zhongyong*.[155] The collective measure of goodness in forms of *ren*, *li*, and *yi* can be lived out by a consideration of *zhongyong*: doing what is perfectly suitable in any situation. *Ren*, rather than living out in a generic sense, should be exercised depending on the people one is dealing with (Analects 4:3). *Li*, though highly recommended, should also be done according to proper measure and not amounting to flattery (Analects 3:18). Therefore, it is not surprising that Confucius recommends it for an exemplary person: a well-balanced mixture of substance (质) and refinement (文; Analects 6:18). The Analects 15:28 similarly suggests an attitude of moderation instead of following the talk of people. Confucius himself admits that he has to "keep hammering at the two sides of questions

---

152. Slingerland, *Confucius Analects*, 32–33. According to Slingerland, Confucius' approval of his conventionally tabooed son-in-law (Analects 5:1) and his suspicion of unexamined social judgments in 13:4 serve as practical illustrations of this principle.

153. Chen, *Sishu Duben*, 101.

154. According to Analects 6:29 and also *the Doctrine of the Mean* (chapter 3), "The Master said, 'Supreme indeed is the Mean as a moral virtue. It has long been rare among the common people.'"

155. It has been suggested that, if one renders the two opposing extremes as point A and point B, there are four ways of *zhongyong* taught in Analects: 1) It is neither A nor B, not invariably for or against anything (Analects 4:10); 2) It is both A and B, depending on political circumstances (Analects 8:13); 3) It is A and then B, depending on the primary importance supported by secondary depiction (Analects 7:38); and 4) It is A but not B, where B represents a total contrast of A, recommendations to choose for the desirables against the undesirables (Analects 17:18; 20:2). See Zhu, *Yu Kongzi Duihua* [Dialogue with Confucius], 47–53.

until he gets something out of it" (Analects 9:8). Hence, the middle path is not exactly another ethical idea, but a method of practicing virtuous governance that encompasses humanness, propriety, and righteousness.

The middle path should be misunderstood neither as compromise nor as ambiguity As the term suggests itself, it means the opposite of extremes. It is neither too much of an action nor none at all. It is an appropriate action taken at any point around the medial, doing what is suitable in any given context. The Analects 11:16 tells of how Confucius evaluates two of his students, "Shi overshoots the mark; Shang falls short." For Confucius, neither Shi nor Shang should be considered better than another because Shi overexerts things and Shang underdoes them. One can tell, therefore, *zhongyong* is the wisdom to find balance.[156] Through learning and observation, one can master the middle path in dealing with people and matters in politics (not being too simple nor too complicated; the Analects 6:2), economics (spending necessarily without being extravagant; the Analects 20:2), natural science (proper way of agriculture maneuvering), personality (a well-balanced of substance and refinement; the Analects 6:18), and behavior (moderation instead of being undisciplined or overly scrupulous; the Analects 13:21).[157] From this understanding of *zhongyong*, corresponding ideas are being developed: standing firm without compromising, *zhongli* (中立), acting in accordance to harmony, *zhonghe* (中和), and distinguishing between right and wrong, as well as true and false, *zhezhong* (折中).[158] Perhaps one can conclude that *zhongyong*, including its corresponding ideas, is a consciousness of behaving according to what experiences and observations have perceived to be appropriate. This attitude of *zhongyong* distinguishes the exemplary person from the inferior. *Zhongyong* guides one's personal cultivation in a dynamic, time-sensitive, and flexible way according to circumstantial conditions.[159] In short, *zhongyong* is a method for exercising wisdom to decide when (the appropriate time) and how (the degree and frequency) to exercise a certain virtue.

Virtuous Living as a Way of Life—The Analects 2:21 and 7:11

Analects 2:21—Someone asked Confucius, saying, "Master, why you are not involved in politics?" The Master replied, "*The Book

---

156. Shang et al., *Zhongguo Ruxue Fazanshi* [History and Development], 37.
157. Du and Gao, "Zhongyong" [Moderation], 371-2.
158. Ibid., 373-83.
159. An idea of *zhong* with dynamic or action, and circumstantial ethics which are mentioned in Zhu, *Yu Kongzi Duihua*, 45, 11.

of History says, 'By being filial to your parents and friendly to your siblings, one can exert an influence upon government.'[160] This then is also an involvement in politics. Why should there be *official duty* in order to be considered having involved in politics?"[161]

Analects 7:11—The Master said to Yan Yuan, "Only you and I have the ability to go forward when called to be in office, and stay out of sight when not appointed."

In Confucius' articulation, virtuous living is an attitude. Being virtuous is a way of life applicable in all aspects of life, including in the arena of politics. Hence in the Analects 2:21, whether or not one has an official duty in government is not an issue to qualify for practicing attributes of filial piety and hospitality. Slingerland brings in the idea of *Wuwei* (无为) here, suggesting "one should 'do government' through 'not doing'"—by establishing the "root" of virtue, and letting the rest follow naturally through the power of one's virtue.[162] Here, Confucius asserts a way of life whereby, through one's virtue in daily living, a person can be influential in society. The Analects 7:11 is therefore complementary to the understanding of the Analects 2:21. When virtuous living represents a way of life for him, Confucius is ready to take office anytime when appointed. When he is not appointed, he will remain hidden.

Similarly, Confucius commends virtuous lifestyles of people even when they are not appointed to government office. Hence in the Analects 15:7, Qubo Yu (蘧伯玉) is lauded as *junzi*—he takes office when there is social order, and stays out of sight when there is social chaos. Confucius often conveys that there is a time of order and a time of chaos, such as here in the Analects 15:7, again in the Analects 14:1, 14:3, 8:13, and 16:2. At times, people should discern the difference between social order and chaos and act appropriately in response to the situation. At other times, however, a person who stands for what he believes in times of order *and* chaos— such as Shi Yu (史鱼) in the Analects 15:7—is commendable. Confucius

---

160. Lau states that this part is from a lost chapter of *The Book of History*, or *Shang Shu* (尚书), incorporated in a modified form into another chapter. See Yang and Lau, *Lunyu*, 21. Many commentators point to the possibility of mis-division. For example, Chen, *Sishu Duben*, 77 prefers the exclamation of filial not to be included in the original text of *The Book of History*.

161. "Official duty" is my addition to make the point clear, thus is italicized. This understanding reflects that of most commentators, perhaps informed by Zhu Xi's reading. Cf. Slingerland, *Confucius Analects*, 15, "What need is there, then, to speak of 'participating in government?'"

162. Slingerland, *Confucius Analects*, 15.

nevertheless advocates virtuous living every time. Then, when a virtuous person is appointed to official duty in a time of order, he can make a difference in society.

Furthermore, the Analects 2:20 brings out the importance of cultivation in shaping attitudes in life, in order that people may be filled with enthusiasm. According to this passage, cultivation can nurture unlearned people to be diligent in seeking virtues in life. In addition, the Analects 13:9 calls attention to the need for education, apart from being well fed.[163] Food comes first, as it is a necessity in life. Yet when the basic human need is fulfilled, the need for virtuous cultivation is specified as well. Confucian education hence aims to shape one's virtuous lifestyle. This is a visionary solution to shape a learned culture, one that well suits Confucius' idea of social refinement.

A Reading of the Analects Political Wisdom

Humanness (仁 Ren): the Essence of One's Political Maneuver

The Analects communicates a political philosophy based on both personal and collective practices of humanness. De Bary avers that *ren* is an undefinable, open-ended concept that suggests the essence of a common humanity.[164] Though the Analects does not give a definition of *ren*, it is clear on where to begin to nurture *ren*.[165] *Ren* is a lifestyle. Political leaders, namely, rulers and government officials, are required to manifest this lifestyle. In the Analects 7:30, Confucius makes *ren* so important that if one wills to be virtuous, one can be a person of virtue. On virtuous governance, political leadership is typified by exemplary moral standard and leadership. Such political leadership entails respect and trust from the people. Therefore, regarding politics, Confucius promotes character building especially by cultivation of humanness. It appears that no one before him had advocated the value of humanness in relation to politics. The inculcation of humanness generates the moral consciousness of people and is constructive and preferable to reinforcing punishment.

---

163. As noted by Slingerland, *Confucius Analects*, 143, it is food first and education second here (in contrast to 12:7, which states food second and trust from the people as the first). As a "proto-Mencian" theme, the people need to be materially comfortable before they can be educated, presumably in virtue as maintained by most commentators. Cf. *Mencius* 3:A3.

164. De Bary, *Trouble with Confucianism*, 38–39.

165. Ibid., 39.

Ren is required of all people. Confucius' political ideal elaborates on the ruler-minister relationship in all human ethics, for it comprises the most important mechanism of political survival to ensure society's subsistence and national well-being. Since *ren* inculcates mutual respect within civic life and ensures political stability in a state, it alleviates the tension between the ruling class and subjects.[166] Hence it is virtuous governance, but not legalism, that is given preference in Confucian politics.

Confucius' emphasis on leading with a prerequisite of humanness is a sign of progress in his time. He has directly pointed out the reason for political chaos and power corruption among the ruling class. Due to his conviction for virtuous governance, Confucius encourages virtuous people, not the royalty's families or relatives, to be assigned important duties. Therefore, the Analects recommends the Yao and Shun ideal of succession based on virtue rather than on lineage (Analects 20:1). Personal cultivation, according to the Analects, therefore, is essentially related to the public political sphere. This political wisdom is the extension and application of Confucius' emphasis on personal cultivation of *ren*.[167] The Analects communicates that people of *ren* should be placed in the leadership position of a state. As such, Confucius' idea of a virtuous government brings advantage to the people as a whole. *Ren* therefore is a decisive political imperative in the wisdom of the Analects.

Propriety (礼 Li): Proper Political Behavior

A substantial amount of political teaching in the Analects weighs on the endorsement of propriety. Politically speaking, rectification of roles and functions according to the order of ruler-noble-minister-commoner entails distinctive proper political behavior. Political leaders are concerned with government matters according to their offices (Analects 8:14). Rectification, *zhengming*, thus becomes the most important function of government to ensure political unity in a state.[168] Rectification will eventually lead to the centralization of power in which the ruler occupies the apex of hierarchy and supremacy. The role and function of the ruler comprises the highest authority, status, and power. The role and function of ministers also entail different ministerial responsibilities and duties. Not only do the personal

---

166. Lin, "Lun Kongzi de Zhengzhi Sixiang," 258.

167. Zhu, *Lunyu Benyi* [New Interpretation on the Original Meaning of the Analects], 154.

168. Hsü, *Political Philosophy of Confucianism*, 46–59, 61.

qualities of both rulers and ministers' matter but also the way they carry out their functions, namely, *li*.

In ancient Chinese, *li* is treasured as a social norm and cultural expectation. It was the prescribed behavior for everyone born into a particular social class. *Li* ranges from one's inward self-control of speech and behavior to one's outward dress code, inter-personal addresses at home, in a clan, in society and in royal court, and further to the governance of a nation. *Li* goes well with music, *yue* (乐). In pairs, both *li* and *yue* signify the quintessence of a civilization. In practice, *li* qualifies the manner in which *ren* (仁) is to be carried out. Confucius did not invent the concept of *li*, nor did he design a society based on its principle.[169] Historically, the idea of propriety had effectively brought about political stability and harmonious society, namely, in the Zhou dynasty. The political structure and kinship community designed by Duke Zhou (周公) was one that established the Zhou emperor as the universal king under heaven.[170] The emperor was called "the son of heaven," and his family was the primary clan. Subsequently, every noble family was constructed on the same clan principles. The socio-political system was hence designed into a hierarchical structure to combine the ruler, nobles, ministers, other officials, intellectuals, and commoners into an entity. But the Zhou political order surviving during Confucius' time collapsed due to corruption of the moral standard among the ruling class, giving rise to political chaos. Confucius determined to rectify such lawlessness and restore social order by restructuring the feudal values toward a social institution modeled upon Zhou's *li* (Analects 3:14). Instead of handing down the aristocratic feudal values naturally from parents to children, Confucius systematized and universalized them according to a system of moral imperatives.[171] Therefore, Confucius' political ideas revolved around the concern about how to interpret, justify, and adapt such a system.[172] From then, Confucian thinkers strived to contribute political ideas that suggested ways of reinstalling orderliness in society. This movement stimulated a hundred schools of thought that emphasized distinctive aspects of political administration, some even dismissing the idea of *li* altogether.[173]

---

169. Jones and Culliney, "Confucian Order at the Edge of Chaos," 398.

170. Chen, "Modernity and Confucian Political Philosophy," 95.

171. Blocker, "Chinese Philosophy," 231.

172. Chen, "Modernity and Confucian Political Philosophy," 96.

173. The Mohist, Daoist, and Legalist, for example, rejected the idea of *li*, which was more often than not in accompaniment with the emphasis of music to form a culture that upheld propriety and music together. This culture is promoted in the Confucian tradition. See Yu, "Rujia Zhengzhi Sixiang," 146.

Confucian political wisdom is expressed in a time-consuming cultivation of *li* and rectification of name. Socially speaking, the observance and affirmation of *li* is relevant, even today in the preservation of modern society.[174] Moral chaos and role confusion necessitate propriety as a harmonious integration of individuals into society.[175] To restore propriety, one does not necessarily revive the feudalistic political system, which tends to be oppressive in nature. It is because Confucius' notion of *li* and the rectification of name are transformative. His political ideas on the appointment of government offices based on virtue—rather than descent partiality—and his establishment of home-school education were revolutionary. Therefore, it is even paradoxical to say of Confucius that he was trying to restore Zhou *li*.

In the core of his reform, Confucius aimed to correct corrupt political mismanagement and a functionally confused social system. The abuse of socio-political protocols of his time resulted in disorder. To resume proper order, Confucius suggested a centralization of power, where the emperor stands supreme as the head of a state and also as the ultimate commanding figure. Therefore, in his conception of a political vision, Confucius affirms a monarchical and patriarchal system.[176] He assumes a pyramid power structure, as well as proper authority of the ruler-noble-minister-commoner. In contemporary words, Confucius is a political thinker who is pro-establishment. His political ideas are not entirely conservative, but transformative and progressive. Consequently, in my judgment, Confucius is quite avant-garde, for he promotes everyone, rulers and commoners alike, to act according to *li* as social norms that are drawn out beforehand. As such, everyone in a state is bound by expectations of the moral standard and requirement of virtue. The rulers who do not act in accordance with customary anticipations should then be replaced. Also, despite having the supreme authority, power in the hands of the ruler is never meant to be absolute (contra the Legalist) and is never intended to be abused for personal gain. The point is that Confucius' political thoughts recorded in the Analects reflect a reformist's ideas of social transformation. A segregation of hierarchical status, a feudalistic social system, and a monopolization of power are generally assumed in the Analects. This makes the Confucian political ideal appear less practical in the postmodern democratic world. However, one should never examine Confucian political thought from the democratic perspective of later human history. The essence of the Confucian political ideal can still

---

174. Jones and Culliney, "Confucian Order at the Edge of Chaos," 399.
175. Leys, *Analects of Confucius*, 178.
176. De Bary, *Trouble with Confucianism*, 4.

serve as the inner dynamic within a political body to necessitate order and spirit of unity.

Righteousness (义 Yi): Doing the Right Things and Doing Things Right

In the Analects, *yi* represents what is just and appropriate. A political leader knows what the right thing to do is and should act upon it. As long as an action qualifies as necessary, *yi* strives to do the appropriate, and vice versa. This behavior is expected of people in general, especially of *junzi*, one who often hold a political duty in the government office. When a minister finds himself unable to assert what is thought to be right and instead is driven to do otherwise, he should resign. Such is the Confucian principle of ministerial responsibility.[177] According to Leonard Shihlien Hsü, when a ruler is too corrupt to stay on the throne or when he is too old to attend to public affairs, the minister may act as the regent of the government based on *bona fide*—approval by heaven and by the people.[178] In this circumstance, a lower-ranking authority figure functions in supremacy to sustain national balance. As de Bary also has argued, the public trust and the personal commitment to serve humankind enable someone with the mandate to rule.[179] This mandate represents heaven's imperative for leaders to claim their political and moral conscience.[180] It differs from toppling a ruling figure in the name of following the mandate of heaven. Confucius approved this ministerial duty as a way to *yi*, simply because of its appropriateness in benefitting the people at large.

Righteousness involves a process of personal dynamic in decision making. At its most fundamental level, "*yi* denotes the importation of aesthetic, moral, and rational significance into personal action in the world."[181] In other words, one would decide to do what constitutes as right and just whenever one sees the necessity. Therefore, *yi* is also doing the right thing at the right time, when the situation and timing requires one to do so. If coupled with *li*, *yi* expresses the right action through appropriate manner. Righteousness is important even in a tedious matter, for "people who spend the whole day together, indulging themselves in showing petty cleverness

---

177. Hsü, *Political Philosophy of Confucianism*, 89.

178. Ibid. Such was the case with Duke Zhou, who executed authority as a regent when the ruler who succeeded the throne from his father (Duke Zhou's demised brother) was too young to rule.

179. De Bary, "Prophetic Voice," 354.

180. Ibid.

181. Yu, "Yi: Practical Wisdom," 336; see also Hall and Ames, *Thinking through Confucius*, 90.

without ever touching on the subject of righteousness in conversations, are surely difficult to teach" (Analects 15:17). Empty chatter is inappropriate and hence not recommended.

Confucius places a high regard on *yi* to substantiate an exemplary person. In the reading of the Analects, *yi* is inseparable with the practices of other qualities mentioned earlier namely, *ren* and *li*. These qualities constitute a collective attribute toward Confucius' political ideals. Exercising humanness (仁), propriety (礼), and righteousness (义) is a prerequisite for virtuous governance. Humanness represents the substance of a virtuous government, whereas propriety in its visible forms and righteousness are the motive. To sum up, virtuous governance is the basis of political rule. Humanness is the essence of such virtuous governance, whereas propriety is the tool, and righteousness, the attitude. Humanness, propriety, and righteousness will collectively lead to effective political leadership. Politics can progress in a healthy manner if it derives from Confucian ideas of *ren*, *li*, and *yi*. A government works best if these virtues precede law and punishment.

The Exemplary Person (君子 Junzi): A Moral and Political Construct

The Analects offers no fewer than 106 passages that deal with the subject of *junzi*.[182] It communicates the distinctiveness between the exemplary person (*junzi*) and the inferior person (*xiaoren*), using a similar figure of speech from ancient wisdom literature of contrasting the righteous and the wicked or the wise vs. the fool. In the Analects, the term "*junzi*" always refers to a person with moral quality and often points to a political leader. *Junzi*, literally "son of the ruler," denotes a descendant of the ruling house and thus indicates an aristocrat.[183] Before Confucius, *junzi* always denoted those of higher socio-political status. To this social status of political leaders, Confucius introduced notable ethical content, qualifying a *junzi* as one with high moral awareness in addition to serving in the royal court as minister and official.[184] The meaning of *junzi*, accordingly, has changed from an emphasis

---

182. De Bary, *Trouble with Confucianism*, 6.
183. Waley, *Analects of Confucius*, 28.
184. Leys, *Analects of Confucius*, 105–106. When the ethical dimension was substantially developed unto the notion of *junzi*, it has remarkably changed how one understands the term: a commoner can be called a *junzi* if having a commendable moral standing; likewise, an aristocrat can be disqualified as a *junzi* for lacking in moral stature. In Confucius' oratory in Analects, *junzi* is essentially an aristocrat, or political leader. Without a title or function in a political organization, *junzi* still exists as one who lives high moral standard in society.

on high social standing to an emphasis on high moral standard.[185] The new interpretation has far-reaching implications for fundamental aristocratic stature.

The political functioning and moral gravity of *junzi* are hence spelled out at the beginning of the Analects. In Confucius' rhetoric, *junzi* who possess high social status at the same time as being morally upright will command trust and deference. The Analects 13:26 speaks of political leaders being at ease without arrogance, whereas the commoner lacks such gravity. A political leader agrees with others without echoing what they say, but a commoner lacks such weight (Analects 13:23). Elsewhere, a political leader is at ease of mind, whereas a commoner is full of anxiety (Analects 7:37). A political leader, being far-sighted, aspires to morality while a commoner aspires only to one's native land. Similarly, a political leader has respect for the verdict, whereas a commoner is concerned only with receiving generosity (Analects 4:11). A political leader empowers others to achieve what is good and does not help them to effect what is bad; a commoner does not possess such authority (Analects 12:16). In terms of purpose-seeking, a political leader aims above, believably to imply moral standard; a commoner aims down below, probably meaning profit (Analects 14:23). Even if a learned person, people are advised to choose the path of a political leader instead of commoner (Analects 6:13). Confucius' discussions of *junzi* in the Analects include the fulfillment of personal moral mission even in political adversity, in order to preserve one's self-respect and to remain true in one's sense of right and wrong.[186]

Again, the difference of interpretations of *junzi* and *xiaoren* should be kept in mind. In the Analects, *junzi* occurs ninety-three times. *Junzi* is always one who lives with high moral standards, as opposed to the one who is morally questionable (Analects 7:37; 12:16 and 14:23), and is often the political leader as opposed to the civilian who is the subject (Analects 16:6, 17:4 and 12:19). Many of their occurrences in the Analects are set in the context of political leadership, though it is deliberately connected to morality. In the passages where a moral standard is not meant, *junzi* taken as a political leader still works. In my opinion, Confucius himself does not distinguish between the two possible meanings of *junzi* (between morality and political leadership). Since *junzi* is in the position of political leadership, *junzi* should live with the qualities of *ren*, *li*, *yi* and *de*. Moreover, the various qualities that convey the character, knowledge, depth, and width of

---

185. De Bary, *Trouble with Confucianism*, 6.
186. Ibid., 7.

a *junzi* are Confucius' concepts of the archetypal person who is needed to actualize his political ideals.[187]

Based on Confucius' rhetoric in the Analects, *junzi* is therefore a moral and a political term. The moral aspect of *junzi* is often acknowledged over the political aspect by people. Therefore, this chapter stresses the importance of its political aspect. Since *junzi* is in political leadership, *junzi* is bound by certain codes of morality and manners, signifying higher social status and superiority of character.[188] That makes *junzi* the leader whereas *xiaoren* are the subjects, the commoners, and the followers. Self-cultivation of *de* (德), *ren* (仁), *li* (礼), and *yi* (义) is highly prized and is strongly promoted for political leadership. Confucius' educational goal is to cultivate *junzi*: one who is morally suited to be an effective leader in society. Not only is it politically constructed, *junzi* is a practical objective to achieve compared to *shengren* (圣人; saint), a person of perfect moral character, which appears remarkably less in the Analects.[189]

Political Wisdom in the Analects: An Assessment

Although much discussion has been rendered on topics of virtuous governance, the political wisdom in the Analects does not rely entirely on the qualities of *de, ren, li,* and *yi*. The political organization in the Analects weighs substantially on management knowhow and administrative strength as well. Dongfang Shuo and Lin Hongcheng, who argue for a separation of politics and morality in the Analects, insist on "independent spheres of and differences between morality and politics."[190] Quoting various passages from the Analects, they establish that the wisdom of management proficiency should stand as a separate entity, not necessarily replying on moral agency. Quoting the Analects 4:13 and 12:11, they illustrate that proper duties and obligations are required as essentials of politics.[191] Work ethics—as pointed out in the Analects 12:14, 12:17, 13:1, 13:3 and 15:38—too is not a moral issue, but involves responsibilities and priorities consistent with appropriate posts in political involvement. Further, proper delegation according to abilities and character, depicted in the Analects 2:19 and 6:8,

187. Liu, "Lun Kongzi de Zhengzhi Sixiang," 266.

188. Waley, *Analects of Confucius*, 28.

189. Taylor, "Study of Confucianism as a Religious Tradition," 148, has nevertheless argued that the goal of sagehood (it is called "sainthood" in this book) is at the root of Confucian religious life.

190. Shuo and Lin, "Separation of Politics and Morality," 402.

191. Ibid., 404.

reflects popular management theory. Likewise, national steadiness will be ensured if the administration of political affairs in food supply, armed forces, gross productivity, and budget is run with an attitude of diligence and seriousness. According to the Analects 1:10, Confucius does not solely embrace a moral ideal for all political concerns. Rather, Confucius' politics is concerned primarily with political legitimacy, on how the ruler and his government, as representatives of the collective interest, should perform their roles and functions effectively.[192] Once again, the political wisdom depicted in Analects underlines management savoir-faire in addition to moral guidance of the ruler. As Shuo and Lin have pointed out, the enrichment of a state, military force, and establishment of political orders are fundamental principles of politics.[193]

The differentiation between politics and morality does not mean that both are completely separate from each other, as Shuo and Lin also remarked.[194] Confucius appears to identify more with the practice of collective attributes in political articulation, for there are times when a moral standard is required to execute political leadership. Yet there also are times when what is required represents a wise performance of duties related to the theory of organizational behavior, work ethics, and management. One should therefore be thoughtful when summarizing Confucius' political ideas as depicted in the Analects. Essential management theories like planning, organizing, delegation, control, and leadership style for the purpose of accomplishing a goal are actually engaged in the Analects. The way to organize human resources and national reserves also is conveyed brilliantly. Shuo and Lin are therefore right to maintain that the consultancy of morality and the consultancy of politics in the Analects have their own boundaries and features, and that "the clue and contents of Confucius' answers cannot be generally treated as a substitution of moralities for politics."[195]

To sum up, Confucius reasoned that the evils of his day came from a decay of morals, especially among the ruling class. Against this setting, Confucius advocated moral management, *dezhi* (德治), and virtuous governance, *renzheng* (仁政). In Confucian political understanding, the word "*junzi*," apart from being a term for people who meet Confucius' moral standard, is indeed a political construct. Confucius' political wisdom communicates that *junzi*, as a leader in political realm, should cultivate *ren*, *li*, *yi*, and *de* because the rectification of those he governs begins with him. As

192. Chen, "Modernity and Confucian Political Philosophy," 96.
193. Shuo and Lin, "Separation of Politics and Morality," 402.
194. Ibid., 407.
195. Shuo and Lin, "Separation of Politics and Morality," 416.

such, Confucius' political thoughts are valuable. Its concepts on qualities of *ren*, *li*, *yi*, and *de* weigh up to strengthen the political efficiency. Among Confucian thinkers themselves, Confucius' political philosophy has the onerous task of providing solutions to the political reconstruction of contemporary Chinese society.[196]

Nevertheless, the person of *junzi* and its corresponding Confucian attributes appear to be idealistic. Confucius' politics faces challenges of being institutionalized into a functional political system.[197] One could not institutionalize virtuous governance on a measurement of morality, humanness, propriety, and righteousness. Further, Confucius' politics cannot solve the problems of having rulers who are ineffectual, oppressive, and morally corrupt.[198] Moreover, virtuous governance is time-consuming. A true *junzi*-type ruler takes a generation to cultivate (Analects 13:12), and an actualized virtuous state requires one hundred years to eliminate the violence and cruelty (Analects 13:11). In reality, there is no political body in Chinese history that executes virtuous governance based on the teaching of the Analects. Confucius' evaluation of the virtue of political leaders was perhaps too optimistic.[199] No one among the rulers of Confucius' time followed his political thoughts. Many of the post-Confucius emperors in ancient China who proclaimed to adapt a Confucian way of governance in fact practiced legalism. Han Wu Di (汉武帝; 156–87 BCE) of the Han dynasty, for instance, recognized the effectiveness of Confucian political thought in consolidating his rule. He held Confucian teaching in the greatest esteem by rejecting all other schools, yet also reinforced harsh punishment on his officials and violence on his people. In later historical developments, Confucian rhetoric also was employed as propaganda in political manipulations.[200] Absolute political power is more desirable in most cases, and humans are easily corrupted by it. For these reasons, Confucius' political philosophy either was distorted or not actually practiced in Chinese history.[201] Yet, one should never dismiss Confucius' political thoughts as futile philosophical conceptions or null ethical formats. Confucius' political portrayal of *junzi* is attractive, and his political ideals are engaging. Such ideals become the driving force of Confucius' pedagogical vocation in the later part of his life, when he recruited many other disciples and nurtured them toward

---

196. Chen, "Modernity and Confucian Political Philosophy," 94.
197. Jiang, "Lunyu de Zhengzhi Gainian," 225.
198. Ibid.
199. Zhao, "Axiological Rules," 167.
200. Kam, *Critiques of Confucius*, 548.
201. Zhao, "Axiological Rules," 167.

actualizing his political aspirations. The extent to which Confucian political thought could impact the political reconstruction today is dependent on the influence of scholars and the adaptation of political leaders who firmly believe in its significance.

Conclusion

The political cornerstone of the Confucian vision of a good governing body is one outlined by virtuous strength and competence. The ultimate reason for such a government is the well-being of the people: to be rid of oppression, violence, and tyranny. Yet Confucian political thought is a multifaceted entity. Functionally, Confucius' governing wisdom encompasses a leadership substance that is preceded by virtue, an administrative awareness that weighs on righteousness, and an organizational method outlined by propriety.[202] The political wisdom of Confucius is therefore distinctive. It stresses collective attributes instead of law and punishment for political effects, without compromising the emphasis on skills and capabilities. A government led by *junzi*(s), who are virtuous on one hand and proficient on the other, is certain to accomplish political order and social harmony leading to national transformation. Confucius, as depicted in the Analects, is consequently a political reformer. His political ideas are visionary and wise. In short, the purpose of political organization according to the Analects is to ensure orderliness and functionality in a human society. This assessment merits a mark of wisdom for the Confucian political ideals depicted in the Analects.

---

202. Li, "Rujia Guanli Zhexue [Confucian Management Philosophy]," 373–85.

4

Ecclesiastes and the Analects at a Crossroads

THIS CHAPTER ILLUSTRATES A cross-textual approach to interpreting Ecclesiastes and the Analects in parallel. The "crossing"[1] of these two texts will help an interpreter go beyond the canonical boundaries to discover wider human quests. As a cross-textual reader, I attempt to engage the biblical text that speaks for my faith and, at the same time, engage a native text wherein I was culturally nurtured. The metaphor of a "crossroads" in this chapter is chosen to encapsulate two meanings. First, it is a place where one reading crosses another. Second, it points to a new direction in one's understanding of the crossings. This cross-textual reading is predicated upon a conviction that new understandings may be obtained through mutual enrichment of two texts. In the past, Ecclesiastes has been placed in conversation with *Mencius* and the *Daode Jing*. The Analects too was frequently compared to the biblical Proverbs. Such endeavors are insightful. This study represents another effort, by focusing on political wisdom through the reading of Ecclesiastes and the Analects. Observable commonalities and disparities between the two inspire a dialogical imagination. The purpose of this study is to show how a cross-textual reading of Ecclesiastes and the Analects directs one to live wisely, as a common human quest in a politically disordered world.

Criteria for Establishing Correspondence between Texts

There are several approaches to genuine correspondence between texts. Most comparative studies undertake to engage in exchanging thoughts or ideas based on similar themes expounded from the written records. Cross-textuality, however, engages more than textual correspondences.[2] According

---

1. Lee, "Cross-textual Hermeneutics on Gospel and Culture," 47.

2. For instance, a reader compares the etymology of Confucian *ren* (仁) with biblical *agape*, and explores their corresponding philology, semantic field, and meaning.

to P. D. Miscall, a reader, as an agent of meaning, "must decide what limits are to be placed on what is to be read and how it is to be read."[3] As a reader, I recognize the links between Ecclesiastes and the Analects based on three criteria.

First, the occurrence of key terms that share similar ideas is compared and discussed. For instance, words in Ecclesiastes such as ṣedek (צֶדֶק), "righteousness," and mišpāṭ (מִשְׁפָּט), "justice," are compared to the term yi (义), "righteousness," in the Analects. Second, like concepts are considered in both texts. The basis for claiming similarities is admittedly subjective and interpretive. On the above two criteria, a link or links should be established between Ecclesiastes and the Analects.[4] The meaning of a text, therefore, is not only found in the text within Ecclesiastes and the Analects respectively, but also is found in the space "between" the texts.[5] By reading the two texts in parallel, a reader forms an understanding of the fabric of the texts, which gives them meaning.

Third and most importantly, their sapiential nature connects Ecclesiastes and the Analects, even though their basic assumptions are different. Ecclesiastes is concerned more with survival in an unsettling socio-political reality, a form of descriptive wisdom. The Analects, on the other hand, is concerned with advocacy for change in such reality, a form of prescriptive wisdom. Yet wisdom connects both reflective and prescriptive types. As has been said before, instructions and reflections are pointers to how one can cope in life. Wisdom is didactic in essence. Thus, descriptive wisdom (observations and reflections) and prescriptive wisdom (instructions and admonitions) are both didactic. I submit that political wisdom contains both instructions for political organization *and* reflections on how to survive politically. Also, the line of difference between reflective wisdom and prescriptive wisdom in each text is not very clear at times. As one can see from previous chapters, Ecclesiastes and the Analects in turn communicate both types of wisdom to different extents. One can only say, therefore, that Ecclesiastes deals more on reflective wisdom and less on the prescriptive wisdom. The Analects, on the other hand, is preoccupied more with

---

Based on their similarities as well as differences, a reader finds connections where a text enlightens the other.

3. Miscall, "Texts, More Texts," 252; Miller, "Intertextuality," 294. This idea is in favor of a reader-oriented approach.

4. Miller, "Intertextuality," 294. Miller is relating to the intertextuality within the Old Testament per se, yet his idea here serves as a general guidance.

5. Therefore, the outcome of this cross-textuality will enhance the understanding of the two texts individually. See Miscall, "Texts, More Texts," 14 and Miller, "Intertextuality," 299.

prescriptive wisdom and not as much of the reflective type. Moreover, the political wisdom meant in this study is universal: it is the ability to cope with living life within a socio-political structure.[6] Taken together, both Ecclesiastes and The Analects communicate political wisdom for surviving in an imperfect world. The main body of this chapter illustrates such ability from a cross-textual reading of both texts.

A Cross-Textual Reading of Ecclesiastes with the Analects

From their Social Political Background

The Need for Order

In the thought of Ecclesiastes as well as the Analects, there should be a proper order for governing socio-political living.[7] The expressions of such order are done through the perspective of time (in Ecclesiastes) and dao (in the Analects). In Ecclesiastes, Qoheleth points out a social disorder in which fools are placed in high positions, and the rich are lowly stationed (10:5–7). Instead of social order, Qoheleth witnesses a disordered world. Hence, he questions the social order that he once he thought he knew. Similarly, Confucius observes the times when the dao does not prevail, when feudal lords violate the authority of the ruler to take power into their own hands (Analects 16:2). Confucius is therefore concerned with the establishment of a just society or "the restoration of a lost order—based on moral leadership and persuasion."[8]

Qoheleth and Confucius face different levels of socio-political disorder in the land. For both of them, people need to uphold the socio-political order. The oppression inflicted by government officials in society are real. But both Qoheleth and Confucius believe that the better alternative is having political leaders who govern well (5:8–9 [Hebrew 5:7–8]; Analects 12:19; 20:2). Qoheleth is preoccupied with coping with this reality; Confucius is engrossed in managing the situation. Qoheleth makes an imperative of the theological assertion to fear God, whereas Confucius offers a way of ethics

---

6. Wisdom in general is not confined to the Israelite community, nor is it necessarily associated with a covenantal relationship.

7. While the word "order" does appear in Analects, namely "*xu*" (序), it does not occur in Ecclesiastes. Qoheleth's belief of such an order is reflected, for example, in Eccl 3:1–15, as well as in his theological articulation in Ecclesiastes. Further, the wisdom theology of its ancient Near Eastern context does expect an order, which is evidently implied in the divine work of creation.

8. Ching, *Confucianism and Christianity*, 183.

in addition to proper management approaches. A sharp distinction in the overall aim between these two texts is clear. While Confucius' goal is to improve human character by setting up a moral order, Qoheleth's fundamental aim is theological. He stresses God's order in the history of humanity (in light of Eccl 3:1–8).

The theological assertion is evident in Qoheleth's articulation. Qoheleth seems to discern an order of time and events in 3:1, "For everything there is a season, and for every matter under heaven there is a time." Qoheleth comments also in 8:6, "For every matter there is time and judgment." He appears to suggest that people are to live appropriately according to an order. But the order in the world is elusive, despite impressions to the contrary.[9] God, however, represents the determining factor. The order of time and events in 3:1–8 is sandwiched between God's giving of wisdom (2:26) and God's making of things (3:14–15), wherein God is the subject. The order of historical events is indeed determined by God, as evident in 3:9–15. Yet how God determines this order is beyond human grasp. Qoheleth even questions God on how it works in the human realm. Human activities instead—in toiling, accumulating wealth, and exercising authority—have inevitably yielded disorderliness. Thus, for Qoheleth, order works well only in God's hands, not so much in the hands of mortals, as advocated by Confucius. Nevertheless, Qoheleth expects people to live prudently. This human effort is part of the civic wisdom that Qoheleth has advocated for in Ecclesiastes.

As for Confucius, humans can maintain social order by living an ordered life. Confucians have various theories for interpreting natural and social phenomena and for handling questions like how the universe runs its course, what kind of position humans have in the universe, and whether or not the world can be known.[10] Human moral capacity is hence much accentuated for the maintenance of social order. Such order is expressed through the idea of moral conduct and observance of propriety in the Analects. In the Analects 2:1, order in the universe is depicted through an imagery of a myriad of stars surrounding the Pole Star, a metaphor for the moral capacity of a political leader. An order is thus discernible from one's moral strength: in commanding power, in commanding deference, and in holding the central influence. Similarly, in the Analects 12:19, there is imagery of the grass bending over with the wind blowing. It indicates that the moral quality of a ruler signifies one's strength in asserting influence. This suggests that the morality of political leaders will create a desirable social norm. This belief of "matching nature with morality," *yide peitian* (以德配天), is a Confucian

---

9. Seow, *Ecclesiastes*, 49.
10. See Yao, *REC*, 5.

view of the way of living. "Guide the people by morality" (Analects 2:3) is therefore the typical moral order of Confucius' political ideal. On this basis, morality and propriety are preferred over law and punishment. Regulations are still needed nonetheless, but self-cultivation lasts longer. It rectifies human behavior in the quest for political stability.

In short, both Qoheleth and Confucius discern the need for order. This need is expressed through the ideas of time (in Ecclesiastes) and the Way (in the Analects). While Ecclesiastes points to the acknowledgment of the divine order, the Analects promotes a workable moral order on earth. From the reading of Ecclesiastes *and* the Analects respectively, the order in the human world does assume a distinction of social class that enhances the hierarchical power structure. People of different stature—the rich and the poor, a slave and a prince—are expected to be treated differently. Qoheleth *knows* that there should be order in human living as well, but he *sees* a reversal of such order. For Confucius, *li* represents a much-valued idea for ensuring mutual respect and orderliness in society. Thus, in the terminology of the Analects, Qoheleth expects *li* in the reality of the lack of *li*. *Li* is questioned as much as *li* is needed, for the world that Qoheleth keeps "seeing" demonstrates a total reversal of *li*. Yet, regardless of how Qoheleth questions the way God works in the human world, Qoheleth asserts a theological imperative: to trust in divine sovereignty. This theological imperative, decisively absent in the Analects, is much needed to put things into perspective when one stresses moral imperatives. And the moral order in the Analects, fundamentally absent in Ecclesiastes, is a proactive measure one can adhere to in pragmatic living.

The Need for Justice and Righteousness

Political ethics for maintaining justice in society can be traced back to the *Instruction of Ptahhotep,* which was written during the Egyptian Old Kingdom.[11] Here, as in many other ancient Near Eastern texts and the Bible, the ruler is depicted as a shepherd. A Babylonian proverb says, "People without a king are (like) sheep without a shepherd."[12] In the prologue of *The Code of Hammurabi*, the king depicts himself as one who "causes justice to prevail in the land, to destroy the wicked and the evil, and that the strong might not oppress the weak."[13] And in its epilogue, Hammurabi takes up the role of a shepherd, as Marduk had committed to him. A general understanding

11. Black, *World History of Ancient Political Thought*, 25.
12. Lambert, *BWL*, 229, 232; lines 14–15.
13. Pritchard, ed., *ANET*, 164 and 177.

in the ancient world is that by prescribing ordinances and justice, political leaders deal fairly with subjects. This ancient Near Eastern background is crucial to the expectation of justice and righteousness in Ecclesiastes.

Despite its proper function in prescribing justice, the political establishment easily can be the source of the violation of justice. The background reflected in Eccl 4:1 communicates such violation, "I turned and saw all the oppressions which are done under the sun. And look! Tears of the oppressed! But they have no comforter." The power structure in Qoheleth's time housed the powerful, who were often the source of evil (3:16–17). The hierarchy of the power structure too reflected levels of corruption and power abuse (5:8–9 [Hebrew 5:7–8]). Thus, one sees familiar pictures of ordinary people being intimidated by their unruly, yet powerful, governors. In such circumstances, Qoheleth enunciates political advice like that proffered in Eccl 5:8 and 8:2–5 and in the Analects 8:13 and 12:17.

> **Eccl 5:8 [Hebrew 5:7]**—If you see an oppression of the poor, and a violation of justice and righteousness in a province, do not be astounded over the matter. For a high official watches over high official, and high officials are above them.
>
> **Eccl 8:2–5**—I say, keep the command of the king as over the word of oath to God. Do not be dismayed before his presence and leave. Do not stand in a harmful matter, for he will do whatever he delights. As which the word of the king is power, and who can say to him, "what are you doing?" The one who keeps a command will not experience harm. As for the time and judgment, a wise heart knows.
>
> **Analects 8:13**—Do not enter a state that is in peril, nor dwell in a state that is in chaos. Let yourself be visible when the way prevails in the world, but let yourself be invisible when there is not.
>
> **Analects 12:17**—To govern is to correct. Should you lead correctly, who would dare to be incorrect?"

On the issues of justice and righteousness, two Hebrew words are noted to be in dialogue with *yi* (义) from the Analects: *ṣedek* (rightness) and *mišpāṭ* (judgment). The word "*ṣedek*" has a range of meanings, stemming from "what is right or normal" to "what is just" to "justice."[14] Whereas *mišpāṭ* is a *mem*-noun derived from *šapāṭ*, it is found in Ugaritic and Phoenician with the meaning of "government, authority."[15] In Hebrew, it means

---

14. Brown et al., *BDB*, 841. Holladay, "צֶדֶק," *HALOT*, 303. This root basically connotes conformity to an ethical or moral standard. See Waltke et al., "צַדִּיק," *TWOT*, 72.

15. Botterweck et al., "מִשְׁפָּט," *TDOT*, 87.

"legal decision,"[16] with its focal point in the realm of justice, judgment, and law.[17] *Mišpāṭ* also is an "attribute of the *šopēṭ* : justice, right or rectitude."[18] Both *ṣedek* and *mišpāṭ* often are used in parallel but are not synonymous.[19] The semantic field of "decision, judgment, law" attaches to *mišpāṭ*, while the root *ṣdk* focuses on the principle of "what is right, and correct."[20] Both terms appear in parallel in Eccl 3:16 and 5:8 [Hebrew 5:7], ironically referring to examples of human injustice.[21] The term *mišpāṭ* occurs in Eccl 11:9 and 12:14 however, meaning divine judgment in occurrences of injustice. These occurrences suggest divine reward and punishment. This notion makes possible Qoheleth's idea that God is just, even though the world he observes is full of injustices (3:16; 5:8 [Hebrew 5:7]). This paradox weighs on the contradictions of which Qoheleth is already aware.[22] Qoheleth does not hastily affirm divine justice in life's injustices. Neither does Qoheleth propose a revolutionary utopia.[23] In a pragmatic way, Qoheleth advises people therefore not to be over-confident about being righteous (7:16),[24] with the underlying assumption that people still will do the right thing. One needs to stress that Qoheleth does "assume the natural working of justice" by considering some consequences deriving from a cause of foolishness (7:17; 10:12, 15).[25] And God appears to bring every deed into *mišpāṭ*, whether good or evil (12:14).

This advice of Qoheleth appears to cast a somewhat passive implication when compared with Confucius' proactive dynamic of righteousness, *yi*, which Confucius highly advocated (Analects 17:23). According to the Analects, *yi* is doing what is ethically correct and, at the same time, what is reasonable. In its political meaning, *yi* is required of *junzi*. As political leader, a *junzi* should uphold justice on the land. As such, the *junzi* is to do what is correct and reasonable as required according to one's own responsibility. In the Analects 15:18 and 17:23, righteousness is associated with the character

---

16. Holladay, "מִשְׁפָּט," *HALOT*, 221.

17. Botterweck et al., "מִשְׁפָּט," *TDOT*, 87. The word has expanded semantic functions that include concrete commandments or actions. See Botterweck et al., "צֶדֶק," *TDOT*, 248.

18. Brown et al., *BDB*, 1048.

19. An even more frequent juxtaposition associates *mišpāṭ* and *ṣĕdākâ*. See Botterweck et al., "צֶדֶק," *TDOT*, 247.

20. Ibid., 248.

21. Fox, *Time to Tear Down and a Time to Build Up*, 52.

22. Ibid., 51.

23. Lohfink, *Qoheleth*, 13.

24. Seow, *Ecclesiastes*, 252–54 and 267.

25. Fox, *Time to Tear Down and A Time to Build Up*, 53.

of a political leader. If political leaders are for righteousness, the people will obey their authority (Analects 13:4). Righteousness naturally comes with the courage to act as well (Analects 2:24). A caution remains that courage in itself is dangerous. It can be the source of tyranny and injustice (Analects 17:23). Courage therefore should have *yi* as its motive to substantiate a political action. Here one observes that the Analects confronts human oppression with a more proactive measure. This is due to the fact that the Analects derives from the perspective of political establishment, suggesting workable ways of rectifying injustice and unrighteousness. This proactive, corrective notion of *yi* is remarkably absent in Ecclesiastes.

Qoheleth communicates Confucius' *yi* through *ṣedek* (rightness) and *mišpāṭ* (judgment) in different facets. Ecclesiastes emphasizes the time factor of *yi*.[26] In Eccl 8:5, *'ēt wûmišpāṭ* is "the appropriate time" or "proper time." A wise person such as Qoheleth knows that there is an appointed time for every human event (3:1). Yet as a human, Qoheleth is unable to discern when a given moment is the right time (3:11, 8:17). So, he expresses his frustration that life is the way it is: human existence has tampered with the human inability to control and know the appropriate time to do the right thing.[27] One should therefore do what constitutes as right at a given time, moment by moment. This notion is nevertheless analogous to Confucius' idea of *yi* (Analects 2:24).

Elsewhere, Qoheleth does not engage *yi* affirmatively as Confucius does. In Eccl 7:16–18, for instance, Qoheleth seems to commend half-hearted righteousness. This leaves him open either to the advocacy of the Confucian golden mean or the allegation of teaching immorality. In my judgment, both perspectives are overstated. R. N. Whybray has suggested that the passage depicts Qoheleth's warning against self-righteousness, neither against an excess of righteousness nor against an excess of striving after it.[28] The particle adverb *harbēh*, from the word *rābâ*, is always "much, many, great" or "numerous" but never "too" or "over."[29] The particle adverb *harbēh* here, according to Whybray, does not express any value judgment such as "too righteous" in Eccl 7:16, but an ironical sense, that is, a "self-styled *ṣaddîq*."[30] Whybray then asserts that Qoheleth is no immoralist. On the contrary, he

---

26. The *yi* (义) according to Analects too encapsulates the idea of proper time as discussed in the earlier chapter.
27. Longman, *Book of Ecclesiastes*, 33.
28. Whybray, "Qoheleth the Immoralist?," 191.
29. Brown et al., *BDB*, 915.
30. Whybray, "Qoheleth the Immoralist?," 195–96.

is "the enemy of false righteousness."[31] Seow disagrees with Whybray's reading, suggesting instead that it is overconfidence in righteousness that is at stake in Qoheleth's dissent.[32] Taken together therefore, it is *not* an aspect of moral agent that is absent in Ecclesiastes (the moral agent is repeatedly accentuated in the Analects). Qoheleth's warning is directed against the case of a person who lays claim to righteousness to the effect that righteousness is absolutely attainable. The passage thus does not advocate the Confucian golden mean applicable to *yi*, purportedly to navigate an adequate amount of morality. Rather, unlike Confucius' confidence in upholding *yi* to alleviate social injustice and unrighteousness, Qoheleth perceives a realistic human limitation in living out *ṣaddîq*.

It is certain that both Ecclesiastes and the Analects point out the reality of injustice and unrighteousness, and both suggest different reasons for that. Ecclesiastes implies a hierarchy of political structure (4:1–3; 5:8–9 [Hebrew 5:7–8]) and a corrupt judicial system (3:16–17) as the causes. The Analects posits moral decay and violence among the ruling class as possible sources (Analects 12:19; 20:2). "Courageous acts" without a sense of righteousness is a further reason: a *junzi* too will cause disorder (Analects 17:23). These reasons of injustice and unrighteousness had inevitably brought about social disorder in the *Sitz im Leben* of Ecclesiastes and the Analects. Ecclesiastes therefore speaks of divine *mišpāṭ*, whereas the Analects asserts *yi* as a quality for re-ordering individual and communal life. There is mutual enlightenment here, where one has what the other lacks. The Analects brings in the dynamic of human initiative toward righteousness and justice. This dynamic is a proactive measure lacking in Ecclesiastes. Ecclesiastes, on the other hand, affirms divine judgment. Both *mišpāṭ* and its time belong to divine dominance. The point is that the deity does care about *ṣedek*, *mišpāṭ* or *yi*. It is important to have Qoheleth's theological conviction confronting the reality of injustice and unrighteousness, inasmuch as it also is important to suggest Confucius' ways for guiding human behavior.

The Merging of Pedagogics and Politics

Wisdom has much to do with pedagogic endeavors evident in universal sagacity as with the ancient world. Ancient Near Eastern didactic wisdom texts merge pedagogics and politics.[33] In Ecclesiastes, Qoheleth counsels on

---

31. Ibid., 202.

32. Seow, *Ecclesiastes*, 267.

33. To name a few, *The Instructions of Anii, Ankhsheshonqy, Ahiqar, Amenemope* and the biblical *Proverbs*.

civic life (for example, Eccl 8:2–9; 10:4–7). In the epilogue, he is depicted as a wisdom teacher who teaches the people knowledge by writing, studying, and arranging many proverbs (12:8–11). The Analects, on the other hand, conveys Confucius' political wisdom. It, too, reflects Confucius as a teacher who imparts wisdom by teaching and learning. Qoheleth's commitment to wisdom articulation and Confucius' enthusiasm in teaching-learning have a recognizable similarity: they merge pedagogy and politics.

Qoheleth is preoccupied with acquiring knowledge by observing and reflecting on life under the sun (Eccl 1:13; 2:3, 11–12, 20; 7:13–15; 8:16; 9:1; 12:9). He imparts that knowledge through teaching and compiling literature (12:9–11). The most recurring verb associated with Qoheleth is to see, *rā'â*.[34] The repetition of this verb reflects a sage's activities of constant observation and reflection. Qoheleth does so to seek wisdom (2:12, 19; 7:23–25; 8:1, 16–17). Qoheleth and Confucius are both ancient sages who display the quality of sages to impart a pedagogy tradition of learning and thinking. But unlike Proverbs-like prescriptive wisdom, the pedagogics in Ecclesiastes are more reflective. He weighs on observations compared to instructions. In Qoheleth's pedagogy, the "yes-but"[35] reality in life is highlighted. Wisdom is no doubt better than folly. But wisdom is limited, not least by mortality. Also, enjoyment of life is good. Yet it is short-lived and not guaranteed.

This "yes-but" reality is accentuated in Qoheleth's political counsel. Qoheleth observes that the power of governance is divinely decreed upon a ruler's coronation. But such power can be a source of injustice. In Eccl 8:2–5, Qoheleth highlights this possible injustice. He alludes to the supremacy of the ruler and the powerlessness of his subjects. Therefore, he advises on how to behave in a royal court for survival. Elsewhere in 4:13–16, a young ruler who possesses wisdom certainly gains an upper hand. His wisdom, however, only gains temporary popularity. No one survives political takeovers. In 9:13–16 also, a man's wisdom has the advantage to deliver the under-sieged city from a great threat. The deliverer, however, is forgotten. Therefore, Qoheleth says that wisdom is better than might. Yet such wisdom is despised when the deliverer is a commoner.

One can take note, therefore, that Qoheleth's "yes-but" rhetoric is remedial to the conventional prescriptive civic advice. Qoheleth holds two existing political phenomena in juxtaposition. Scenario A (the decreed power of governance) exists alongside Scenario B (the abuse of such power). Both scenarios exist in tension. Qoheleth acknowledges the tension therein.

---

34. The word appears forty-seven times in Ecclesiastes, for example, in Eccl 1:14; 2:13,24; 3:10, 16, 22; 4:1,4, 7, 15; 5:12,17; 6:1; 7:15; 8:9–10,17; 9:13; 10:5,7; 12:3 and the like.

35. An exegetical solution for recognizing the "yes, but" saying, *zwar-aber Tatsache*, see Seow, *Ecclesiastes*, 40, and Murphy, *Ecclesiastes*, xxxiv.

Despite the tension, Qoheleth appears to affirm the reality of both. This "both-and"[36] scenario, just like the *hebel* complaint and carpe-diem motif, is essentially built into Ecclesiastes' literary work. Thus, in Ecclesiastes, both "the injustice" is set in view with "the place of justice" (5:8-9). "No judge" in the place of righteousness, but then "God will judge" (3:16-17). Both "wisdom is better" and "wisdom is despised" are set in perspective of political survival (9:13-16). Accordingly, Qoheleth teaches how to align one's political attitude to properly respond to both scenarios. Therein Qoheleth teaches the mastery of political living. Occasionally, his teaching is embedded in anecdotes and proverbial sayings (4:13-16; 10:16-20), suggesting room for reflection and caution when confronting the unknown.[37] Also in Qoheleth's pedagogics, political counsel is tactfully and sometimes ironically conveyed: through double entendre, political satire, and proverbial caution (5:8-9 [Hebrew 5:7-8]; 8:2-9; 10:4-7; 10:16-20).

Comparatively in the Confucian tradition, education aims to mold character through "normative recommendations" of motivation, mentoring, and self-examination.[38] The Analects 2:15 mentions, "Learning without thinking will lead to the bewilderedness. Thinking without learning, on the other hand, will lead to imperil." The Analects emphasizes an evocative teaching to inspire students to think widely, and "to respond with three more ideas" (Analects 7:8). Active learning, therefore, is the crux of Confucian learning. Self-reflection, likewise, constitutes proper learning in order to grow in character and maturity, as the Analects 1:4 suggests.[39] Such an emphasis on learning is evident in the Analects' political articulation. The Analects make learning an imperative for anyone who is politically involved. Training in skills will not work without accumulating wisdom. A scholar (仕 *shi*) is skillful and also knowledgeable, combining physical strength as well as intellectual aptitude. *Junzi* at the time of Confucius were educated persons who served in the royal court and fought in battlefields. Based on the emphases of knowledge, as well as management competence, Confucius nurtures his disciples toward a political career.

---

36. I am indebted to Seow, *Ecclesiastes*, 40, for this insight. Earlier, this book has stated that Qoheleth does not think of issues in terms of "either-or" propositions. This book is taking it a step further, avowing this "both-and" scenario, in view of the connection of Seow's discussion on the Chinese concept of yin-yang: both are ever present.

37. As maintained before, wisdom is didactic; reflective wisdom is therefore didactic as well.

38. Kupperman, "Fact and Value in the Analects," 408-9.

39. Analects 1:4 reads, "I examine myself on three counts. Have I failed to do my best in what I have undertaken for others? Have I failed to be trustworthy in my dealings with friends? Have I failed to practice repeatedly what I have learned?"

In addition, the rhetoric of the Analects aims at virtuous governance. Social disorder is a result of a breakdown in the moral standard, particularly among the ruling class. Such moral failure can be remedied through pedagogy. Therefore, Confucius advocates for the fundamental necessity of self-cultivation to shape *junzi*(s) in political leadership. In the Analects, moral requirements are intentionally connected to political involvement (Analects 2:1, 3, 19). Personal cultivation, in addition to knowledge and skills, will ensure political functioning. Attributes of *de, ren, li, and yi* are therefore central in Confucian pedagogics for shaping political leaders. With the socio-political order at stake, the Analects records Confucius' attempts to influence political powers in combining pedagogics and political organization. His language in the Analects is largely didactic. His political portrayal of the *junzi* is insistent. The moral exemplar and political ideal of the *junzi* become the driving force of modern Confucian pedagogy, aiming to shape characters to live rightly.

Ecclesiastes and the Analects convey an unanimity that politics has to do with pedagogy. But both of them have merged pedagogics and politics in their discrete ways. Ecclesiastes engages pedagogics and politics through "yes-but" rhetoric and political satire against the political establishment. The Analects engages pedagogics and politics through a learning imperative deriving from the perspective of political establishment. An obvious distinction between the approaches is the fundamentally different perspectives they each derive. Taking a closer-to-the-public perspective, Ecclesiastes criticizes the power structure of its time. He observes the realities of power corruption (5:8–9 [Hebrew 5:7–8]), tyranny in the hands of kings (8:2–9), self-indulgence at a high level (10:16–17), and sluggishness in handling political duty (10:18–19). Qoheleth draws out the division between the powerful and the powerless intentionally. He uses parody to convey his criticism toward the powerful indirectly. The Analects too contains political rhetoric, through comparisons between regulation-punishment and morality-propriety as in The Analects 2:3. The political counsel in the Analects, however, is conveyed in a more direct manner, to instruct political leadership toward practical re-organization. Therefore, in Analects, one has to be virtuous and wise and, at the same time, skillful to ensure political functioning. But in Ecclesiastes, a reader has to discern the civic wisdom behind its literal sense. The wisdom in both texts works well according to their practical platforms: they engage political wisdom in their dissimilar, but functional, ways. Their distinct ways of civic survival are teachings for different people located in different political contexts. In the end, through writing, compiling, and editing the texts of their time, both Qoheleth and Confucius have appropriated wisdom writings in pedagogics and politics.

On Political Leadership

There are many valuable political ideas in Analects on governance and leadership. In Analects, the first principle for governing effectively is to live correctly (Analects 12:17; 13:13; 13:6). A good example of political leadership rebuffs violence and dismisses brute force (Analects 12:19). Besides, Confucius prioritizes the rectification of name (Analects 13:3). This rectification of name contains definitions of role and official duty. It goes along with proper protocols in any political functioning. Further, moral principles are prerequisites for political leadership (Analects 2:1; 12:19). A political leader should administer duty by following moral guidance (Analects 2:3; 2:19) and by setting examples (Analects 12:17, 19; 13:2). Besides moral capacity, one's skill and proficiency are crucial to the entrustment of government duties (Analects 6:8). In addition, personal cultivation, in addition to knowledge and skills, will make one perform effectively in political functions (Analects 15:10; 3:19). Furthermore, political leadership looks after the civilian's well-being. Political leaders appoint skilled labor at appropriate times to the greatest advantage for the people (Analects 20:1–3). Humanness is their dynamic of executing duty (Analects 12:22). They treat all people fairly (Analects 2:21) and clothe themselves with propriety (Analects 13:4; 14:41). They respect the able and are tolerant to all people (Analects 19:3). They raise upright and competent people over government posts (Analects 13:2). Those who have political power manage a nation well—by taxing the people lightly (Analects 12:9), by making the people affluent and by providing education (Analects 13:9), by being diligent (Analects 13:1), and by being generous (Analects 20:2). Last but not least, political leaders should secure the trust of the people at large (Analects 1:5; 12:7). In general, political leaders should rule over people with dignity and treat people with kindness (Analects 2:20). In short, Confucius' principle of a good government is essentially based on virtuous governance *and* managerial competence. Since the *junzi* is a political construct, sayings in Analects that teach the way of the *junzi* can be applied to political management.

The elaborations above may be Confucius' ideals, but Qoheleth appears to doubt their practicality and certainty. Indeed, there are relatively few passages in Ecclesiastes that elaborate on political leadership. Ecclesiastes rather deals more with perspectives against the political establishment. But Qoheleth too suggests some feasible political options in the civic wisdom he conveys. Ecclesiastes 5:8–9 [Hebrew 5:7–8] introduces an idea of rulership: a well-managed nation is a result of one who governs well. One should not miss Qoheleth's double entendre here, however, that there is an ironic meaning by implying a state of undermanaged government. Besides, levels of government bureaucracy in 5:8–9 [Hebrew 5:7–8] too imply layers of corruption. The passage could be taken to mean that if the political leader manages the nation properly, lower-level corruption can be subdued; the people would benefit from political management and oppression could be eradicated. Qoheleth may have implied that the reality was exactly the opposite. Qoheleth uses a figure of speech here in 5:8–9 [Hebrew 5:7–8] to convey an offensive opinion—without having the risk of facing action taken from the political establishment.

Further, Qoheleth asserts the value of having mature political leaders who govern wisely rather than indulge in feast, drunkenness, and greed (10:16–17). As long as a mature leader rules the nation with the help of diligent officials who feast at a proper time for the right reason, blessings entail. Conversely, if an immature ruler governs with sluggish officials who feast at inappropriate time for self-indulgence, disasters will follow. Politically motivated criticism is discernible here in 10:16–20, as feasts are intentionally associated with princes (10:16–17). Greed and corruption are implied therein, as "money occupies everyone" (10:19). The idea from 10:18–19 also implies laziness of politically powerful people, for their laziness will crumble a state. Ecclesiastes 10:19 aims to deliver a political ridicule against the lifestyles of the political establishment, which includes feasting, drinking, and being preoccupied with money. It is evident that Qoheleth is pressing against the self-indulgence of the ruling class as well as the elite. Ecclesiastes 10:20 is the most satirical and, under the sapiential pretense of "do not curse the king and the rich," Qoheleth solicits discreet political criticism. This criticism has to be packaged under proverb-like wisdom teaching, for anti-government sentiments are highly sensitive in the royal court. Words may be spread through informants who report to the authorities about subversive speech. In short, one can observe that Ecclesiastes is concerned specifically with political misbehavior in wisdom thought. And Qoheleth delivers such satirical comments in 10:16–20.

On account of civic life, Qoheleth observes the evils of injustice and unrighteousness (3:16–17) and the danger of absolute political power (8:2–9). He seems to assert a divine political leadership by pointing to the One who judges (3:17). Unlike a human leader, ʾĕlōhîm judges the wicked. Thus, judgment is valid, Qoheleth asserts. He too persuades his reader about the idea of the appropriate time for such judgment. In fact, he insists on an appropriate time for everything that happens under the sun. Also, ʾĕlōhîm is the One whose presence is remembered (cf. 4:13–16), whose wisdom is not despised, and whose words are heeded (cf. 9:13–16).[40] On account of

---

40. While humans have only short-lived political popularity in Eccl 4:13–16 and a

human effort, Qoheleth reckons that there is a problem of injustice over which humans simply do not have control. But he assures that there is a time for everything, including judgment of the wicked (and the righteous). So, the divine judgment represents the ultimate comfort. One can therefore observe that the consistency in Analects' prominence on corrective political measures are evidently lacking in Ecclesiastes. There are two different kinds of wisdom ideas on political leadership in the cross-textual reading here. One aims at managing (Analects) and the other at coping (Ecclesiastes). Both however, aim to survive the civic living. They have drawn on contrasting viewpoints and made converse suggestions.

On Political Behavior

Relationship

Ren is prized in the textual world of the Analects, especially with regard to political constitution. As mentioned before, in its etymology, humanness is a cognate of *ren* as human. The cognates, taken together, designate the reciprocity of human relationship. In its functionality, *ren* (仁) is multi-faceted for various political situations. Being the basis that intrinsically connects all of Confucian ethics, *ren* overlooks kinship and family connection in favor of the love for all people (Analects 12:22). Virtuous governance in the Confucian tradition is constructed through a fundamental emphasis on *ren*. Since the central idea of Confucius' moral teachings is *ren*, harmonious human relationship is at the forefront of the Analects' political behavior. This standpoint naturally and inevitably connects *li* and *yi* with the practice of *ren*. They collectively contribute toward common good in the public sphere. In short, *ren* represents the basic guideline for building an enriching inter-personal relationship. It is also the basic requirement for political relationship.

The idea of trust in the Analects covers another perspective in the Confucian notion of political leadership. The relationship between the leader and the people often is highlighted by underlining the word "trust," *xin* (信). Its etymology points to a person who stands by one's word. A political leader who stands by his word can be trusted. When the overall advantage of the people is considered foremost, the government is trustworthy (Analects 1:5; 12:7; 20:1–3). Hence, one needs to be trusted in order to govern effectively. Faith in the governing body entails general well-being among the people. Conversely, all forms of corruption and malpractice will bring

---

fleeting advantage of wisdom in 9:13–16.

about distrust among the people. In the Analects, when the political leader is trustworthy, the people will be sincere in return (Analects 13:4). When a nation stands by its word, people from other states will be attracted to it (Analects 13:16).[41] In sum, governance is people-oriented. The idea of trust is regarded as one of the fundamentals in political organization. Apart from the Analects' notion of *ren*, *xin* is another direct instruction to mold political behavior.

The idea of humanness (*ren*) and trust (*xin*) on account of relationship is cast in a somewhat negative light in Ecclesiastes. Qoheleth sighs at the presence of *rešaʿ* (wickedness) and the lack of *mišpāṭ* (justice) in civic life. He sees wickedness stemming from human actions. The wickedness occurs ironically in places of justice and righteousness wherein people are expected to be protected by law (3:16). Evidently, there is no kindness and trust in civic life. Qoheleth calls into question Confucius' value of *ren*: a stranger (not the next-of-kin) inherits the fruit of one's wealth, possessions, and honor (Eccl 6:1–2 cf. 4:7–8). Qoheleth protests against appropriating one's fruit of labor from another, contra Confucius' advocacy of an extensive love. He describes such behavior as *rāʿâ* and *heḇel* (6:1–2; 4:7–8), as if a common good does not engage Qoheleth's recommendation. Elsewhere, Qoheleth examines a common wickedness done to one another, which is the reverse of *ren* and *xin*. The oppression of the poor and the violation of justice and right (3:16–17; 4:1–3) make no *ren* (humanness) in civic life and certainly no *xin* (trust) in the judicial system. When Qoheleth sees the same fate—death comes to both the righteous and the wicked (9:2–3)—he calls it an evil, *rāʿâ*. For some, Qoheleth appears to revoke the value of having *ren* and *xin* in one's lifetime.

It is important to note, however, that Qoheleth does not actually invalidate the idea of *ren* and *xin*. The rhetorical question in Eccl 4:8, "For whom am I toiling and depriving myself of good?" implies that one's toil is for the benefit of someone else. As such, there is actually a creative tension arising between "toiling" and "good." Qoheleth is saying that there is no use toiling and denying oneself of pleasure, if one has no one to share the benefits either in the present or the future.[42] When another person shares in one's fruit of labor, one's toil has an added meaning. For this, I believe that Qoheleth values the idea of *ren*. Further, in the numerical proverbs in 4:9–12, Qoheleth affirms partnership in contrast to being solitary. One who has a companion (that is, *šěnayim* "two" in the Hebrew, cf. the essence of *ren* that comprises

---

41. Reading from the literary sequence of Analects 13:15–16. Some passages in Analects connect to the idea of the text before or after, like this one.

42. Seow, *Ecclesiastes*, 188.

of "two persons") has a benefit in their toil: "good" (4:9). And here one sees that the idea of companionship in Eccl 4:9–12 connects with the root meaning of *ren* (仁), which suggests people and twoness. Qoheleth makes the good of duality apparent through three instances in subsequent illustrations (4:10–12), implying that people are better able to cope with crises if they help one another.[43] Instead of being selfish, one should get together with companions or turn over to the needy a portion of one's liberality (4:9–12; 11:1–2).[44] So the idea of *ren* is still recommendable for Qoheleth. There is value in doing good for others in Ecclesiastes. Qoheleth validates *ren* in human relationships. He merely sighs at the lack of it in the socio-political reality. As for *xin*, it is equally elusive in the human socio-political reality. The trust of the people toward a ruler either does not endure (as in the case of 4:13–16) or is unpredictable (as in the case of 9:13–16). Since the wisdom and greatness of mortals is elusive, Qoheleth points toward the deity, whose wisdom and judgment is trustworthy.

Qoheleth's usage of the terms *hebel* and *rā'â* are means, therefore, not ends, to deliberately draw out tensions in the reality of life.[45] He points out the tension within living circumstances, wherein the sovereignty of God lies also.[46] So in Eccl 3:16–17, there is a lack of *ren* in civic life, and a lack of *xin* in the judicial system. Confucius too, shares these common shortages of *ren* and *xin* in his time. These shortages drive Confucius to advocate for their cultivation in the Analects. For both Ecclesiastes and the Analects, the tension between the "place of justice–source of injustice" is real in civic life. Because of the "use and abuse of power" in political sphere, the absence of *ren* and *xin* are evident in both texts. But for Qoheleth, he simply describes the tensions of the "powerful-powerless" and the "oppressor-oppressed" without hastily solving them. One may even toil in vain looking in Ecclesiastes for a human solution to the lack of *ren* and *xin*. For Qoheleth, life under the sun occurs in this way. It is marked by tensions and paradoxes. It is *hebel*—inscrutable and uncontrollable.

---

43. Seow, *Ecclesiastes*, 189.

44. Krüger, *Qoheleth*, 1.

45. I am indebted to Fox for this reading. See Fox, *Qohelet and His Contradictions*, 28; and Fox, *Time to Tear Down and A Time to Build Up*, 3. Fox believes that Qoheleth marshals his readers to tear down meaning and then to build up meaning, for Qoheleth discovers "paradoxical truths" that lead to greater meaning.

46. For example, in Eccl 6:1–2 and 4:7–8, Qoheleth expects someone closer, not a stranger, to share in one's benefit. But it happens sometimes that a stranger enjoys one's outcome as well. Humans have no control of this either.

Discretion

In Ecclesiastes, the supreme authority of the king and the powerlessness of the subjects are perceivable from the reality of life. With this perception, Qoheleth counsels on how to behave appropriately in the royal court. Qoheleth teaches not to challenge this absolute power, but to adhere to it by a self-adjustment of behavior. A closer position near the central political power is influential, and it is unwise to renounce one's post hastily (Eccl 8:3; 10:4). Remaining at the position would amend situations, for defiance is dangerous in the reality of tyranny. As a way of proper courtly behavior, negative sentiment should be avoided. For Qoheleth, an immediate clash is simply inappropriate. It is dangerous to act tactlessly, especially when a political leader possesses absolute power. In the face of challenging political autocracy, a wise person knows to act with diplomacy.

From the above, one can ascertain that Qoheleth warns against direct confrontation with the political establishment. He encourages instead a prudent handling of courtly matters. This position appears to be unlike Confucius in the Analects. For Confucius, direct confrontation appears to be a necessary act at times. The Analects necessitates ethics to serve in the government. Yet if one cannot see to it that ethics is being practiced as believed, one should resign from an official post. In the case of the Analects 16:1, warring against Lu's kinfolks without a valid reason is essentially wrong. If political leaders know it, yet pursue the crusade nonetheless, it is ethically questionable. Confucius' disciples are rebuked for knowing the right thing to do yet not doing it. Elsewhere in the case of the Analects 11:24, a great political leader serves in the government by way of virtue. But when virtuous governance cannot be implemented whatsoever, one should resign from political leadership. In short, the consciousness of *yi* (义) demands a *junzi* to do the right thing in the Analects 16:1 and 11:24. The Analects promotes resignation, a discretion justifiable on the firm belief in the motive, *yi*.

Here the Analects records a sharp contrast to the political advice of Ecclesiastes, although political oppression is a reality in both Ecclesiastes and the Analects. In the Analects, since the idea of *yi* substantiates an action by its motive, political leaders should by all means act upon the matters that are perceived to be right. Lower ranking officials, however, are incapable of going against rulers' decrees. In the event that an official no longer has the capacity to shun political evil, but is compelled to do otherwise, one should leave the political post. Ecclesiastes, on the other hand, advocates to "keep the command of the king" (8:2) and "do not be dismayed before his [the king's] presence and leave" (8:3). To Qoheleth, *yi* is to remain in the political position. To Confucius conversely, *yi* is to resign.⁴⁷

In Ecclesiastes, since God is the endorser of kings, it is justifiable to remain in the political position because of the oath of allegiance before God (8:2).⁴⁸ Moreover, by remaining in the position, one will not experience harm (8:5) because the king's power is supreme.⁴⁹ This obedience of subjects to the supreme authority of the king constitutes what is right, *yi*. Therefore, Qoheleth advises that no one should hastily resign from a position, even with good cause. Even though part of Ecclesiastes' literary purpose is possibly to expose the harmful nature of oppressive political power (by repeatedly rendering key words like *rā'â*), it is passive in Ecclesiastes in terms of suggestions for how one can respond to it. Not until the later part of Eccl 8:2–9 does one notice an assertive thought: it is harmful to have an absolute political power system. And a king's death ends his autocracy.

Ecclesiastes and the Analects record very different attitudes toward political discretion aimed at different points of departure. In a nutshell, both texts have totally different approaches to *yi*. It is not the intention of this study to force the Analects' instinct of *yi* into Ecclesiastes' advocacy of courtly obedience. Such endeavor will inevitably be forced and unnecessary. The teachings on political discretion for both Ecclesiastes and the Analects have contextual bases and their cultural considerations. For Ecclesiastes, religious basis of political power is asserted. For the Analects, ethics is at stake in the justification of a crusade (Analects 16:1) and in materializing virtuous governance (Analects 11:24). Nevertheless, both Ecclesiastes and the Analects uphold political wisdom on courtly behavior using distinct approaches. Each of the texts is proper according to the demand of context. Different qualities of *yi* are required for different circumstances. In essence, *yi*, as its cognate suggests, represents what is right and appropriate at a given time.

---

47. The political power during the time of Qoheleth and Confucius respectively could be the main reason behind these distinctive approaches. Qoheleth was addressing the Israelite community under the foreign Persian rule, while Confucius was speaking to his own Chinese people.

48. The "command" of the king, literally "mouth of the king," is of an unquestionable authority recalling "mouth of YHWH" (cf. Num 14:41; 22:18; 1 Kgs 13:21). This does not change even though foreign kings, Persians, are set in view. Isaiah 45:1 speaks of Cyrus favorably as the LORD's "anointed" and, in Isa 44:28, as his "shepherd."

49. *The Proverbs of Ahiqar* from Elephantine during the period of Ecclesiastes shares the same obedience vis-à-vis the king's wrath, in order to face no harm.

On Political Rhetoric

Qoheleth and Confucius affirm monarchy and the status quo rather than advocate for radical reformation. This does not mean, however, that both do not have a critical attitude toward the establishment. Both Qoheleth and Confucius indirectly press against the misbehavior of the ruling class, as well as the rest of the elite. Their critiques are communicated through their comparable political rhetoric. For instance, it is typical of wisdom literature to draw on anecdotes. Ecclesiastes 4:13–16 and 9:13–16 are anecdotes for making comparisons. The former points out the short-lived realities of political power; the latter informs the limits of wisdom in political survival. From these anecdotes, Qoheleth conveys that the political world is unstable and ironic. Wisdom is better than folly, but it ironically cannot guarantee one's durability in the royal court. Soon, there will be another taking over one's power. This "yes-but" rhetoric points to the political irony in Ecclesiastes.

A similar "yes-but" rhetoric is discernible through Confucius' carefully constructed speech. In the Analects, Ji Kangzi is subtly confronted on his way of governance. Two perspectives are set in "yes-but" contrast: governance by way of law-punishment vs. governance by way of morality-propriety (Analects 2:3). In this passage, the way of law-punishment is laid out first, but it contains a negative evaluation. Then the way of morality-propriety is asserted by highlighting its advantage. These two different ways of governance are further contrasted by employing wordplay on dao (道) and dao (导). Whereas in the Analects 12:17, Confucius draws out the idea of governance (政 *zheng*), "to correct" (正 *zheng*), both are cognate, to make a similar point. There are some other comparable literary skills Qoheleth and Confucius employ to deliver political counsel. The following section presents some of those in both Ecclesiastes and the Analects.

Metaphors and Imageries

The Analects is written with a rich engagement of metaphors and imagery.[50] In articulating his love of nature, Confucius uses water and mountain metaphors (Analects 6:23). He uses the imagery of a flowing stream of days and nights to signify fleeting time (Analects 9:17). The imagery of making a heap by filling a basketful of dirt is employed to recommend perseverance (Analects 9:19). Commenting on the simple lifestyle of a disciple, Yan Yuan,

---

50. Lo, "Finding the Self in the Analects," 15. It says that in Analects, many moral concepts were still going through a process of conjectural definition. Yet many scholars have agreed that Analects as a wisdom text displays fine literary skill.

Confucius uses the analogy of "a bowlful of rice, a ladleful of water and a mean dwelling place" (颜渊; the Analects 6:11). Confucius likens Zhong Gong (仲弓) to "a bull born of plough cattle that has a sorrel coat and well-formed horns" (Analects 6:6). He did so to encourage Zhong Gong to excel in society despite having a low family background. In addition, the frequent use of the term dao (道), a root word as "way" or "path," is customary in the Analects to signify a way of governance. For instance, the three generations of Xia, Shang, and Zhou had straight political paths worthy of Confucius' ideals (Analects 15:25). Elsewhere, Confucius uses the imagery of sailing out to the sea if his political ideals are not heeded (Analects 5:7). The imagery of having to walk through the front door of a house also is used to question the lack of followers for Confucius' political ideals (Analects 6:17). The use of metaphors and imagery is a persuasive tool in the Analects for adopting its political ideology. By employing these metaphors and imagery, the Analects also presents lively insights into the actual exchange of political ideas.

Despite the "mainly prosaic outlook" of the book,[51] the use of metaphors and imagery in Ecclesiastes conveys Qoheleth's poetic depiction of his thought world. The opening chapter of Ecclesiastes displays imagery of the nature world (1:4–7). Subsequent chapters use metaphors of a pit, a wall, and a serpent (10:8–11). Then trees, rain, wind, and clouds are used (11:3–4), as well as the sun, moon, and star (12:2). Grinding and singing imagery appears in Eccl 12:3–4. The rich depiction of nature in Eccl 12:5 follows, "the almond tree blossoms, the grasshopper dragging itself along; all going to their eternal home, and the mourners will go about the streets." One also notes the silver cord, golden bowl, pitcher, and wheel in Eccl 12:6. Qoheleth's portrayal of 12:1–7 here represents a possible allegory of aging or an allegory of death; both are consistent with Qoheleth's perspective that often derives from the end of things.[52] In Qoheleth's political articulation, metaphors and imagery are richly rendered as well. To name a few, the place of justice and righteousness (3:16), tears (4:1), the dead (4:1), the poor (5:8 [Hebrew 5:7]), the land and cultivated field (5:9 [Hebrew 5:8]), a commoner but wise youth and an old but foolish king (4:13), death (8:8), a small city and a great king (9:13), servants on horses while princes walk (10:7), eating and drinking (10:16–17), beam-work and a house (10:18), and a bird in the sky (10:20). Besides, Qoheleth's physical depiction is frequent:

---

51. Barton, *Critical and Exegetical Commentary*, 51.

52. For discussions of the allegories, see Fox, *A Time to Tear Down and a Time to Build Up*, 344–48.

heart,[53] hand,[54] mouth,[55] and voice,[56] alongside their related verbs: walk,[57] know,[58] see,[59] and eat.[60] Many of those physical illustrations are reflections, decisions, speeches, and behaviors associated with political living. Fox notes that an allegory requires the reader to give careful attention to images while simultaneously calling to mind the realities signified.[61] The allegories used in Ecclesiastes' thus call to mind the following realities of political living. There is no justice at the place of justice. Tears of the oppressed and oppression of the poor are real. A properly managed nation is ideal. Disordered political functioning is due to a reversed position of prince-servant. Feasts and drinking are engaged in at inappropriate times. A political structure collapses as a result of laziness. Information will be spread by government spies.

Parallelism

Parallelism refers to the grouping of lines or half lines with the intention to echo, enhance, compare, or contrast. The purpose of parallelism is to communicate the wider thoughts of the writer. The Analects frequently uses poetic parallelisms typical of the ancient Chinese to accentuate a point. To illustrate only a few, in the Analects 4:11 below, a balanced structure is constructed. Not only does it aim to contrast political leaders vs. civilians but also it distinguishes the distinct personalities and typical concerns of both categories:

53. The word for "heart" occurs forty times in thirty-four verses: Eccl 1:13, 16–17; 2:1, 3, 10, 15, 20, 22–23; 3:11, 17, 18; 5:1, 19; 7:2–4, 7, 21, 22, 25,26; 8:5, 9, 11, 16; 9:1, 3, 7;10:2–3; 11:9–10.

54. The word for "hand" occurs thirteen times in thirteen verses: Eccl 2:11, 24; 4:1, 5; 5:5, 13,14; 7:18, 26; 9:1, 10; 10:18and 11:6.

55. The word for "mouth" occurs seven times in six verses: Eccl 5:1, 5; 6:7; 8:2; 10:12–13.

56. The word for "voice" occurs six times in five verses: Eccl 5:2, 5; 7:6; 10:20; 12:4.

57. The verb "to walk/to go" occurs thirty times in twenty-five verses; among which those associated with human actions are: Eccl 2:14; 3:20; 4:15, 17; 5:14 [twice]; 5:15; 6:4,6,8; 7:2 [twice]; 8:3,10; 9:7,10; 10:3,7,15,20; 11:9; 12:5.

58. The verb "to know" occurs thirty-six times in thirty verses: Eccl 1:17; 2:14, 19; 3:12, 14, 21; 4:13, 17; 6:5, 8, 10, 12; 7:22, 25; 8:1, 5, 7, 12, 16–17; 9:1, 5, 11–12; 10:14–15; 11:2, 5–6, 9.

59. The verb "to see" occurs forty-seven times in forty-three verses: Eccl 1:8, 10, 14, 16;2:1, 3, 12–13, 24; 3:10, 13, 16, 18, 22; 4:1, 3–4, 7, 15; 5:7, 12, 17; 6:1, 5–6; 7:11, 13–15, 27, 29; 8:9–10, 16–17; 9:9, 11, 13; 10:5, 7; 11:4, 7; 12:3.

60. The verb "to eat" occurs fifteen times in fourteen verses: Eccl 2:24–25; 3:13; 4:5; 5:10–11, 16–18; 6:2; 8:15; 9:7; 10:16–17.

61. Fox, *A Time to Tear Down and A Time to Build Up*, 344.

Analects 4:11—A *junzi* thinks of virtue // A *xiaoren* thinks of comfort.
A *junzi* thinks of consequences // A *xiaoren* thinks of favors.

In the Analects 4:16, the *junzi-xiaoren* contrast is conveyed through antithetical parallelism by the choice of subjects, verbs, and nouns. The comparison intends to point out the fundamental concern of righteousness that is required of a political leader:

Analects 4:16—The mind of *junzi* is accustomed to righteousness //
The mind of *xiaoren* is accustomed to gain.

Whereas in the Analects 7:37, the *junzi-xiaoren* contrast is drawn through the choice of adjectives, signifying gravity between a political leader and a civilian:

Analects 7:37—A *junzi* is genuine and forthright // A xiaoren is full of distress.

Sometimes, the comparisons become intriguing through the mutual exchange of words, yet making clear the sharp differences:

Analects 13:23—A *junzi* is amiable but not sycophantic //
A *xiaoren* is sycophantic, but not amiable.

Analects 13:26—A *junzi* is dignified without arrogance //
A *xiaoren* is arrogant without dignity.

Analects 15:34—A *junzi* cannot be known in little matters, but may be assigned with great task //
A *xiaoren* cannot be assigned with great task, but may be known in little matters.

Analects 19:13—When one is able to excel in official duties, one should then learn //
When one is able to excel in learning, one should then be given official duties.

It is amazing that numerous ideas are communicated through so few words in the parallelisms. Here is a record of the assessment of four of Confucius' disciples:

Analects 11:18—Chai is simple-minded // Shen is slow // Shi is flawed // You is foolhardy.

Politically, Confucius often tells between a time of order, *youdao* (有道), and a time of chaos, *wudao* (无道). Confucius encourages discernment in times of order and chaos so that people are able to tell the difference and act accordingly.

> **Analects 14:3**—When there is order in a state, be bold in your speech and action //
> When there is chaos in a state, be bold in your action but reserve in your speech.
>
> **Analects 16:2**—When there is order in the empire, propriety, music, and punitive expeditions are initiated by the emperor. //
> When there is chaos in the empire, propriety, music, and punitive expeditions are initiated by the feudal lords.
>
> **Analects 8:13**—When there is order in the empire, let yourself be seen. //
> When there is chaos in the empire, keep yourself hidden.
>
> **Analects 8:13**—When there is order in the state, it is shameful to be poor and lowly. //
> When there is chaos in the state, it is shameful to be rich and honorable.

In Ecclesiastes, Qoheleth uses parallelisms extensively. The parallelisms in the catalogue of times and events in Eccl 3:2–8 is observable. Further in 4:6, sandwiched between two political passages in 4:1–3 and 4:13–16, is a proverb among the series of "better-than" sayings (4:1–16). It compares and suggests what is more desirable:

> **Eccl 4:6**—Better is a handful with quietness // than two handfuls with toil, <u>and a chasing after wind.</u>[62]

The antithetic parallelism in Eccl 10:12 contrasts the wise from the foolish before leading to a political parody in 10:16–20:

> **Eccl 10:12**—Words from the mouth of the wise bring favor // but the lips of a fool devour him.

Further, Eccl 10:16 is parallel to 10:17. It communicates two political scenarios in relation to two different kinds of rulers:

> **Eccl 10:16**—Woe to you, O land, whose king is a boy, while your princes feast in the morning! //

---

62. The underlining is intended to highlight the disproportionate part of this parallelism.

Eccl 10:17—Blessed are you, O land, whose king is a noble, while your princes feast in the proper time, <u>for strength and not for drunkenness!</u>[63]

And, in Eccl 10:18, a synonymous parallel conveys an image of a collapsed political structure as a result of sluggishness:

Eccl 10:18—By sluggishness the beam-work collapses //
by slackness of hands the house leaks.

Literary Contrast

A contrast in a literary work is a rhetoric to set two distinctive aspects in view in order to emphasize the differences between them. It is alternately called binary opposition. In any literary contrast, two clearly defined concepts are set against one another. Such contrast is present in both the Analects as well as in Ecclesiastes. The Analects depicts "the exemplary person in contrast to the inferior person" extensively (for instance, the Analects 4:11; 7:37; 12:16; 13:23, 26; 14:23; 15:34).[64] Similarly, there is a dichotomy between "life and death" (Analects 2:5; 11:12; 12:5), "poverty and richness" (Analects 14:10), "good and bad" (Analects 4:3; 12:16; 20:2), "ruler and minister" (Analects 3:19; 12:11), as well as "father and son" (Analects 12:11; 13:18). In addition, "morning and evening" (Analects 4:8), "out and in" (Analects 9:16), "big and small" (Analects 13:17; 15:27, 34), "old and young" (Analects 14:43), "down and up" (Analects 14:35), and "many and few" (Analects 2:18) display Confucius' rhetoric in asserting his perspective. Finally, different functional spheres like "word and deed" (Analects 2:18), "thinking and learning" (Analects 2:15), and "human in contrast to heaven/spirits" (Analects 11:12; 14:35) also are set in comparison. In conclusion, the literary contrast in the Analects' political passages entails several meanings. First, it draws a contrast between the ruler and the ruled. Second, contrast imposes personal judgment between good and bad models of governance. As such, personal judgment is conveyed through a contrast between *junzi* and *xiaoren*. Finally, the contrasts in the Analects encourage preferred attitudes in political functioning: virtue and cultivation over law and punishment.

The contrast between *junzi* and *xiaoren* in the Analects finds its correspondence in the comparisons of the wise vs. the fool in Ecclesiastes. It also is true in the political sense. As it has been suggested in this study, in

---

63. Again, the underlining is intended to highlight the disproportionate part of this parallelism.

64. Other occurrences include Analects 2:14, 4:16, 6:13, 12:19, 13:25, 14:6, 15:2, 21.

the Analects, *junzi* is essentially a political leader as opposed to *xiaoren*, the civilian. The word "*junzi*" often is connected to moral principle. Its occurrences of ninety-three times frequently are set in the context of political leadership. The rhetoric of *junzi-xiaoren* therefore aims to point out expected qualities of political leaders in different circumstances. In Qoheleth's thoughts, the dichotomy to contrast "the wise vs. the fool" occupies substantial passages in Eccl 2:12–16, 4:13–16, 7:4–7, and 9:17–10:15. The wise do not necessarily represent political leaders in Ecclesiastes. Yet "the king" (*hamelek*), which is in 2:12, appears in the subsequent comparison of the wise vs. the fool (2:12–17). Similarly, Qoheleth's proverbs on wisdom in 4:13–16 point out the disparity between the wise ruler and the foolish one. Also, Eccl 7:7 implies the bribes taken in political handling, and in 7:12, suggests "the protection of money" in political survival.

Qoheleth's comparisons of people occur too between "the righteous and wicked" (8:14; 9:2), "the good and the sinful," and "the clean and unclean" (both in 9:2).[65] Moreover, the dualistic "life and death" is obvious as Qoheleth commends the dead more than the living (4:2). This dualistic idea continues, where he questions the advantage and goodness of life in view of death in 6:11–12. He commends the day of death more than the day of birth in 7:1. The notion of "life and death" is at work again in 9:3–6. Qoheleth thus recommends "carpe diem" in 9:7–9 in view of the co-existence of life and death. Further, Qoheleth speaks about "light and darkness" in 2:13–14, where light exceeds darkness as wisdom exceeds folly. On this "light-darkness" dichotomy, Eccl 2:22–23 describes one's toil *under the sun* yet *even at night* his minds do not rest." And *light is sweet* but one has to remember *the days of darkness* (11:7–8). Furthermore, a series of contrasting parts is identifiable in the catalogue of time and events in 3:2–8. "Life and death," "killing and healing," "tearing and building," "weeping and laughing," "keeping quiet and talking," "to love and to hate," as well as "war and peace," and the like are depicted in view, side by side. Adding to the list of dichotomies are the views of "heaven and earth,"[66] "God and mortal" (both in 5:2), "love and hate" (9:1, 6), and "morning and evening" (11:6).

---

65. Literary contrast appears to be a literary device of wisdom literature. A similar dichotomy is known in other ancient Near Eastern literature. Babylonian writings have spoken of two realms of heaven-earth, Marduk is the "lord of heaven and earth." See Lambert, *BWL*, 113; lines 17 and 30. Elsewhere, *the Harper's Song*, the realm of the dead or the afterlife, "over there," is distinct from "on earth." See Pritchard, ed., *ANET*, 467.

66. In the heaven-earth dichotomy, Qoheleth divides reality into two realms: one is the dwelling place of God and the other of human. Expressions that frequently rendered human activities—namely "under the sun," "under heaven," "on earth" and the like—convey an underlying assumption that "God is in heaven, and you upon the earth" (Eccl 5:2) throughout the book. See Eaton, *Ecclesiastes*, 44.

Literary contrast in Ecclesiastes reflects Qoheleth's inner disputation rhetoric. It heightens the "yes-but" tensions Qoheleth intends to convey, where "human activity and enjoyment are equally enabled and restricted."[67] In Qoheleth's rhetoric, for instance, wisdom is strongly acclaimed, yet wisdom has its limitations also. As Eccl 8:17 points out, some people are wise, but they too cannot find out what God is working under the sun. Qoheleth's "yes-but" rhetoric simply cautions the reader against the "absolute goodness" of wisdom in the political realm. It is not surprising, then, that "*hebel*" and "to fear God" represent yet another deliberate contrast as evident in Eccl 7:15–18, 8:10–13, and 12:8–13. This contrast repeatedly validates Qoheleth's anthropology of "puff of breath" and his theology "to fear God."[68]

The contrast in Ecclesiastes heightens Qoheleth's quest for understanding life under the sun. Qoheleth's pursuit, represented through two verbs for "searching," *dāraš* (1:13) and *tûr* (7:25), puts life's tensions into perspective. Other regular expressions, such as, "seeking" *bâqaš* (3:6; 7:25) and "finding" *māṣā'* (five occurrences in 7:27–29), reinforce Qoheleth's chasing after the meaning of life. When a tension occurs between two comparing perspectives, it is either harmonized by recommending enjoyment that goes with one's toil, or it is harmonized by recommending the fear of God in view of *hebel*.[69] Consequently, Qoheleth exhorts his readers to live moment by moment, despite the fact that the political world is perilous. The same quest for understanding is helpful in resolving the tensions entrenched between the ruler and the ruled. Opposing views, in Qoheleth's rhetoric, "is a powerful cohesive force ... to bring into focus the book's central concern: the problem of meaning in life."[70] The contrast in Ecclesiastes, therefore, enhances the pursuit of political survival: its loss (because of injustice and tyranny) and its partial recovery (by fearing God).

Religious Consciousness in Politics

The word for Qoheleth's God, *'ĕlōhîm*, occurs forty times in total in Ecclesiastes. In all occurrences, Qoheleth refers to God by the generic *'ĕlōhîm*, never by a personal name in the Bible, YHWH.[71] The *'ĕlōhîm* in Ecclesiastes is

67. Krüger, *Qoheleth*, 2.

68. Lohfink, *Qoheleth*, 2.

69. The question of whether the tensions between all the dualistic dichotomies are ever solved, or are left to stand in tension, is yet to be conclusive among interpreters.

70. Fox, *A Time to Tear Down and A Time to Build Up*, 3.

71. The name by which YHWH represents and by which Qoheleth abstains from using, recalls a covenantal relationship that invokes warmth and closeness. See Longman, *Book of Ecclesiastes*, 35.

powerful (3:14–15) but keeps humans in ignorance (3:11). *'Ĕlōhîm* controls the details of human life but keeps a distance from the mortals.[72] Therefore, Qoheleth never addresses God in dialogue, neither in prayer nor lament.[73] Yet Qoheleth is concerned with religious matter, as he advances lengthy religious remarks in Eccl 5:1–7 [Hebrew 4:17–5:6]. He solicits obedience and reverence to the divine being before touching on the issues of oppression, injustice, and governance in 5:8–9 [Hebrew 5:7–8]. Qoheleth identifies the religious by whether they give sacrifices, although he too thinks they have the same fate as the non-religious (9:2).

The *'ĕlōhîm* in Ecclesiastes, unlike the *Tian* in the Analects, is "an active God."[74] *'Ĕlōhîm* is the subject of these frequently rendered verbs in Ecclesiastes: *natān* "give" (1:13; 2:26; 3:10,11; 5:18–19; 6:2; 8:15; 9:9; 12:7) and *'āśâ* "do or make" (3:11,14; 7:14,29; 8:17; 11:5). *'Ĕlōhîm* is the God who judges (3:17; 11:9). *'Ĕlōhîm* may be angry (5:6). Thus, humans are advised to fear *'ĕlōhîm* in all that they do (3:14; 5:6; 7:18; 8:12; 12:13). However, the dialectic in Qoheleth's thought is that "God is utterly present at the same time utterly absent" in the human world.[75] Even though *'ĕlōhîm* is active, humans cannot figure what *'ĕlōhîm* is doing (3:10–11) nor what *'ĕlōhîm* has done under the sun (8:17). The moves and motives of God are mysterious. And, like other ancient Near Eastern literature, Ecclesiastes relates the idea of political leadership closely with religion (5:1–9 [Hebrew 4:17–5:8]). It is not surprising that Qoheleth advances testimonials about God, to the effect that God is the endorser of kings (8:2). Such a relation between politics and religion, however, does not necessarily entail a harmonious political organization. Rather, social oppression and power corruption occur frequently.

On the other hand, the Analects too conveys a religious worldview. Rodney L. Taylor, among many others, has argued that the Analects is fundamentally religious.[76] Even though the Analects seldom offers a theological articulation, its religious element is real. To begin, heaven or *Tian* (天) has religious uniqueness.[77] It represents a supernatural force that guides the

---

72. Fox, *Ecclesiastes*, xxxi.
73. Crenshaw, *Old Testament Wisdom*, 124.
74. Murphy, *Ecclesiastes*, lxviii.
75. Ibid.
76. See Taylor, *Religious Dimensions of Confucianism*, 1–12. The book presents Confucian tradition as a religious one, by identifying aspects of the tradition that can be described as religious, including the cultivation of the sagehood, *sheng* (圣) as religious heroes, and by identifying major religious themes in Confucian texts.
77. Here, heaven (天*Tian*) is understood in a religious peculiarity. Elsewhere in Analects, it is understood as a natural phenomenon, and represents the cosmos in which human live and act. *Tian* is regarded here as distinctive from dao (道) especially

order of the universe. *Tian* is described as "great" in the Analects 8:19, which Emperor Yao had modeled after. *Tian* is the source wherein the moral values and fundamental principles of humans are established. In this regard, *Tian* is sometimes understood in parallel with the Way (道 dao), meaning the decreed way of life. The concept of "the way of heaven" (天道 *tian dao*) and "the mandate of heaven" (天命 *tian ming*) derive from this understanding.[78] As *Tian* shoulders the overarching position of power, all major changes— such as the defeat of an inferior state by a higher political power—derive from the influence and determination of its will.[79] Failure to manifest ethical virtues also leads to the downfall of a ruler.[80] Ethics therefore derives from this way of *Tian*. Confucius discerns an order that *Tian* will communicate its course through nature, "What does Heaven have to say? There are four seasons going around a year and there are hundreds of things growing. What does Heaven have to say?" (Analects 17:19) Confucius acknowledges that his virtue was given by *Tian* (Analects 7:23). His disciples likewise concede that one's life and death, as well as one's wealth and honor, were matters of destiny depending on *Tian* (Analects 12:5). The sense of reverence toward *Tian* reflects one's cultivation. And the observance of *li* conveys such cultivation.

Confucius' commitment to the practices of rites and sacrifices further suggests a religious undertone in his sayings in the Analects. Julia Ching maintains that, "Confucius' philosophy is clearly grounded in religion— the inherited religion of the Lord on High or Heaven, the supreme and personal deity."[81] Ching calls attention to the classical writing for *li* (禮), which etymologizes sacrificial vessels.[82] Thus, the word has religious origin. Confucius' speech in the Analects conveys similar religious undertones. For instance, he addresses issues cautioning against the religious belief of

---

when dao is explained in terms of faculties of human experience, especially humanness (仁 *ren*) and propriety (礼 *li*). The most comprehensive analysis classifies *Tian* into four categories of meanings: 1) rightness; 2) virtue; 3) nature; and 4) a willful personal God. See Zhang and Li, *Ruxue Yuanliu*, 186.

78. According to the theory of the "mandate of heaven" in ancient China, heaven gives the mandate to deserving man as the ruling figure, to govern wisely and humanely. According to Ching, *Chinese Religions*, 45–6, this theory developed with the emergence of the classical texts, including Confucian.

79. Cheng, "Origins of Chinese Philosophy," 500. Whether Confucius' *Tian* is a personal deity remains debatable to the present day. Most Confucian thinkers hesitate to claim that *Tian* is a personal deity.

80. Ching, *Chinese Religions*, 46, reasons that the mandate of heaven gives justification to the rise and fall of many dynasties in Chinese history. See also Yao, *REC*, 5.

81. Ching, "What is Confucian Spirituality?" 65.

82. Ibid.

his time, "To offer sacrifice to the spirit of an ancestor not of one's own, is flattering" (Analects 2:24). He maintains an attitude of honesty in religious affairs by saying, "If I am not participating at the sacrifice, I do not sacrifice at all" (Analects 3:12). In addition, Confucius' attitude toward gods is reverence, *jing* (敬), evident in the Analects 6:22.[83] Therefore, it is against the background of cultic worship that Confucius cautions on these proper religious attitudes. Furthermore, Confucius appears to be open to the idea of destiny or decree. He professes, "It is destiny if my way prevails, it is also destiny if my way fails" (Analects 14:36). He comments that anyone who does not know the destiny cannot be an exemplary person (Analects 20:3). To Confucius, humans seem to possess the potential to know the decree of *Tian* and to live accordingly. The religious consciousness again is clearly embedded in Confucian thought.

Whether *Tian* embodies a religious essence in Confucius' thought is out of the question. But Confucius's *Tian* is hardly a personal deity. Confucius insists on *Tian* as a distant and over-arching Order in his wisdom articulations. And in the Analects, Confucius appears to be more concerned with the pragmatic dimension of human activities and less on the thoughts of gods. In spite of this, to suggest that Confucius is an atheist and to discard the religious elements in Confucius' philosophy all together is far-fetched.[84] On the other hand, many Confucian thinkers today are hesitant to present Confucian philosophy as religion, despite the fact that many Confucian temples in China are built to worship Confucius and his disciples as gods.[85] For them, Confucian philosophy appears more to be a philosophy of life in pursuit of virtue and the formation of community.[86] For this reason, the question of whether heaven or *Tian* is personal or not, is not so simple. This issue remains largely debatable. A religious worldview is nonetheless embedded in the Analects' articulation of ethics, including that of political ideas. Yeo is correct to argue for a theological dimension in Confucian ethics, "that every ethic, culture, or religion—which of course overlap and interact with each other—contains a theology by which it is shaped and directed."[87] The phrase "theological ethics" that Yeo has invoked therefore encapsulates both Confucian ethics and Confucius' religious consciousness.

---

83. Confucian of later development suggests such reverence toward *Tian*, yielding the idea of *Jingtian* (敬天).

84. For example, Yuan, "Kongzi de Zhihui" [Confucius Wisdom], 34 suggests that Confucius is an atheist.

85. Yeo, *Musing with Confucius and Paul*, 80.

86. Ibid.

87. Ibid.

Both Ecclesiastes and the Analects have religious consciousness. Although Qoheleth's impression of God and Confucius' impression of *Tian* are distant, their religious consciousness is honest. At base, each of these wisdom texts express their theological meanings uniquely. And both connect religion with political living. Ecclesiastes and the Analects acknowledge a higher order of events above the human realm. They both affirm an ultimate order, *'ĕlōhîm* (in Ecclesiastes) and *Tian* or dao (in the Analects), to guide the socio-political order on earth. This higher and ultimate order appears to be mysterious for Qoheleth and Confucius for factors beyond human grasp. Qoheleth's understanding of *'ĕlōhîm* directs a fear of the deity, whereas Confucius' understanding of *Tian* leads to moral principles. This point of departure is evident in the distinct political ideas of Ecclesiastes and the Analects, respectively.

How Ecclesiastes and the Analects Enlighten Each Other

Ecclesiastes

The association of Qoheleth with the political establishment only lasts for the first two chapters in Ecclesiastes. Most of the book depicts Qoheleth as one who identifies more with civic life. Oppression and injustice therefore are perceived from the public eye. Human toil, responsibilities, and activities "under the sun" are also surveyed. Qoheleth paints a picture of helpless and oppressed civilians in the hand of the politically powerful. Criticism toward the establishment only can be discerned from rhetoric, political satire, and double entendre indirectly. To Qoheleth, no human, not even the wise, can settle the problem of socio-political disorder. Even if a wise one stands a chance of solving it, he needs to be given a chance. Yet Qoheleth assures his readers that there is a time and judgment for every human work, even though he too warns how its works may be mysterious. God will judge, despite the reality that how and when God judges may remain unknown. This notion of God's judgment is remarkably lacking in the Analects. Yet, in Ecclesiastes, it conveys a profound theology for one who questions the advantage of living in the midst of social disorder. God will *šāpaṭ* in the place where wickedness abounds, precisely in places of *mišpāṭ*. It is comforting to acknowledge that there is a time when God judges the wicked (and the righteous). In this regard, Ecclesiastes enlightens the Analects by introducing theology. This theology is rooted in its political context as a way to cope with challenges of social injustice and tyranny. God not only will guide human history but also will judge human activities at the appointed time. This aspect of theology, namely, an active deity, is absent in the Analects, yet is profoundly true in ancient wisdom thought.[88]

As humans, therefore, one behaves prudently toward authority to avoid trouble. One also can work within the political structure and use their position and ability to influence political decision. Unlike the Analects, which prizes wisdom absolutely, the practical value of wisdom in Ecclesiastes is conditioned and transient. Wisdom merely has a relative advantage, not an absolute one. Wisdom is not always good, though it is always better than folly. For wisdom enables one to cope in an unstable political environment. It helps one to survive political maneuvers. Therefore, a wise person makes political survival worth living: by seizing the moment, by making wise choices, and by embracing acceptable courtly behavior.

The Analects

In the Analects, the political organization is set as the main concern in Confucius' teaching. Therefore, the focus of the Analects aims at political leadership, dealing more with how to manage governmental duty. As such, the Analects communicates a political philosophy based on virtuous governance. Human efforts are accentuated in this political philosophy in order to mold people of *ren*, *de*, *li*, and *yi*. In its core, *ren* (humanness) is to be cultivated to respect and love all people despite social distinctions. *De* (morality) is a person's influence in commanding deference. *Li* (propriety) encompasses the centralization of power, rectification of roles and functions, proper execution of responsibilities and meeting social expectations, all of which are essentials. Further, political leaders should embrace *yi* (righteousness): to do the just and appropriate at the right time. In short, if virtuous governance is the ideal of political rule, then humanness is its essence, morality is its power, propriety is its tool, and righteousness is its motive or attitude. A political leader is a *junzi* who has moral quality and who possesses the qualities of humanness, propriety, and righteousness. Such a political leadership ideal is a Confucian educational goal in the Analects.

Like Ecclesiastes, the Analects has pointed out directly the reason for political chaos and power corruption among the ruling class. Yet unlike Ecclesiastes, the Analects suggests righting the situation based on inculcating humanness, moral principles, propriety, and righteousness. For this idea, virtuous governance is accentuated as decisive political vision. Confucius aims to mold characters for the advancement of the nation. Therefore,

---

88. The aspect of dealing with a personal and active deity is true in ancient wisdom thought, although it is found to a lesser degree in Ecclesiastes.

Confucius does have a vision for change. In the core of his reform, Confucius aims to correct a corrupt political misadministration and disordered social system. His political thought is considered wise, even radical. It is a sign of breakthrough and advancement in its historical background. The Analects is hence intended to contribute to the reinstatement of orderliness in society. Confucius believes that people can live in proactive ways that challenge the destructive power in the socio-political world. He suggests a dynamic of self-organization amidst political chaos, proposing order within a disordered world. The essential ideas are found in the complex and related attributes of *de, ren* and *yi,* and *li.* How these attributes relate to each other remains a scholarly debate in Confucian circles.

A Dialogical Imagination

The cross-textual endeavor undertaken in this study has located several interwoven connections between the textual worlds of Ecclesiastes and the Analects. In terms of similarities, both wisdom texts concern socio-political survival. They propose attitudes to live authentically as humans in two distinct socio-political contexts. Both Confucius and Qoheleth advocate proper behavior, either for future betterment (the Analects) or simply for coping with reality (Ecclesiastes). As part of the wisdom tradition, they combine pedagogics in politics. In terms of difference, both wisdom texts begin at different points of departure: one from the political establishment (the Analects) and the other largely from the civilian (Ecclesiastes). The former perspective identifies problems of moral corruption and social disorder among rulers, feudal lords, and government officials. The latter identifies oppression and suffering of the civilian amid socio-political evils. On the grounds of this dissimilarity, the Analects and Ecclesiastes record distinctive political wisdom on how to survive consequentially.

The Analects encompasses a proactive attitude toward correcting the existing disorder. Its political ideal has a specific and concrete methodology that accentuates human actions. And it highlights most parts of what is silent in Ecclesiastes: what need to be done to ensure social order. Such a perspective derived from the political establishment explains the presence of direct instructions and confrontations against the political establishment. Corrective measures are asserted. The Analects is indeed more direct in pointing out the wrongs in the power structure. It is also more directive in its instructions for change.

On the other hand, Ecclesiastes asserts a theology. Qoheleth does not advocate proactive and corrective measures for change. Nevertheless, he upholds an attitude of prudence and caution to avoid further peril. Qoheleth's seemingly passive perspective comes from the general perception of human limitation and an acknowledgment of human ignorance of how God works in the human world. There is no direct confrontation with the political establishment in Ecclesiastes; instead, there are anecdotes, political satires, and double entendre. Such political wisdom is upheld because Qoheleth perceives several realities in a socio-politically disordered world. First, the powerlessness on the part of people is real; they are at the mercy of the rich and the political establishment. Second, political power is short-lived and will soon be over. Third, wisdom ensures general political survival, yet wisdom is not absolutely advantageous every time. Therefore, instances of socio-political disorder only can be handled one at a time. It cannot be solved once and for all. Qoheleth nevertheless points toward an attitude of fearing God in view of disorder. The theology in Ecclesiastes thus has directed people to engage sensible thinking and wise praxis. As humans, people are informed by the reality of political challenges like tyranny, absolutism of rulership, and power corruption.

Judging from the above similarities and differences, both wisdom texts can speak meaningfully at the same time. A dialogical imagination takes into account each perspective for the elucidation of another. The exchange of ideas brings about enlightenment and enrichment. I suggest a corresponding need to fill The Analects with Ecclesiastes' theological assertion, and to gratify Ecclesiastes with the Analects' proactive ethics. This dialogical imagination can be made first by appropriating Qoheleth's fear of God as the motive and dynamic of Confucius' vision of virtuous governance. The fear of God entails an acknowledgment of the divine being, who ultimately judges how humans have run the world. Human effort therefore will have its value before the ultimate ruler and judge. On this account, Yeo has suggested the idea of "theological ethics," an intertwined relationship to connect Confucius' ethics with Pauline theology communicated through the Book of Galatians.[89] "Theological ethics" represents a similar idea here to communicate Qoheleth's and Confucius' pursuit of surviving politically.

The socio-political evil can be dealt with through parallel efforts combining virtuous living and the fear of God. As such, virtuous governance and managerial competence are not merely human efforts, but efforts with theological motives. A higher, personal deity will make human effort meaningful in its appointed time. Wisdom as a quest for becoming authentically human is evident in both Ecclesiastes and the Analects. Both texts convey

---

89. Yeo, *Musing with Confucius and Paul,* 88–89, 110–76. Yeo uses the Confucian notion of *de* (morality or virtue) in reading Paul's understanding of God's Spirit; he uses Paul's understanding of the Spirit as the initiator of ethics when reading Confucian *de*.

anthropological specifics on how to be meaningfully human. The theological anthropology in Ecclesiastes and the anthropological theology in the Analects aim at the same objective: to uphold order in the human world in line with the ultimate Order above. Moreover, theology or religion does not depart from practical life. Both elements are intact in wholesome human living. As one can see from the reading of Ecclesiastes and the Analects, Qoheleth and Confucius express their religious beliefs based on socio-political realities respectively. Such religious beliefs make their wisdom thoughts all the more pragmatic and down-to-earth.[90] In a nutshell, by combining Ecclesiastes' theological assertion and the Analects' proactive ethics, one secures a theological anthropology or anthropological theology that conveys "political wisdom in a disordered world" powerfully.

As Roger Ames and Henry Rosemont have pointed out, Chinese philosophers in general, and Confucius in particular, do not concern themselves much with describing knowledge about the world, but are more concerned with how to get on in the world.[91] Wisdom is how people should steer their living. The way or dao, literally referring to a physical path or road, also refers to a "way" of doing things. So, the "way" in the Analects, endorsed by *Tian* (the ultimate Way), is the path that people should embark on to steer their lives.[92] Because of the corruption of ritual practice and culture, people easily are led astray from the way one should live.[93] Re-establishment of a proper "way" of living hence becomes imminent and imperative in the Analects. This concern explains why establishing a moral order preoccupies the exchange of political ideas in the Analects. This proactive measure also explains why it should be gratified in the reading of Ecclesiastes. With this dialogical imagination, one would not dismiss the Analects' political thoughts as futile philosophical ideas or invalid ethical theories. Neither would one write off Ecclesiastes' political ideas as mere escapism. Each of these two wisdom texts is practical in its own milieu.

As Archie Lee has appropriated it, there are liberating elements as well as enslaving ones in the two texts, where "the negative or enslaving elements can be challenged and judged."[94] In the cross reading of Ecclesiastes and the Analects, each text provides the necessary contour against the other, such that one can be seen in a greater light. Ecclesiastes strengthens the

90. Although they therefore emphasize the realm of human living more than the realm of the supernatural and the unknown.

91. Ames and Rosemont, *Analects of Confucius*, 33.

92. Slingerland, *Confucius Analects*, xxii.

93. Ibid., xxiii. Moral decay in Confucius' time, apart from human weaknesses, is also due to the quality of tradition into which people are acculturated.

94. Lee, "Cross-textual Hermeneutics," 61–62.

understanding of the Analects, and vice versa.[95] In short, Ecclesiastes and the Analects represent mirrors to one another with regard to articulating political wisdom. Ecclesiastes needs the Analects to introduce proactive measures and assertive behavior. Likewise, the Analects needs Ecclesiastes to advance theology that affirms the ultimate value of human effort. In short, wisdom texts are situated in constant dialogues with each other. More cross-textual dialogues will enrich aspects of faith-native understanding to the point that the strength of one text supplements the blind spot of the other. Such an approach does not attempt to eliminate differences between texts, but to appropriate both texts in the proper perspective.

The Crossings: In Search of Political Wisdom

This part of "crossings" derives from the dialogical imagination resolved as above. Wisdom includes making choices amid socio-political challenges. Sometimes it involves good judgment, determining what is morally acceptable or obligatory. Other times wisdom is a good sense of relation to others.[96] In the socio-political realities of Malaysia, many are affected by the presence of repeated wickedness—right in the places where justice and righteousness are to be expected. Some incidents in recent years have sparked an outrage across the nation upon the political power and have communicated a quest for justice.[97] Apparently, the governing political leadership has raised doubt about its credibility. Besides, oppression is sometimes encountered in Malaysia at certain political events, in the media and in publications, and with the distribution of religious texts. Moreover, power corruption in the form of nepotism and financial fraud have been recurrently brought to public awareness. There is hence a general growing distrust about the moral standard of some political leaders. It appears that social values and power structures no longer function meaningfully. Such phenomena are disturbing today as much as they were in the ancient world of Qoheleth and Confucius. Oppression will likely recur as long as there is the existence of a power structure. In this regard, the call for political wisdom in Ecclesiastes

95. I am indebted to Lee, "Cross-textual Hermeneutics," 61–62, for this perspective.

96. Baltes and Smith, "Toward a Psychology of Wisdom," 95; Sternberg and Jordan, *Handbook of Wisdom: Psychological Perspectives*, 250.

97. For instance, the supposedly independent commission body of anti-corruption in the country (Malaysian Anti-Corruption Commission) is questioned about its failure to conduct investigations into the financial scandals of some government-owned operations. On the other hand, it is also allegedly responsible for the death of a political aide of the Opposition on 16 July 2009, while conducting investigations on an alleged corruption.

and the Analects is necessary. It is the hope of the author of this study, as a Malaysian Chinese Christian, to seek pragmatic measures in order to live authentically amid this challenging situation.

The Necessity of Political Leadership and Wise Management

The recent results of the general election of Malaysia has accelerated the necessity for a just government and sound management.[98] Before and after the general election, many people are looking for ways to combat serious moral decay in the government system. Christians too are searching for means to cope with an oppressive human establishment that involves activities such as high-handedness on campaigning, media control, misappropriation of funds, and ballot manipulation. Living in the present contexts scarred by power abuses, one can examine the similar oppressive socio-political reality reflected in Ecclesiastes and the Analects. They correctly point out the agonizing pain resulting from the problem of evil. Nevertheless, they both suggest that political establishment is necessary. In the case of fund misappropriation, for instance, Christians should insist on responsible management, beginning with the example of church leadership. Informed by the teachings of biblical and native texts, Malaysian Chinese Christians can impress upon the society the concept that God-fearing leadership can possibly relieve social evil. The God-fearing motive is professed repeatedly in Ecclesiastes. In this regard, management knowhow also is crucial, as evidenced in the Analects. Management knowhow and the God-fearing motive are both needed for meaningful survival in todays' socio-political world.

In light of the political wisdom of both Ecclesiastes and the Analects, teachings of organizational behavior, work ethics, and proper management are to be promoted, lived out, and taught in schools and churches. Essential management theories like planning, evaluating, organizing human resources, and distributing national reserves (as in the Analects) can be exemplified among Chinese churches. Crucial surviving skills like diplomatic conduct, courtly behavior, observance of protocol and prudence (as in Ecclesiastes) can likewise be nurtured at large. Through wisdom, national stability is ensured due to the wise administration of food supply, armed forces, gross productivity, and budget (Analects 12:7; 20:1–3). Through wise defenses, a country facing invasion from a foreign nation can be delivered (Eccl 9:13–16). Therefore, wisdom is important in political leadership. Though

---

98. The general election of Malaysia meant here was held on May 5, 2013. There after, the next general election of Malaysia was held on May 9, 2018 which recorded a change of government.

one is reminded from Qoheleth's articulation that wisdom has its limitations, wisdom is still relatively good for political living.

Theological Anthropology

It is an irony that one of the sources of socio-political disorder today derives from the political establishment itself. Yet the political establishment intrinsically bears a duty to maintain socio-political order. Qoheleth and Confucius expect a socio-political order that reflects the cosmic order. Even in contemporary wisdom thought, creation itself is a divinely bestowed order. Human conduct has a significant influence on this order. When social disorder occurs, it conflicts with this cosmic order. The goal of wisdom, therefore, is to discover an order so that the people correspond accordingly through proper conduct. The ancient sages construe from their observations which actions lead to good and bad consequences that can affect this order. Christians, therefore, can call for orderly behaviors while, at the same time, believe in divine timing. Chinese, on the other hand, can count on virtuous governance, advocating *li* as a way to comply with the cosmic order. When these two notions are taken together, a theological anthropology is indicative for today.

The expectation of orderliness and functionality in a human society comes from a theological conviction. In Christian belief, God directs human activities (Eccl 3:10–15; 5:19; 8:17; 9:1) and brings human deeds into judgment (12:13–14). While Christians affirm divine sovereignty, they entrust the judgment of social injustice to God's timing. Since God's way is inscrutable, their philosophy of life can be geared toward an anthroposcopic concern, specifically, healthy execution of duties and responsibilities.[99] Most importantly, there is a time for divine judgment. The affirmation of God's sovereignty reminds people to live in a God-fearing manner. Therefore, Qoheleth's theology is as profoundly important as the human endeavor advocated in the Analects. And Chinese Christians should believe that, even today, there is a way for humans to conduct themselves, and there is a way for society to be consolidated.[100] Confucius' anthropological ways should be reassessed in surviving today's world. Likewise, Ecclesiastes' theology should be weighed and put into practice.

---

99. An idea from Barton, *Critical and Exegetical Commentary*, 49–50.

100. See Van Norden, *Confucius and the Analects*, 19. The term "dao" (道), "way," in the sense of "path" or "road" rendered in Analects reflects a common terminology also used by ancient sages in the Near East.

Human Endeavor is Crucial

Wisdom concerns the art of living. To achieve this art of living, human endeavor is underlined. Following the articulations of Ecclesiastes and the Analects, proper behavior is therefore crucial today for Chinese Christians who cope with various socio-political realities. In Malaysia, for instance, Chinese sometimes become the target of heated racist remarks, while the Christian faith is also often challenged. In the midst of searching for meaningful survival, a retrospect on human endeavor is vital. In Ecclesiastes, the term "human" is used forty-eight times, suggesting substantial thought is given to the human spheres. It is 'ādām, "humankind," whose toil, enjoyment, ethics, living, as well as death, occupies Qoheleth's subject matters.[101] In the Analects, on the other hand, it is also human effort that is largely advocated in the cultivation of *junzi*—to guide human behavior toward political order. Therefore, both texts speak powerfully to uphold human effort. Efficacious leaders, the *junzi*(s), who are morally acceptable on one hand and competent on the other, are needed to ensure order and harmony. Diligence, wise speech, courtly protocol, and necessary attitude are likewise needful for the official to handle issues tactfully. In short, edifying human endeavor, informed by both Ecclesiastes and the Analects, can be advocated among Chinese churches. Wisdom, in general, communicates similar emphases on this concern of human endeavor. It is essentially a mastery of life.

This Worldliness in Focus

Even though the present realities are challenging, it is nevertheless helpful to be mindful of this-worldly responsibilities. Qoheleth clearly adopts an anthroposcopic view in articulating his theological reflections. Confucius, too, was preoccupied with political praxis in the society of his time, keeping his eyes fixed firmly on this life and this world, especially the social and political.[102] Therefore, human endeavor is preferred more than other-worldly assumptions. In both texts, there are overriding interests in addressing human concerns. As for divine matters, Christians knows 'ĕlōhîm who, as an overarching divine being, appears to be distant and inscrutable (from the reading of Ecclesiastes). And Chinese learn that it is wise to "keep a distance from the gods and spirits of the dead while showing them reverence" (Analects 6:22). Thus, nurtured by both native and faith texts, Chinese Christians

---

101. Seow, *Ecclesiastes*, 54. Qoheleth elaborates at length on human toils and activities "under the sun" before drawing his conclusions (Eccl 1:3, 13; 2:1–10, 18–19; 3:10; 4:1–5; 5:8–17; 6:1–2; 8:5–15; 9:3, 13–18, and so forth).

102. Ching, *Confucianism and Christianity*, 185.

are pragmatists in keeping attention focused on this-worldliness. They can choose to "carpe diem"—to live responsibly for the moment and to enjoy the present. And at the same time, they also can be ethically inclined, pressing toward becoming *junzi*(s) in order to impact society directly.

Conclusion

This chapter has attempted to take two wisdom texts as dialogical partners. As cross-textual hermeneutics suggests, the biblical text and the native text are equally valid. They pose similar human quests. And they address political dimensions of life. Many evils of the present day come from the political establishment. Confronting this reality, Ecclesiastes affirms theological conviction, whereas the Analects necessitates ethics. Qoheleth insists on fearing God, whereas Confucius asserts proactive human action. Both wisdom texts convey valuable, indispensable, and complementary political wisdom. There are areas where Ecclesiastes and the Analects share commonalities. Yet there are also areas in which they record fundamental differences. Such differences have highlighted fundamental faith-native tensions, but they do not suggest superiority on either side. They do suggest, however, that they need each other for mutual enlightenment. Their different approaches are due to "historically-culturally bound conditions."[103] Despite their remarkable differences, they both illustrate a concern with political wisdom in general, and a sense of survival in particular. Both Ecclesiastes and the Analects suggest skills in their distinctive capacity to survive chaotic living conditions. On account of the cross-textual reading of this study, the Analects adds a proactive dimension to the often mistaken *hebel* notion of Ecclesiastes, while Ecclesiastes introduces a theological dimension that is largely silent in the Analects.

---

103. Lee, "Cross-textual Hermeneutics on Gospel and Culture," 46.

Epilogue

IN A CROSS-TEXTUAL HERMENEUTICS between Galatians and the Analects, Yeo comments that the two texts shape the contours of a Chinese Christian identity in a complementary way. Yet, "there are basic differences that are simply irreconcilable, and holding on to them in radical tension is an ever-present challenge."[1] Following this lead, I admit that both Ecclesiastes and the Analects inevitably create a tension within me as a Chinese Christian. I contain both an innately-conditioned Chinese identity *and* a faith-nurtured Christian identity. Both identities inherit two different textual traditions. Both textual traditions have formed an integrated whole in me and have genuinely shaped my true self. For me, a textual tradition is essential for the fulfilment of the other. Reading these two texts together as a Chinese Christian suggests a dialogical empowerment that involves the advantage(s) of both texts. Their differences will continue to be in tension between my faith and my native culture. Yet their crossings are nevertheless surprisingly informative and edifying to a Chinese Christian like me.

A sincere understanding of a native text, in addition to a biblical text, can open up faith-native dialogue within a person. It is true for anyone else whose contours of identity are shaped by two different faith-native traditions. Hwa Yung advocates this understanding for "the communication of the gospel through a cogent Christian apologetic."[2] While Hwa is concerned with the evangelical movement, this study concerns itself with faith-native reconciliation in Chinese Christians. A person who owns both faith-native aspects of identity can engage them more in dialogue, in theologizing, and in biblical hermeneutics. Such faith-native crossings are helpful to a person's reading of Scripture. It also is being responsible for living in a multi-scriptural environment. It is all the more necessary when one's biblical understanding is found in tension with one's nativeness. A closer look into the two different textual traditions in this study is unexpectedly telling and enriching.

---

1. Yeo, *Musing with Confucius and Paul*, 36.
2. Hwa, "Towards an Evangelical Approach to Religions and Cultures," 25.

A cross-reading of Ecclesiastes and the Analects in this study indicates that the sages often are connected to the royal court. Their writings thus necessitate articulation about politics. They sought orderliness in the political realm. They taught about proper conduct to ensure political survival. The cross-textual interpretation undertaken in this study has nevertheless pointed out various distinctions between Ecclesiastes and the Analects. The differences lead to fundamental disparities in their worldviews and ideas. Rather than becoming obstacles to understand each other, however, the disparities are taken as resources to engage in for mutual enrichment and through an attitude of openness. Just as there are real tensions between a native text and a faith text, there are tensions within an individual who holds both native and religious identities. I believe the key lies in how a reader handles and utilizes such differences in an attempt to make meaningful and enriching encounters.

Cross-textual hermeneutics entails reading a text in light of another text. It brings about "crossing" from one text to the other in progressing to a broader understanding. This interpretive approach finds validation from the dynamic and the openness of ancient wisdom texts. Wisdom is didactic. It denotes a universal quest for mastery in life. Personally, this cross-textual reading also represents a journey of self-discovery. In general, Christians are being told to know more about themselves in light of becoming new creations in Christ. Yet they are seldom told to discover themselves in light of their native connection through their home-grown texts. I have embarked on this discovery, and yet find it ever-intriguing and helpful. It is enriching to both my faith as a Christian and my native culture as a Chinese. I hope this study continues to affirm that the Confucian tradition has much to contribute to on-going biblical hermeneutics. I suggest, therefore, this research as a move toward reintroducing Confucian ethics to biblical interpretation. As this study shows, Chinese classics could serve as a resource for biblical hermeneutics. More similar cross-textual hermeneutics will enrich the faith-native aspects to the point that the strength of one text supplements the weakness of another. Rather than trying to eliminate the differences, cross-textual hermeneutics will appropriate the faith-native textual traditions in proper, supplementary, and dialogic engagement.

Bibliography

Ames, Roger T. *The Art of Rulership: A Study in Ancient Chinese Political Thought.* Honolulu: University of Hawaii Press, 1983.
Ames, Roger T., and Henry Rosemont Jr. *The Analects of Confucius: A Philosophical Translation.* New York: Ballantine, 1998.
Anderson, William H. U. *Qoheleth and Its Pessimistic Theology: Hermeneutical Struggles in Wisdom Literature.* Mellen Biblical Press Series 54. Lewiston, NY: Edwin Mellen Biblical, 1997.
Angle, Stephen C. "Tiaozhan Hexie: Dui Rujia He Gainian de Bianhu yu Quanshi" [Confronting Harmony: Defending and Interpreting the Confucian Concept of He]. In *Zhongguo Ruxue Yi* [Chinese Confucianism]. Vol. 1, edited by Wang Zhong-Jiang and Li Cun-Shan. Beijing: Commercial, 2006. 安靖如："挑战和谐：对儒家'和'观念的辩护与诠释"。《中国儒学（一）》。王中江、李存山主编。北京：商务印书馆，2006.
Arnold, Bill T., and Bryan E. Beyer, eds. *Readings from the Ancient Near East: Primary Sources for Old Testament Study.* Grand Rapids: Baker Academic, 2002.
Baltes, P. B., and J. Smith. "Toward a Psychology of Wisdom and Its Ontogenesis." In *Wisdom: Its Nature, Origins, and Development,* edited by Robert J. Sternberg, 87–120. Cambridge: Cambridge University Press, 1990.
Barr, James. *Comparative Philology and the Text of the Old Testament.* 1968. Reprint, Winona Lake, IN: Eisenbrauns, 1987.
Bartholomew, Craig G. *Ecclesiastes.* Baker Commentary on the Old Testament Wisdom and Psalms. Grand Rapids: Baker Academic, 2009
Bartholomew, Craig G., and Ryan P. O'Dowd. *Old Testament Wisdom Literature: A Theological Introduction.* Downers Grove, IL: IVP Academic, 2011.
Barton, George A. *A Critical and Exegetical Commentary on the Book of Ecclesiastes.* ICC. Edinburgh: T. & T. Clark, 1908.
Beentjes, Panc. "Some Notes on Qoheleth 8, 1–15." In *Qoheleth in the Context of Wisdom,* edited by Antoon Schoors, 303–15. Bibliotheca Ephemeridum Theologicarum Lovaniensium 136. Leuven: Leuven University Press, 1998.
Bell, Daniel A. *Beyond Liberal Democracy: Political Thinking for an East Asian Context.* Princeton: Princeton University Press, 2006.
———. *China's New Confucianism: Politics and Everyday Life in a Changing Society.* Princeton: Princeton University Press, 2010.
———, ed. *Confucian Political Ethics.* Princeton: Princeton University Press, 2008.
Bell, Daniel A., and Hahm Chaibong, eds. *Confucianism for the Modern World.* Cambridge: Cambridge University Press, 2003.

Berlejung, A and P. Van Hecke, eds. *The Language of Qoheleth in Its Context: Essays in Honour of Prof. A. Schoors on the Occasion of his Seventieth Birthday*. Orientalia Lovaniensia Analecta 41. Leuven: Peeters, 2007.

Berry, Donald K. *An Introduction to Wisdom and Poetry of the Old Testament*. Nashville: Broadman & Holman, 1995.

Berthrong, John H. *Transformations of the Confucian Way*. Oxford: Westview, 1998.

Berthrong, John H., and Evelyn Nagai Berthrong. *Confucianism: A Short Introduction*. Oxford: One World, 2000.

Black, Anthony. *A World History of Ancient Political Thought*. Oxford: Oxford University Press, 2009.

Blanshard, Brand. "Wisdom." In *Encyclopedia of Philosophy*, edited by Paul Edwards, 8:322–24. New York: Macmillan, 1967.

Blocker, H. Gene. "Chinese Philosophy: Social and Political Thought." In *Encyclopedia of Philosophy*, edited by Donald M. Borchert, 231–38. New York: Thompson Gale, 2006.

Boardman, John, N. G. L. Hammond, D. M. Lewis, and M. Ostwald. *The Cambridge Ancient History*. 2nd ed. Vol 4. Cambridge: Cambridge University Press, 1988.

Boda, Mark J., Tremper Longman III, and Cristian G. Rata, eds. *The Words of the Wise Are Like Goads*. Winona Lake, IN: Eisenbrauns, 2013.

Botterweck, G. Johannes, et al., eds. *Theological Dictionary of the Old Testament*. Translated by John T. Willis, Geoffrey W. Bromiley, David E. Green, and Douglas W. Scott. Grand Rapids: Eerdmans, 1974–2006.

Bowker, John, ed. *The Oxford Dictionary of World Religions*. Oxford: Oxford University Press, 1997.

Bricker, Daniel P. "Innocent Suffering in Mesopotamia." *Tyndale Bulletin* 51 (2000) 193–214.

Brooks, E. Bruce, and A. Taeko Brooks. *The Original Analects: Sayings of Confucius and His Successors: A New Translation and Commentary*. New York: Columbia University Press, 1998.

Brosius, Maria. *The Persian Empire from Cyrus II to Artaxerxes I*. LACTOR 16. London: London Association of Classical Teachers, 2000.

Brown, Francis, S. R. Driver, and Charles Briggs. *The New Brown-Driver-Briggs Hebrew and English Lexicon*. Oxford: Clarendon, 1907.

Brueggemann, Walter. "The Social Significance of Solomon as a Patron of Wisdom." In *The Sage in Israel and the Ancient Near East*, edited by John G. Gammie and Leo G. Perdue, 117–32. Winona Lake, IN: Eisenbrauns, 1990.

Cai, Xi-Qin, Lai Bo and Xia Yu-He. *Lunyu: Zhongwen Yizhu, Yingwen Fanyi* [English Translation and Chinese Annotation to the Analects]. Beijing: Sinolingua, 1994. 蔡希勤、赖波和夏玉和译：《论语》。中文译注、英文翻译。北京：华语教学，1994.

Chai, Ch'u and Winberg Chai. *Confucianism*. Woodbury, NY: Barron's Educational Series, 1973.

Chan, Alan K. L. "Confucian Ethics and the Critique of Ideology." *Asian Philosophy* 10 (2000) 245–61.

Chan, Wing-Tsit. "Chinese Philosophy: Overview." In *Encyclopedia of Philosophy*, edited by Donald M. Borchert, 2:149–60. 2nd ed. Detroit: Macmillan Reference USA, 2006.

Chen, Bin. "Zuowei Zhengzhi Xingdong de Xiushen: dui *Lunyu Weizheng* Diyi zhi Sizhang de Sikao" [Self Cultivation as a Political Activity: Reflections on *Weizheng* Chapter 1-4 in *Lunyu*], in *Zhongguo Ruxue* [Chinese Confucianism], edited by Zhong-Jiang Wang and Cun-Shan Li, 81–107. Vol 3. Beijing: China Social Sciences, 2008. 陈斌："作为政治行动的修身—对《论语·为政》第1-4章的思考。"《中国儒学（三）》。王中江、李存山主编。 北京：中国社会科学，2008，页81-107。

Chen, Cai-Jun, ed. *Zhongyong Quanji* [Complete Collections on the Doctrine of the Mean]. Annotation by Li Jing. Beijing: Tide, 2009. 陈才俊主编：《中庸全集》。李静注释。北京：海潮，2009。

Chen, Chin-Wen. "A Study of Ecclesiastes 10:18–19." *TJT* 11 (1989) 117–26.

Chen, Ji-Zheng, ed. *Sishu Duben* [The Texts of *the Four Books*]. Tainan: New Century, 1982. 陈基政编：《四书读本》。台南：新世纪，1982。

Chen, Li Fu. *The Confucian Way: A New and Systematic Study of the "Four Books."* Translated by Shih Shun Liu. Taipei: Commercial, 1972.

Chen, Ming. "Modernity and Confucian Political Philosophy in a Globalizing World." *Diogenes* 56.94 (2009) 94–108.

Cheng, Chung-Ying. "On *Yi* as a Universal principle of Specific Application in Confucian Morality." *Philosophy East and West* 22 (1972) 272.

———. "The Origins of Chinese Philosophy" In *Companion Encyclopedia of Asian Philosophy*, edited by Brian Carr and Indira Mahalingam, 493–533. London: Routledge, 1997.

———. *New Dimensions of Confucianism and Neo-Confucian Philosophy*. SUNY Series in Philosophy. Albany: State University of New York Press, 1991.

Cheng, Hao, and Cheng Yi. *Erchengji* [Collections of the Chengs]. Vol 1. Beijing: Zhong Hua, 2004. 程颢、程颐：《二程集》上。北京：中华书局，2004。

Chia, Philip P. *Huangmiu yu Zhenli: Lun Chuandaoshu zhi Shenxue Sixiang* [Truth and Absurdity: on the Thought of Qoheleth]. Hong Kong: Alliance Bible Seminary, 2000. 谢品然：《荒谬与真理——论传道书之神学思想》。香港：建道，2000。

Chin, Annping. *The Authentic Confucius: A Life of Thought and Politics*. New York: Scribner, 2007.

Chin, Francis Y. P. *Confucius and Aristotle: A Comparative Study on the Confucian and Aristotelian Political Ideals*. Taipei: The Committee for Compilation and Examination of the Series of Chinese Classics, 1981.

Ching, Julia. *Chinese Religions*. London: Macmillan, 1993.

———. *Confucianism and Christianity: A Comparative Study*. Tokyo: Kodansha International, 1977.

———. *Mysticism and Kingship in China: The Heart of Chinese Wisdom*. Cambridge Studies in Religious Traditions 11. Cambridge: Cambridge University Press, 1997.

———. "What Is Confucian Spirituality?" *Confucianism: The Dynamics of Tradition*, edited by Irene Eber, 63–80. New York: Macmillan, 1986.

Choh, Kwong-Huen. "The Notion of the State in Aristotle and Confucius." http://digitalcommons.mcmaster.ca/opendissertations/htm/.

Clarke, Benjamin. "Misery Loves: A Comparative Analysis of Theodicy Literature in Ancient Mesopotamia and Israel." *Intermountain West Journal of Religious Studies* 2.1 (2010). http://digitalcommons.usu.edu/imwjournal/vol2/iss1/5/htm/.

Clifford, Richard J. *The Wisdom Literature*. Interpreting Biblical Texts. Nashville: Abingdon, 1998.

———. *Wisdom Literature in Mesopotamia and Israel*. Society of Biblical Literature Symposium 36. Atlanta: SBL, 2007.

Cline, Erin. M. "Two Senses of Justice: Confucianism, Rawls, and Comparative Political Philosophy." *Dao* 6 (2007) 361–81.

Clooney, Francis X. *Comparative Theology: Deep Learning Across Religious Borders*. Malden, MA: John Wiley & Sons, 2010.

———, ed. *The New Comparative Theology: Interreligious Insights from the Next Generation*. New York: T. & T. Clark, 2010.

Cobb, John B., Jr., ed. *Christian Faith and Religious Diversity*. Facets. Minneapolis: Augsburg Fortress, 2002.

———. *Transforming Christianity and the World: A Way Beyond Absolutism and Relativism*. New York: Orbis, 1999.

[Confucius]. *The Analects*. Translated by Ezra Pound. Washington, DC: Square, 1957.

[Confucius]. *The Analects*. Translated by David Hinton. Washington, DC: Counterpoint, 1998.

[Confucius]. *The Analects of Confucius*. Translated by Burton Watson. New York: Columbia University Press, 2007.

[Confucius]. *The Analects of Confucius: A New Millennium Translation*. Translated by David H. Li. Bethesda, MD: Premier, 1999.

[Confucius]. *Confucianism: Analects of Confucius*. Translated by Arthur Waley. Edited by Jaroslav Pelikan. New York: Quality Paperback, 1992.

[Confucius]. *Confucius: The Analects*. Translated by D.C. Lau. Taipei: Penguin, 1979.

[Confucius]. *The Philosophy of Confucius*. Translated by James Legge. New York: Peter Pauper, 1956.

[Confucius]. *The Sayings of Confucius*. Translated by James R. Ware. London: The New English Library, 1955.

[Confucius]. *Ta Hsueh and Chung Yung: The Highest Order of Cultivation and On the Practice of the Mean*. Translated by Andrew Planks. London: Penguin, 2003.

"Cong Lunyu Kan Kongzi Zhengzhi Sixiang" [Confucius Political Thought from the Analects]. 从《论语》看孔子政治思想. http://lunwen.5151doc.com/Article/HTML/226566.html.

Coogan, Michael D. *The Oxford History of the Biblical World*. New York: Oxford University Press, 1998.

Cook, J.M. *The Persian Empire*. New York: Schocken, 1983.

Covey, R. Alan. "Political Complexity, Rise of." In *Encyclopedia of Archaeology*, edited by Deborah M. Pearsall, 1842–1853. Amsterdam: Elsevier/Academic, 2008.

Crenshaw, James L. *Ecclesiastes: A Commentary*. OTL. Philadelphia: Westminster, 1987.

———. *Old Testament Wisdom*. Louisville: Westminster John Knox, 1998.

Cua, Antonio S. "Confucian Philosophy, Chinese." In *Routledge Encyclopedia of Philosophy*, 1:536–49. New York: RoutledgeCurzon, 1998.

———, ed. *Encyclopedia of Chinese Philosophy*. New York: Routledge, 2003.

Cui, Da-Hua. *Ruxue Yinlun* [Introduction to Confucianism]. Beijing: People, 2001. 崔大华：《儒学引论》。北京：人民，2001.

Cui, Jian-Lin, ed. *Sishu Wujing* [The Four Books and the Five Classics]. Beijing: Chinese Drama, 2007. 崔建林主编：《四书五经》。北京：中国戏剧，2007.

Dahood, Mitchell J. "Canaanite-Phoenician Influence in Qoheleth." *Bib* 33 (1952) 30–52.

———. "The Phoenician Background of Qoheleth." *Bib* 47 (1966) 264–82.

Day, John, Robert P. Gordon, and Hugh Godfrey Maturin Williamson. *Wisdom in Ancient Israel: Essays in Honor of J. A. Emerton*. Cambridge: Cambridge University Press, 1995.

Dawson, Miles Menander. *The Ethics of Confucius: The Sayings of the Master and His Disciples upon the Conduct of "the Superior Man."* New York: Knickerbocker, 1915.

D'Costa, Gavin, ed. *Christian Uniqueness Reconsidered*. New York: Orbis, 1990.

de Bary, William Theodore, ed. *East Asian Civilizations: A Dialogue in Five Stages*. Edwin O. Reischauer Lectures 1986. Cambridge: Harvard College, 1988.

———, ed. *Finding Wisdom in East Asian Classics*. New York: Columbia University Press, 2011.

———. "The Prophetic Voice in the Confucian Noble Man." In *Confucian-Christian Encounters in Historical and Contemporary Perspective*, edited by Peter K. H. Lee, 352–68. Religions in Dialogue 5. Lewiston, NY: Mellen, 1991.

———. *Rujia de Kunjing* [The Trouble with Confucianism]. Edited by Shui-Ying Huang. Beijing, University of Beijing Press, 2009. 狄百瑞：《儒家的困境》。黄水婴译。北京：北京大学，2009.

———. *Sources of Chinese Tradition*. Vol. 1. New York: Columbia University Press, 2008.

———. *The Trouble with Confucianism*. Cambridge: Harvard University Press, 1991.

Delitzsch, Franz. *Commentary on the Song of Songs and Ecclesiastes*. Translated by M. G. Easton. 1875. Reprint, Grand Rapids: Eerdmans, 1982.

Dell, Katharine J. "Ecclesiastes as Wisdom: Consulting Early Interpreters." *VT* 44 (1994) 301–29.

Denning-Bolle, Sara J. "Wisdom and Dialogue in the Ancient Near East." *Numen* 34 (1987) 214–234.

Ding, Ji. *Lunyu Duquan* [Interpreting the Analects]. Chengdu: Sichuan Education, 2005. 丁纪：《论语读诠》。成都：四川，2005.

Dobe, Timothy S. "Qoheleth and the Lao Tzu: An Experiment with Wisdom." *Ching Feng* 40 (1997) 129–48.

Doeblin, Alfred. *The Living Thoughts of Confucius*. Greenwich, CT: Fawcett, 1965.

Dong, Cong-Lin. *Long yu Shangdi: Jidujiao yu Zhongguo Chuantong Wenhua* [On Dragon and God: Christianity and Chinese Traditional Culture]. Guilin: Guangxi Normal University Press, 2006. 董丛林：《龙与上帝：基督教与中国传统文化》。桂林：广西师范大学，2006.

Dong-Fang, Qiao. *Du Lunyu de Fangfaxue* [The Methodology of Reading the Analects]. Shanghai: Shanghai Books, 2007. 东方桥：《读《论语》的方法学》。上海：上海书店，2007.

Du, Ren-Zhi, and Gao Shu-Zhi. "Zhongyong, Zhongli, Zhonghe and Zhezhong Bianyi." [Moderation, Neutrality and Compromise Resolution Proposed]. In *Kongzi Yanjiu Lunwenji* [Studies on Confucius Research], 368–83. Beijing: Education Science, 1987.杜任之、高树帜："中庸、中立、中和、折中辨议。"《孔子研究论文集》。中华孔子研究所编。北京：教育科學出版社，1987，页 368–83.

Du, Wei-Ming. "Zuowei Tizhengzhiai de Rendao: Quanqiu Lunli Shiye Zhong de Xiao de Tansuo" [The Way of *Ren* as Love in Practice: The Pursuit of Global Ethics on

Filial Piety]. *Zhongguo Ruxue Yi* [Chinese Confucianism]. Vol 1. Edited by Wang Zhong-Jiang and Li Cun-Shan. Beijing: Commercial, 2006. 杜维明："作为'体证之爱'的仁道：全球伦理视野中的'孝'的探索"。《中国儒学（一）》。 王中江、李存山主编。 北京：商务印书馆，2006.

Eaton, Michael A. *Ecclesiastes: An Introduction and Commentary*. Downers Grove, IL: InterVarsity, 1983.

Ellul, Jacques. *Reason for Being: A Meditation on Ecclesiastes*. Translated by Joyce Main Hanks. Grand Rapids: Eerdmans, 1990.

Faulkner, Raymond Oliver. *The Literature of Ancient Egypt: An Anthology of Stories, Instructions, Stelae, Autobiographies, and Poetry*. Edited by William Kelly Simpson. New Haven, CT: Yale University Press, 2003.

Fox, Michael V. *Ecclesiastes*. JPS Bible Commentary. Philadelphia: Jewish Publication Society, 2004.

———. "Frame-Narrative and Composition in the Book of Qoheleth." *Hebrew Union College Annual* 48 (1977) 83–106.

———. "The Inner Structure of Qoheleth's Thought." In *Qoheleth in the Context of Wisdom*, edited by A. Schoors, 225–38. Bibliotheca Ephemeridum theologicarum Lovaniensium 136. Leuven: Leuven University Press, 1998.

———. *Qoheleth and His Contradictions*. JSOT Supplement Series 71. Sheffield: Almond, 1989.

———. *A Time to Tear Down and a Time to Build Up: A Rereading of Ecclesiastes*. Grand Rapids: Eerdmans, 1999.

———. "What Happens in Qoheleth 4:13–16." *Journal of Hebrew Scriptures* 1/4 (1997) 1–8.

———. "Wisdom in Qoheleth." *In Search of Wisdom: Essays in Memory of John G. Gammie*, edited by Leo G. Perdue et al., 115–31. Louisville: Westminster John Knox, 1993.

Fredericks, Daniel C. *Coping with Transience: Ecclesiastes on Brevity in Life*. The Biblical Seminar 18. Sheffield: JSOT Press, 1993.

———. *Qoheleth's Language: Re-Evaluating Its Nature and Date*. Ancient Near Eastern Texts and Studies 3. Lewiston, NY: Mellen, 1988.

Fuerst, Wesley J. *The Books of Ruth, Esther, Ecclesiastes, the Song of Songs, Lamentations: The Five Scrolls*. Cambridge Bible Commentary. London: Cambridge University Press, 1975.

Fu, Pei-Rong. *Lunyu Jiedu* [Interpreting the Analects]. Taipei: Media News, 1999. 傅佩荣：《论语解读》。台北：立绪文化，1999.

———. *Lunyu Sanbai Jiang* [Three Hundred Sermons on the Analects]. 3 Vols. Taipei: Linking Books, 2011. 傅佩荣：《论语三百讲（上、中、下篇）》。台北：联经，2011.

———. *Wo Du Lunyu* [The Analects I Read]. Beijing: Beijing Institute of Technology, 2011. 傅佩荣：《我读《论语》》。北京：北京理工大学，2011.

Gadamer, Hans-Georg. *Truth and Method*. 2nd ed. Translated by Joel Weinsheimer and Donald G. Marshall. London: Continuum, 2004.

Gammie, John G., and Leo G. Perdue, eds. *The Sage in Israel and the Ancient Near East*. Winona Lake, IN: Eisenbrauns, 1990.

Gao, Zhuan-Cheng. *Kongzi. Kongzi Dizi* [Confucius and His Disciples]. Shanxi: People, 1989. 高专诚：《孔子·孔子弟子》。山西：人民，1989.

Gardner, Daniel K. *The Four Books: The Basic Teachings of the Later Confucian Tradition*. Translated by Daniel K. Gardner. Indianapolis: Hackett, 2007.

———. *Zhu Xi's Reading of the "Analects": Canon, Commentary, and the Classical Tradition*. New York: Columbia University Press, 2003.

Garrett, Duane A. "Qoheleth on the Use and Abuse of Political Power." *Trinity Journal* 8 (1987) 159–77.

Garthwaite, Gene R. *The Persians*. Peoples of Asia. Malden, MA: Blackwell, 2005.

Gernet, Jacques. *China and the Christian Impact: A Conflict of Cultures*. Translated by Janet Lloyd. Cambridge: Cambridge University Press, 1985.

Ginsberg, H. L. *Studies in Koheleth*. Texts and Studies of the Jewish Theological Seminary of America 17. New York: Jewish Theological Seminary of America, 1950.

Good, Edwin M. *Irony in the Old Testament*. Philadelphia: Westminster, 1965.

Gordis, Robert. *Koheleth–the Man and His Word: A Study of Ecclesiastes*. 3rd ed. New York: Schocken Books, 1971.

Guo, Qing-Xiang. *YeRu Lunli Bijiaoyanjiu: Minguo Shiqi Jidujiao yu Rujiao Lunlisixiang de Chongtu yu Ronghe* [Comparative Study on Ethics of Christianity and Confucianism: Ideological Conflict and Integration between Christian and Confucian Ethics in the Republic of China]. Beijing: China Social Sciences, 2006. 郭清香：《耶儒伦理比较研究：民国时期基督教与儒教伦理思想的冲突与融合》。北京：中国社会科学，2006.

Hall, David L. and Roger T. Ames. *Thinking through Confucius*. Albany: State University of New York Press, 1987.

Hallo, William W. and K. Lawson Younger Jr., eds. *Contexts of Scripture*. 3 vols. Leiden: Brill, 1997–2002.

Hamburger, Max. "Aristotle and Confucius: A Comparison." *Journal of the History of Ideas* 20 (1959) 236–49.

Hart, Trevor. "Imagination and Responsible Reading." In *Renewing Biblical Interpretation*, edited by Craig Bartholomew, Colin Greene and Karl Möller, 307–34. Scripture and Hermeneutics Series 1. Grand Rapids: Zondervan, 2000.

Heard, R. Christopher. "The *Dao* of Qoheleth: An Intertextual Reading of the *Daode Jing* and the Book of Ecclesiastes." *Jian Dao* 5 (Jan 1996) 65–93.

He, Lin. "Hewei Ruzhe" [What Does *Ruzhe* Mean?]. In *Weida Chuantong: Rujia Shier Jiang* [The Great Tradition: Twelve Lessons on Confucianism], edited by He-Xuan Huang (Beijing: Huaxia, 2008) 172–85. 贺麟："何谓'儒者'"《伟大传统—儒家十二讲》。黄河选编；北京：华夏出版社，2008），页172–85.

Holladay, William L., ed. *A Concise Hebrew and Aramaic Lexicon of the Old Testament*. Grand Rapids: Eerdmans, 1971.

Hong, En-Ci. *Zheren yu Xianzhi de Jiazhi Zhuiqiu* [Axiology of Confucianism and Hebrew Prophets]. Nanchang: Jiangxi Education, 2009.

Hong, Qing-Fu. *Bijiao Wenhua Zhong de Ruxue* [Confucianism in Comparative Cultural Studies]. Shanghai: Shanghai Educational, 2004. 洪庆福：《比较文化中的儒学》。上海：上海教育，2004.

Hsiao, Kung-Chuan. *A History of Chinese Political Thought: From the Beginnings to the Sixth Century A.D.* Translated by F. W. Mote. Princeton: Princeton University Press, 1979.

Hsü, Leonard Shihlien. *The Political Philosophy of Confucianism: An Interpretation of the Social and Political Ideas of Confucius, His Forerunners, and His Early Disciples.* New York: Dutton, 1932.

Huang, Chichung. *Analects of Confucius (Lun Yu): A Literal Translation with an Introduction and Notes.* Oxford: Oxford University Press, 1997.

Huang, Huai-Xin and Li Jing-Ming, ed. *Rujia Wenxian Yanjiu* [Studies on Confucian Literature]. Jinan: Qilu, 2004. 黄怀信、李景明编：《儒家文献研究》。济南：齐鲁书社，2004.

Huang, Nansen. "Confucius and Confucianism." In *Companion Encyclopedia of Asian Philosophy,* edited by Brain Carr and Indira Mahalingam, 535–52. London: Routledge, 1997. Reprinted, 2001.

Huang, Wei. "Chuandaoshu Yanjiu Zongshu Jiqi Wenti [A Summary of Studies and Problems in Ecclesiastes]." *Kuayue Wenben de Bianjie: Li Chi-Chang Jiaoshou Liuzhishou Qingwenji* [Beyond Textual Boundaries: Studies in Honor of Professor Archie C. C. Lee on the Occasion of His Sixtieth Birthday], edited by Lo Lung-Kwong, 18–27. Hong Kong: Chung Chi CUHK, 2010. 黄薇："《传道书》研究综述及其问题"。《跨越文本的边界：李炽昌教授六秩寿庆文集》。卢龙光编；香港：崇基，2010，页18–27.

Hubbard, David Allan. *Chaoyue Xukong: Chuandaoshu Zhong Panwang de Xinxi* [Beyond Futility: Messages of Hope from the Book of Ecclesiastes]. Chinese Translation. Hong Kong: Logos, 1982. 赫戴维：《超越虚空——传道书中盼望的信息》。中译。香港：基道，1982.

———. *Ecclesiastes, Song of Solomon.* Communicator's Commentary. Dallas: Word, 1991.

Hwa, Yung. "Towards an Evangelical Approach to Religions and Cultures." In *Christianity and Cultures: Shaping Christian Thinking in Context,* edited by David Emmanuel Singh and Bernard C. Farr, 17–29. Oxford: Regnum, 2008.

Ingram, Doug. *Ambiguity in Ecclesiastes.* Library of Hebrew Bible/Old Testament Studies 431. New York: T. & T. Clark, 2006.

Jennings, William. *The Confucian Analects: A Translation, with Annotations and an Introduction.* New York: Routledge, 1895.

Jiang, Yi-Hua. "Lunyu de Zhengzhi Gainian ji Qi Tese" [Political Ideas and Its Characteristics in the Analects]. *Zhengzhi yu Shehui Zhexue Pinglun* [Political and Social Philosophy Review]. Vol 24 (2008 March) 191–233. 江宜桦："《论语》的政治概念及其特色"。《政治与社会哲学评论》第24期（2008年3月），页191–233.

Jin, Jing-Fang, Lu Shao-Gang and Lu, Wen-Yu. *Kongzi Xinzhuan* [New Biography of Confucius]. Hunan: Hunan, 1991. 金景芳、吕绍纲、吕文郁：《孔子新传》。湖南：湖南，1991.

Jones, David, and John Culliney. "Confucian Order at the Edge of Chaos: The Science of Complexity and Ancient Wisdom." *Zygon* 33 (1998) 395–404.

Jones, Scott C. "Qoheleth's Courtly Wisdom: Ecclesiastes 8:1–9." *CBQ* 68 (2006) 211–28.

Kaiser, Otto. "Qoheleth." In *Wisdom in Ancient Israel: Essays in Honor of J. A. Emerton,* edited by John Day et al., 83–93. Cambridge: Cambridge University Press, 1995.

Kaiser, Walter C. Jr. *Ecclesiastes: Total Life.* Chicago: Moody, 1979.

Kallas, Endel. "Ecclesiastes: Traditum et Fides Evangelica. The Ecclesiastes Commentaries of Martin Luther, Philip Melanchthon, and Johannes Brenz Considered within the History of Interpretation." PhD diss., Graduate Theological Union, 1979.

Kam, Louie. *Critiques of Confucius in Contemporary China*. Hong Kong: Chinese University of Hong Kong Press, 1980.

Khu, John B., Vincente B. K. Khu, William B. S. Khu, and Jose B. K. Khu. *The Confucian Bible: Book 1. Analects*. Original Chinese, English and Modern Chinese Versions. Manila: Granhill, 1991.

Kidner, Derek. *A Time to Mourn and a Time to Dance*. Downers Grove, IL: InterVarsity, 1976.

———. *The Wisdom of Proverbs, Job and Ecclesiastes: An Introduction to Wisdom Literature*. Downers Grove, IL: InterVarsity, 1985.

Koh, Yee-Von. *Royal Autobiography in the Book of Qoheleth*. Beihefte zur Zeitschrift für die alttestamentliche Wissenschaft 369. Berlin: de Gruyter, 2006.

Kong, Fan-Ling. *Kongzi Yanjiu* [Studies of Confucius]. Confucianism in the 20th Century Series, edited by Fu Yong-Ju and Han Zhong-Wen. Beijing, Zhonghua, 2003. 孔凡岭：《孔子研究》。20世纪中国儒学研究大系。傅永聚，韩钟文编。北京：中华书局，2003.

Kittel, Rudolf. *Biblia Hebraica Stuttgartensia*. Stuttgart: Deutsche Bibelgesellschaft, 1968–76.

Kramers, Robert P. *International Review of Mission* 46.181 (1957) 94–99.

Krüger, Thomas. "Meaningful Ambiguities in the Book of Qoheleth." *The Language of Qoheleth in Its Context: Essays in Honor of Prof. A. Schoors on the Occasion of his Seventieth Birthday*, edited by A. Berlejung and P. Van Hecke, 63–74. Orientalia Lovaniensia Analecta 41. Leuven: Peeters, 2007.

———. *Qoheleth: A Commentary*. Hermeneia. Translated by O. C. Dean Jr.. Minneapolis: Fortress, 2004.

Kugel, James L. "Qoheleth and Money." *CBQ* 51 (1989) 32–49.

Kuhrt, Amelie. *The Persian Empire: A Corpus of Sources from the Achaemenid Period*. 2 vols. New York: Routledge, 2007.

Küng, Hans, and Julia Ching. *Christianity and Chinese Religions*. New York: Doubleday, 1989.

Kung, Te-Cheng. *Confucius: His Life, Thought, and Influence*. Taipei: Government Information Office, 1991.

Kupperman, Joel J. "Fact and Value in the *Analects*: Education and Logic." In *Educations and Their Purposes: A Conversation among Cultures*, edited by Roger T. Ames and Peter D. Hershock, 405–19. Honolulu: University of Hawaii Press, 2008.

Kwok, Pui-Lan. *Discovering the Bible in the Non-Biblical World*. New York: Orbis, 1995.

Lambert, W. G. *Babylonian Wisdom Literature*. Oxford: Clarendon, 1960.

Lee, Archie C. C. "Biblical Interpretation in Asian Perspective." *AJT* 7 (1993) 35–39.

———. "Cross-Textual Hermeneutics." In *Dictionary of Third World Theologies*, edited by Virginia Fabella, M. M., and R. S. Sugirtharajah, 60–62. Maryknoll, NY: Orbis, 2000.

———. "Cross-Textural Hermeneutics and Identity in Multi-Scriptural Asia." In *Christian Theology in Asia*, edited by Sebastian C. H. Kim, 179–204. New York: Cambridge University Press, 2008.

———. "Cross-Textual Hermeneutics on Gospel and Culture." *AJT* 10 (1996) 38–48.

———. "Kuayue Bianjie: Xibolai Shipian yu Zhongguo Shijing dui Renxing de Xiangxiang [Crossing Boundaries: A Study on Human Nature from the Readings of Hebrew *Psalms* and Chinese *Shijing*]." *YeRu Duihua Xinlicheng* [A New Turn in Confucianism-Christianity Dialogue], edited by Lai Pin-Chao and Lee Jing-Xiong, 197–221. Hong Kong: Chung Chi CUHK Press, 2001. 李炽昌：" 跨越边界：希伯来《诗篇》与中国《诗经》对人性的想象，"《儒耶对话新里程》。赖品超、李景雄编；香港：中文大学崇基学院，2001.

———. "Naming God in Asia: Cross-Textual Reading in Multi-Cultural Context." *Quest* 3.1 (2004) 21–42.

———. "The Recitation of the Past: A Cross-Textual Reading of Ps. 78 and the Odes." *Ching Feng* 39.3 (1996) 173–93.

———. "Reclaiming Asian Resources for Christian Theology in Asia." *PTCA Bulletin* 10 (1997) 3–4.

———. "Syncretism from the Perspectives of Chinese Religion and Biblical Tradition." *Ching Feng* 39.1 (1996) 1–24.

———. "Theological Reading of Chinese Creation Stories of *P'an Ku* and *Nu Kua*." In *Doing Theology with Asian Resources: Ten Years in the Formation of Living Theology in Asia*, edited by John C. England and Archie C. C. Lee, 230–36. Auckland: Pace, 1993.

———, ed. *Yazhou Chujing yu Shengjing Quanshi* [Asian Contexts and Biblical Interpretation]. Hong Kong: Christian Literature, 1996. 李炽昌编著：《亚洲处境与圣经诠释》。香港：基督教文艺，1996.

Lee, Eunny P. *The Vitality of Enjoyment in Qohelet's Theological Rhetoric*. Berlin: de Gruyter, 2005.

Lee, Peter K. H., ed. *Confucian-Christian Encounters in Historical and Contemporary Perspective*. Religions in Dialogue 5. Lewiston, NY: Mellen, 1991.

Legge, James. *The Chinese Classics: with Preliminary Essays and Explanatory Notes*. London: Kegan Paul, Trench & Trubner, 1895.

Leys, Simon. *The Analects of Confucius*. New York: Norton, 1997.

Li, Chi-Chang and Zhou, Lian-Hua. *Chuandaoshu Yage* [Ecclesiastes and Song of Songs]. Chinese Bible Commentary Volume 17. Hong Kong: Christian Literature, 1990. 李炽昌、周联华：《传道书·雅歌》。中文圣经注释第十七卷。香港：基督教文艺，1990.

Li, Dian-Yuan and Yang, Mei. *Lunyu Zhimi* [The Mystery of the Analects]. Chengdu: Sichuan Education, 2000. 李殿元、杨梅：《《论语》之谜》。成都：四川教育，2000.

Li, Dao-Sheng. *Shengjing yu Zhongguo Wenhua* [An Encounter between the Bible and Chinese Culture]. Taipei: Caituanfaren, 1987. 李道生：《圣经与中国文化》。台北：财团法人，1987.

Li, Fu Chen. *The Confucian Way: A New and Systematic Study of 'The Four Books.'* Translated by Shih Shun Liu. New York: KPI, 1986.

Li, Hong-Lei. "Rujia Guanli Zhexue de Jiben Jingshen [The Basics of Confucian Management Philosophy]." In *Zhongguo Ruxue Disanji* [Chinese Confucianism Vol. 3], edited by Zhong-Jiang Wang and Cun-Shan Li, 373–85. Beijing: China Social Sciences, 2008.

Li, Xue-Qin. "Jingmen Guodian Jian Zhong de Zisizi" [The Master Zisi in the Bamboo Strips of Guodian, Jingmen]. In *Wenwu Tiandi* [Cultural Relics] 2 (1998) 28–30.

———. *Zhongguo Zhexue* [Chinese Philosophy] Vol. 20 (1999) 75–80.

Li, Yu-Hua and Ma Yin-Hua. *Lunyu, Daxue, Zhongyong* [The Analects, The Great Learning and The Mean]. Shanxi: Ancient Scroll, 2003. 李浴华、马银华译注：《论语·大学·中庸》。山西：古籍，2003.

Liang, Jia-Lin. *Paihuai yu YeRu Zhijian* [Hover between Christianity and Confucianism]. Taipei: Cosmic Light, 1997. 梁家麟：《徘徊於耶儒之間》。 台北：宇宙光，1997.

Lichtheim, Miriam. *Ancient Egyptian Literature.* 3 vols. Berkeley: University of California Press, 1973–80.

Lin, Yu-Sheng. "The Evolution of the Pre-Confucian Meaning of *Jen* and the Confucian Concept of Moral Autonomy." *Monumenta Serica* 31 (1974–75) 184.

Lindbeck, George A. *The Nature of Doctrine: Religion and Theology in a Postliberal Age.* Louisville: Westminster John Knox, 1984.

Lindenberger, James M. *The Aramaic Proverbs of Ahiqar.* Baltimore: Johns Hopkins University Press, 1983.

Littlejohn, Ronnie L. *Confucianism: An Introduction.* New York: Tauris, 2011.

Liu, Honghe. *Confucianism in the Eyes of a Confucian Liberal: Hsu Fu-kuan's Critical Examination of the Confucian Political Tradition.* Asian Thought and Culture Series no. 43. Edited by Sandra A. Wawrytko. New York: Peter Lang, 2001.

Liu, Xiao-Feng, ed. *Dao yu Yan: Huaxia Wenhua yu Jidu Wenhua Xiangyu* [Way and Word: An Encounter of Chinese Culture with Christian Culture]. Shanghai: Joint, 1995. 刘小枫：《道与言：华夏文化与基督文化相遇》。上海：三联，1995.

Liu, Zuo-Chang: "Lun Kongzi de Zhengzhi Sixiang" [On Confucius' Political Ideas]. In *Kongzi Yanjiu Lunwenji* [Studies on Confucius Research], edited by China Confucius Institute, 249–68. Beijing: Educational Science, 1987. 刘祚昌："论孔子的政治思想。"《孔子研究论文集》。中华孔子研究所编；北京：教育科學出版社，1987，页249–68.

Lo, Hing Choi. *Chuandaoshu Fansi: Cong Huangmiu Dao Fengsheng* [From Vanity to Enrichment: Ecclesiastes and Life]. Hong Kong: Chinese Baptist, 2009. 罗庆才：《传道书反思——从荒谬到丰盛》。 香港：浸信会，2009.

Lo, Lung Kwong, ed. *Jidujiao yu Zhongguo Wenhua de Xiangyu* [The Encounter between Christianity and Chinese Culture]. Hong Kong: Chung Chi CUHK, 2001. 卢龙光主编：《基督教与中国文化的相遇》。 香港：崇基：2001.

Lo, Yuet Keung. "Finding the Self in the Analects: A Philological Approach." *Occasional Papers in Chinese Studies, Department of Chinese Studies in the National University of Singapore,* no. 142 (August 2000) 1–21.

Loader, J. A. *Ecclesiastes: A Practical Commentary.* Translated by John Vriend. Grand Rapids: Eerdmans, 1986.

———. *Polar Structures in the Book of Qohelet.* Beihefte zur Zeitschrift für die alttestamentliche Wissenschaft 152. Berlin: de Gruyter, 1979.

Loewe, Michael. *The Cambridge History of China: Volume 1, the Ch'in and Han Empires, 221 BC-AD 220.* Cambridge: Cambridge University Press, 1986.

Loewe, Michael, and Edward L. Shaughnessy, eds. *The Cambridge History of Ancient China: From the Origins of Civilization to 221 B.C.* Cambridge: Cambridge University Press, 1999.

Lohfink, Norbert. *Qoheleth.* Translated by Sean McEvenue. Continental Commentaries. Minneapolis: Fortress, 2003.

Longman, Tremper III. *The Book of Ecclesiastes*. NICOT. Grand Rapids: Eerdmans, 1998.

———. "Chuandaoshu de Shenxue" [Theology of Ecclesiastes]. *Zhengzhu Shengjing Shenxue Cidian* [Zhengzhu Theological Dictionary]. Chinese Translation, edited by Yang Qing-Qiu, 77–81. Hong Kong: Christian Communication, 2001. 朗文："传道书的神学"。《证主圣经神学辞典（上）》。杨庆球编；香港：福音证主，2001，页77–81.

———. *Kuayue Wenben de Bianjie: Li Chi-Chang Jiaoshou Liuzhishou Qingwenji* [Beyond Textual Boundaries: Studies in Honor of Professor Archie C. C. Lee on the Occasion of His Sixtieth Birthday]. Hong Kong: Chung Chi CUHK, 2010.

Lu, Ri-Xing. *Chuandaoshu Zhong de Diaogui* [The Paradox in the Book of Ecclesiastes]. Taizhong: Carmel, 2007. 吕日星：《传道书中的吊诡》。台中：迦密文化，2007.

Luo, Bing-Xiang. "Lun Rujia de Ren Zhuti ji Ronghe zuowei Jibentizhi de Ren, ji Shenai yu Ren jiehe de Chujingshenxue zhi Qianjing he Wenti [On the Theme of *Ren* in Confucianism: the Challenges of Its Contextual Theological Understanding with the Divine Agape]." *Jidujiao yu Zhongguo Wenhua: Guanyu Zhongguo Chujingshenxue de Zhongguo* [Christianity and Chinese Culture: Concerning Contextual Theology of China]., edited by Luo Ming-Jia and Huang Bao-Luo, 125–42. Beijing: Chinese Academy of Social Sciences, 2004. 罗秉祥："论儒家的'仁'主题及融合作为基本题旨的仁，及神爱与仁结合的处境神学之前景和问题"。 罗明嘉、黄保罗主编：《基督教与中国文化—关于中国处境神学德中国—北欧会议论文集》。北京：中国社会科学，2004，页125–42.

Mahood, G. H. "Socrates and Confucius: Moral Agents or Moral Philosophers?" *Philosophy East and West* 21 (1971) 177–88.

Matthews, Victor H and Don C. Benjamin. *Old Testament Parallels: Laws and Stories from the Ancient Near East*. 3rd ed. New York: Paulist, 2006.

Ma, Xin-Lai, ed. *Lunyu de Shenghuo Zhexue* [The Analects' Philosophy of Life]. Taipei: Omura Culture, 1997. 马欣来编：《论语的生活哲思》。台北：大村文化，1997.

Mays, James Luther, et al., eds. *Old Testament Interpretation: Past, Present, and Future*. Essays in Honor of Gene M. Tucker. Nashville: Abingdon, 1995.

Mendenhall, George E. *Ancient Israel's Faith and History: An Introduction to the Bible in Context*. Edited by Gary A. Herion. Louisville: Westminster John Knox, 2001.

Meyers, Eric M., ed. *The Oxford Encyclopedia of Archaeology in the Near East*. Vol 4. New York: Oxford University Press, 1997.

Miller, Douglas B. *Ecclesiastes*. Believers Church Bible Commentary. Scottdale, PA: Herald, 2010.

Miller, Fred. "Aristotle's Political Theory." In *The Stanford Encyclopedia of Philosophy*. Spring 2011 Edition. Edited by Edward N. Zalta. http://plato.stanford.edu/archives/spr2011/entries/aristotle-politics/.

Miller, Geoffrey D. "Intertextuality in Old Testament Research." *CBR* 9 (2011) 283–309.

Miscall, P. D. "Texts, More Texts, a Textual Reader and a Textual Writer." In *Intertextuality and the Bible*, edited by George Aichele and Gary A. Philips, 247–60. *Semeia* 69/70. Atlanta: Scholars, 1995.

Murphy, Roland E. *Ecclesiastes*. WBC 23A. Dallas, TX: Word, 1992.

———. "The Sage in Ecclesiastes and Qoheleth the Sage." *The Sage in Israel and the Ancient Near East*, edited by John G. Gammie and Leo G. Perdue, 263–71. Winona Lake, IN: Eisenbrauns, 1990.

———. *The Tree of Life: An Exploration of Biblical Wisdom Literature*. 3rd ed. Grand Rapids: Eerdmans, 2002.

Nacpil, Emerito P. "The Critical Asian Principle." In *What Asian Christians are Thinking: a Theological Source Book*, edited by Douglas J. Elwood, 3–6. Quezon City, Philippines: New Day, 1976.

Nan, Huai-Jing. *Lunyu Biecai* [On the Analects]. 2 Vols. Shanghai: Fudan University Press, 2012. 南怀瑾：《论语别裁（上下册）》。上海：复旦大学，2012.

Newsom, Carol. "Job and Ecclesiastes." In *Old Testament Interpretation: Past, Present, and Future*, edited by James Luther Mays, David L. Petersen, and Kent Harold Richards, 177–94. Essays in Honor of Gene M. Tucker. Nashville: Abingdon, 1995.

Ogden, Graham S. "Historical Allusion in Qoheleth IV 13–16?" *VT* 30 (1980) 309–15.

———. *Qoheleth*. 2nd ed. Readings. Sheffield: Sheffield Phoenix, 2007.

———. "Qoheleth IX 1–16." *VT* 32 (1982) 158–69.

——— and Lynell Zogbo. *A Handbook on Ecclesiastes*. New York: United Bible Societies, 1997.

Oldstone-Moore, Jennifer. *Confucianism*. New York: Oxford University Press, 2002.

Pang, Pu. "KongMeng Zhijian: Guodian Chujian de Sixianshi Diwei" [Between Confucius and Mencius: The Place of History of Philosophy in the Guodian Strips]. In *Zhongguo Shehui Kexue* [Chinese Social Science] 5 (1988) 88–95. 庞朴："孔孟之间：郭店楚简的思想史地位"《中国社会科学第五期》1988年，页 88–95.

Penchansky, David. *Understanding Wisdom Literature: Conflict and Dissonance in the Hebrew Text*. Grand Rapids: Eerdmans, 2012.

Perdue, Leo G. "'Is There Anyone Left of Saul?': Ambiguity and the Characterization of David in the Succession Narrative." *Journal for the Study of the Old Testament* 30 (1984) 67–84.

———. *The Sword and the Stylus: An Introduction to Wisdom in the Age of Empires*. Grand Rapids: Eerdmans, 2008.

———. "The Testament of David and Egyptian Royal Instructions." *Scripture in Context II: More Essays on the Comparative Method*, edited by William W. Hallo, James C. Moyer, and Leo G. Perdue, 79–96. Winona Lake, IN: Eisenbrauns, 1983.

———. *Wisdom Literature: A Theological History*. Louisville: Westminster John Knox, 2007.

———. "Wisdom Theology and Social History in Proverbs 1–9." In *Wisdom, You are My Sister: Studies in Honor of Roland E. Murphy, O. Carm. on the Occasion of His Eightieth Birthday*, edited by M. L. Barre, 78–101. Washington, DC: Catholic Biblical Association, 1997.

Perdue, Leo G., et al. *In Search of Wisdom*. Louisville: Westminster John Knox, 1993.

Perkins, Dorothy, ed. *Encyclopedia of China: The Essential Reference to China, Its History and Culture*. New York: Facts on File, 1999.

Perry, T. A. *Dialogues with Kohelet: The Book of Ecclesiastes: Translation and Commentary*. University Park: Pennsylvania State University Press, 1993.

Pinker, Aron. "Qoheleth 4, 13–16." *SJOT* 22 (2008) 176–94.

Porten, Bezalel, and Ada Yardeni. *Textbook of Aramaic Documents in Ancient Egypt* [*TAD*]. Vol 3. Jerusalem: Hebrew University Press, 1986–93.

Premnath, D. N., ed. *Border Crossings: Cross-Cultural Hermeneutics*. New York: Orbis, 2007.

Pritchard, James B., ed. *Ancient Near Eastern Texts Relating to the Old Testament* [*ANET*]. 3rd ed. Princeton: Princeton University Press, 1969.

Rad, Gerhard von. "The Joseph Narrative and Ancient Wisdom." In *Studies in Ancient Israelite Wisdom*, edited by James L. Crenshaw, 468–80. New York: KTAV, 1976.

———. *Wisdom in Israel*. Nashville, TN: Abingdon, 1972.

Ranston, Harry. *Ecclesiastes and the Early Greek Wisdom Literature*. London: Epworth, 1925.

Rowley, H. H. *Prophecy and Religion in Ancient China and Israel*. New York: Harper & Brothers, 1956.

Rudman, Dominic. "A Contextual Reading of Ecclesiastes 4:13–16." *JBL* 116/1 (1997) 57–73.

Russell, James R. "Sages and Scribes at the Courts of Ancient Iran." In *The Sage in Israel and the Ancient Near East*, edited by John G. Gammie and Leo G. Perdue, 141–46. Winona Lake, IN: Eisenbrauns, 1990.

Ryken, Leland, and Tremper Longman III, eds. *A Complete Literary Guide to the Bible*. Grand Rapids: Zondervan, 1993.

Schoors, Antoon. *The Preacher Sought to Find Pleasing Words: A Study of the Language of Qoheleth*. Orientalia Lovaniensia Analecta 41. Leuven: Peeters, 1992.

———. *The Preacher Sought to Find Pleasing Words: A Study of the Language of Qoheleth*. Part II. Orientalia Lovaniensia Analecta 143. Leuven: Peeters, 2004.

Schoors, Antoon, ed. *Qoheleth in the Context of Wisdom*. Leuven: Leuven University Press, 1998.

Schwartz, Benjamin I. *The World of Thought in Ancient China*. Cambridge: Belknap, 1985.

Seow, Choon-Leong. "'Beyond Them, My Son, Be Warned': The Epilogue of Qoheleth Revisited." In *Wisdom, You Are My Sister*, edited by Michael L. Barré, S. S., 125–41. Washington DC: Catholic Biblical Association of America, 1997.

———. *Ecclesiastes. The Anchor Bible Series* [*ABS*]. New York: Doubleday, 1997.

———. "Linguistic Evidence and the Dating of Qoheleth." *JBL* 115 (1996) 643–66.

———. "Theology When Everything is Out of Control." *Interpretation* 55 (2001) 237–49.

Shang, Bin, Ren Peng and Li Ming-Zhu. *Zhongguo Ruxue Fazanshi* [The History and Development of Chinese Confucianism]. Lanzhou: Lanzhou University Press, 2008. 尚斌，任鹏和李明珠：《中国儒学发展史》。兰州：兰州大学，2008.

Shao, Han-Ming, Liu Hui and Wang Yong-Pin. *Rujia Zhexue Zhihui* [The Wisdom in Confucian Philosophy]. Jilin: Jilin People's, 2005. 邵汉明、刘辉、王永平：《儒家哲学智慧》。吉林：吉林人民，2005.

Sharp, Carolyn J. *Irony and Meaning in the Hebrew Bible*. Bloomington: Indiana University Press, 2009.

Shaughnessy, Edward L. *Chinese Wisdom: Philosophical Insights from Confucius, Mencius, Laozi, Zhuangzi and Other Masters*. London: Duncan Baird, 2010.

———. *Rewriting Early Chinese Texts*. Albany: State University of New York Press, 2006.

Shields, Martin A. *The End of Wisdom: A Reappraisal of the Historical and Canonical Function of Ecclesiastes*. Winona Lake, IN: Eisenbrauns, 2006.

Shi, Heng-Tan. *Dongfeng Po: Lunyu de Linglei Jiedu* [An Alternate Reading on the Analects]. Jinan: Shandong, 2009. 石衡潭：《东风破：《论语》的另类解读》。济南：山东画报，2009.

Shuo, Dongfang and Lin Hongcheng. "Separation of Politics and Morality: A Commentary on the Analects of Confucius." Translated by Huang Deyuan from *Journal of School of Chinese at Nanjing Normal University. Frontiers of Philosophy in China* 1, no. 3 (2006) 401–17.

Sim, May. *Remastering Morals with Aristotle and Confucius*. Cambridge: Cambridge University Press, 2007.

Sinaiko, Herman L. "The *Analects*: Confucius' Claim to Philosophical Greatness." In *Reclaiming the Canon: Essays on Philosophy, Poetry and History*, edited by Herman L. Sinaiko, 154–77. New Haven: Yale University Press, 1998.

Singh, David Emmanuel and Bernard C. Farr eds. *Christianity and Cultures: Shaping Christian Thinking in Context*. Oxford: Regnum Books, 2008.

Slingerland, Edward. *Confucius Analects: with Selections from Traditional Commentaries*. Indianapolis: Hackett, 2003.

Smart, N. "Comparative-Historical Method." In *Encyclopedia of Religion*. Vol 3, edited by M. Eliade, 571–74. New York: Collier Macmillan, 1987.

Smits, Gregory James. "Later Confucianism." *East Asian History*. http://www.east-asian-history.net/textbooks/PM-China/ch9.htm.

Snell, Daniel C., ed. *A Companion to the Ancient Near East*. Blackwell Companions to the Ancient World. Oxford: Blackwell, 2005.

Soanes, Catherine and Angus Stevenson, eds. "Politics" and "Political." *Oxford Dictionary of English*. 2nd ed. Oxford: Oxford University Press, 2005.

Song, Choan-Seng. *The Compassionate God: An Exercise in the Theology of Transposition*. London: SCM, 1982.

Song, De-Xuan. *Xin Ruxue* [New Confucianism]. Taipei: Yangzhi Culture, 1994. 宋德宣：《新儒学》。台北：扬智文化，1994.

Song, Yan-Shen and Xiao Guo-Liang. *Kongzi yu Ruxue Yanjiu* [Studies on Confucius and Confucianism]. Jilin: Jilin Educational, 1993. 宋衍申、肖国良：《孔子与儒学研究》。吉林：吉林教育，1993.

Song, Zhi-Ming and Liu Cheng-You. *Pikong yu Shikong: Ruxue de Xiandai Zouxiang* [Confronting and Releasing Confucius: Modern Trends of Confucianism]. Chinese Philosophy and Cultural Research Series of the Twentieth Century. Shanghai: Huadong Normal University Press, 2004. 宋志明、刘成有：《批孔与释孔—儒学的现代走向》。廿世纪中国哲学与文化研究丛书。上海：华东师范大学，2004.

Sparks, Kenton L. *Ancient Texts for the Study of the Hebrew Bible: A Guide to the Background Literature*. Peabody, MA: Hendrickson, 2005.

Starr, Chloë, ed. *Reading Christian Scriptures in China*. New York: T & T Clark, 2008.

Starr, Frederick. *Confucianism: Ethics, Philosophy and Religion*. New York: Covici-Friede, 1930.

Sternberg, Robert J. and Jennifer Jordan, eds. *A Handbook of Wisdom: Psychological Perspectives*. Cambridge: Cambridge University Press, 2005.

Sugirtharajah, R. S. *Asian Hermeneutics and Postcolonialism: Contesting the Interpretations*. Maryknoll: Orbis, 1998.

———, ed. *The Postcolonial Bible*. Sheffield: Sheffield Academic, 1998.

Sun, Qin-Shan. *Lunyu Benjie* [The Original Meaning of the Analects]. Beijing: Joint, 2009. 孙钦善：《论语本解》。北京：三联书店，2009.
Swidler, Leonard. "A Christian Historical Perspective on Wisdom as a Basis for Dialogue with Judaism and Chinese Religion." *Journal of Ecumenical Studies* 33 (1996) 557–72.
Talmon, Shemaryahu. "Wisdom in the Book of Esther." *VT* 13 (1963) 419–55.
Tang, Ming-Gui. *Lunyuxue dao Xingcheng, Fazhan yu Zhongshuai: Han Wei Liuchao Sui Tang Lunyuxue Yanjiu* [Studies of the *Analects* in the Six Dynasties of Sui and Tang: Formation, Development and Decline]. Beijing: China Social Sciences, 2005. 唐明贵：《《论语》学到形成、发展与中衰：汉魏六朝隋唐《论语》学研究》。北京：中国社会科学，2005.
Tang, Yi-Jie. "Lun Rujia de Zhixingheyi" [On Confucianism "Knowledge and Action"]. *Rujia Dianji yu Sixiang Yanjiu* [Studies on Confucian Classics and Thoughts]. Vol 1, edited by Center of Collections on Confucian Studies in Beijing University, 139–48. Beijing: Beijing University Press, 2009. 汤一介："论儒家的"知行合一"。"《儒家典籍与思想研究》（第一辑）。北京大学《儒藏》编纂中心编。北京：北京大学，2009，页139–48.
———. *Ruxue Shilun ji Lingwai Wupian* [Ten Lessons on Confucianism and Five Supplements]. Beijing: Beijing University Press, 2009. 汤一介：《儒学十论及另外五篇》。北京：北京大学，2009.
Taylor, Rodney L. *Confucianism*. New York: Chelsea, 2004.
———. *The Religious Dimensions of Confucianism*. Albany: State University of New York Press, 1990.
———. "The Study of Confucianism as a Religious Tradition: Notes on Some Recent Publications." *JCR* 18 (1990) 143–59.
———. *The Way of Heaven: An Introduction to the Confucian Religious Life*. Iconography of Religions. Section XII: East and Central Asia 3. Leiden: Brill, 1986.
Thompson, Kirill O. "The Archery of 'Wisdom' in the Stream of Life: 'Wisdom' in the 'Four Books' with Zhu Xi's Reflections." *Philosophy East & West* 57 (2007) 330–44.
Toorn, Karel van der. "The Ancient Near Eastern Literary Dialogue as a Vehicle of Critical Reflection." In *Dispute Poems and Dialogues in the Ancient and Mediaeval Near East*, edited by G.J. Reinlink and H. L. J. Vanstiphout, 59–75. Leuven: Peeters, 1991.
———. *Sin and Sanction in Israel and Mesopotamia: A Comparative Study*. Studia Semitica Neerlandica Series 22. Assen-Maastricht, The Netherlands: Van Gorcum, 1985.
Torrey, Charles C. "The Problem of Ecclesiastes 4:13–16." *VT* 2 (1952) 175–77.
———. "The Question of the Original Language of Qoheleth." *JQR* 39 (1948) 151–60.
Tse, Mary Wai-Yi. *Chuandaoshu: Shikan Rensheng* [Ecclesiastes: A Contemplation on Life]. Ming Dao Commentary Series 21. Edited by Alvin Kam-Tong Lee. Hong Kong: Ming Dao, 2010. 谢慧儿：《传道书——试看人生》。明道研经丛书21。香港：明道社，2010.
Tu, Wei-Ming. *Confucian Ethics Today*. Singapore: Federal, 1984.
Van Norden, Bryan W, ed. *Confucius and the "Analects."* Oxford: Oxford University Press, 2002.
Waley, Arthur. *The Analects of Confucius: Translated and Annotated*. London: Allen & Unwin, 1949.
———. *Confucius: The Analects*. New York: Knopf, 2000.

Waltke, Bruce K., et al. *Theological Wordbook of the Old Testament.* Chicago: Northfield, 1999.
Walton, John H. *Ancient Near Eastern Thought and the Old Testament: Introducing the Conceptual World of the Hebrew Bible.* Grand Rapids: Baker Academic, 2006.
Wang, Zhi-Cheng. *Jieshi, Lijie yu Zongjiao Duihua* [Interpretation, Understanding and Religious Dialogue]. Beijing: Religious Culture, 2007. 王志成：《解释、理解与宗教对话》。北京：宗教文化，2007.
Wang, Zhong-Jiang and Li Cun-Shan, eds. *Zhongguo Ruxue* [Chinese Confucianism]. Beijing: China Social Sciences, 2008. 王中江、李存山主编：《中国儒学》。北京：中国社会科学，2008.
Weisman, Ze'ev. "Elements of Political Satire in Koheleth 4:13–16; 9:13–16." *Zeitschrift für die Alttestamentliche Wissenschaft* 111 (1999) 547–60.
Wen, Yu-Min. *Lunyu Yanjiu* [Studies on the Analects]. Shanghai: Commercial, 1930. 温裕民：《论语研究》。上海：商务印书馆，1930.
Whaling, Frank. "Jen and Love." In *Confucian-Christian Encounters in Historical and Contemporary Perspective,* edited by Peter K. H. Lee, 255–73. Religions in Dialogue Vol. 5. Lewiston, NY: Mellen, 1991.
Whitley, Charles F. *Koheleth: His Language and Thought.* Berlin: de Gruyter, 1979.
Whybray, R. N. *Ecclesiastes.* NCBC. Grand Rapids: Eerdmans, 1989.
———. "Qoheleth the Immoralist? (Qoh 7:16–17)." In *Israelite Wisdom: Theological and Literary Essays in Honor of Samuel Terrien,* edited by John G, Gammie et al., 191–204. New York: Scholars, 1978.
———. "The Sage in the Israelite Royal Court." In *The Sage in Israel and the Ancient Near East,* edited by John G. Gammie and Leo G. Perdue, 133–39. Winona Lake IN: Eisenbrauns, 1990.
Wong, Yee-Cheung. *Huochu Zhihui Rensheng: Jiuyue Zhihuishu Xinxi Yanjiu* [Living Out Wisdom—an Investigation into the Message of the Wisdom Literature of the Old Testament]. Hong Kong: Tien Dao, 2004. 黄仪章：《活出智慧人生：旧约智慧书信息研究》。香港：天道，2004.
———. *Huo Hao Wo Zhe Yisheng: Cong Chuandaoshu Kan Jingcai de Rensheng* [Living Out a Wise Life: Biblical Insights from the Book of Ecclesiastes]. Hong Kong: Ming Dao, 2009. 黄仪章：《活好我这生：从传道书看精彩的人生》。香港：明道社，2009.
Wright, Addison G. S. S. "The Poor but Wise Youth and the Old but Foolish King (Qoh 4:13–16)." In *Wisdom, You Are My Sister,* edited by Michael L. Barré, S.S., 142–54. Washington, DC: Catholic Biblical Association of America, 1997.
Wright, G. Ernest, ed. *The Bible and the Ancient Near East: Essays in Honor of William Foxwell Albright.* 1961. Reprint, Winona Lake, IN: Eisenbrauns, 1979.
Wu, Ming-Chieh. *Jidujiao yu Zhongguo Wenhua de Jiechudian* [An Encounter of Christianity and Chinese Culture]. Hong Kong: Daosheng, 1990. 吴明节：《基督教与中国文化的接触点》。香港：道声，1990.
Wu, Nai-Gong. *Rujia Sixiang Yanjiu* [Studies of Confucian Thoughts]. Jilin: Dongbei Normal University Press, 1988. 吴乃共：《儒家思想研究》。吉林：东北师范大学，1988.
Wu, Timothy Shan-Jarn. *Chuandaoshu* [Ecclesiastes]. Heaven Bible Commentary Series. Hong Kong: Tien Dao, 2010. 吴献章：《传道书》。天道圣经注释。香港：天道，2010.

Xia, Chuan-Cai. *Lunyu Qudu* [Fun Reading of the Analects]. Taipei: Gold and Silver Tree, 2005. 夏传才：《论语趣读》。台北：金银树，2005.

Xu, Gang. *Kongzizhidao yu Lunyu Qishu* [The Way of Confucius and the Book of the Analects]. Beijing: Beijing University Press, 2009. 徐刚：《孔子之道与《论语》其书》。北京：北京大学，2009.

Yang, Bo-Ju. *Lunyu Yizhu* [Annotation to the Analects]. Beijing: Zhonghua, 2006. 杨伯峻：《论语译注》。北京：中华，2006.

Yang, Bo-Ju, and Lau D. C. *Lunyu* [The Analects]. Contemporary Chinese and English Bilingual Translation. Taipei: Linking, 2009. 杨伯峻、刘殿爵译：《论语》。白话中文、英文双译本。台北：联经，2009.

Yao, Xing-Fu. *YeRu Duihua yu Ronghe: Jiaohui Xinbao Yanjiu* [Dialogue and Integration between Christianity and Confucianism: A Study on *Church Daily* between 1868-1874]. Beijing: Religion and Culture, 2005. 姚兴富：《耶儒对话与融合：教会新报（1868-1874）研究》。北京：宗教文化，2005.

Yao, Xinzhong. *Confucianism and Christianity: A Comparative Study of Jen and Agape.* Brighton: Sussex Academic, 1996.

———. *An Introduction to Confucianism.* Cambridge: Cambridge University Press, 2000.

———, ed. *RoutledgeCurzon Encyclopedia of Confucianism* [REC]. Vol 1. New York: RoutledgeCurzon, 2003.

Ya Se, ed. *Lunyu Daquanji* [Complete Collections of the Analects]. Beijing: New World, 2010. 雅瑟编：《论语大全集》。北京：新世界，2010.

Yeo, K. K. *Kongzi yu Baoluo: Tiandao yu Shengyan de Xiangyu* [Confucius and Paul: An Encounter between the Heaven Path and the Holy Word]. Huadong: Normal University Press, 2009. 杨克勤《孔子与保罗：天道与圣言的相遇》。华东：师范大学，2009.

———. *Musing with Confucius and Paul: Toward a Chinese Christian Theology.* Eugene, OR: Cascade Books, 2008.

Young, T. Cuyler Jr. "Persians." In *Oxford Encyclopedia of Archaeology in the Near East* [OEANE], edited by Eric M. Meyers, 295-300. Vol. 4. Oxford: Oxford University Press, 1997.

Yuan, Shi-Jie "Kongzi de Zhihui he Ershiyi Shiji" [Confucius Wisdom in the Twenty-first Century]. In *Kongzi Sixiang Yanjiu* [Studies on Confucius' Thought], edited by Zhi-Kai Zhu et al., 33-41. Shanghai: Ancient Scroll, 1999. 袁仕杰："孔子的智慧和二十一世纪。"《孔子思想研究》。朱志凯、徐洪兴、潘富恩主编：上海：古籍，1999，页33-41.

Yuan, Zhi-Ming. *Laozi Vs Shengjing: Kuayue Shikong de Yinghou* [Laozi vs. the Bible: An Anticipation beyond Time and Space]. Taipei: Cosmic Light, 1997. 远志明：《老子VS圣经:跨越时空的迎候》。台北：宇宙光，1997.

Yu, Dun-Kang. "Rujia Zhengzhi Sixiang: Dezhengshuo" [On Moral Governance: Confucian Political Thoughts]. In *Zhongguo Ruxue Baikequanshu* [Encyclopedia of Chinese Confucianism], 148-150. China Confucius Foundation Series. Beijing: Encyclopedia of China, 1996. 余敦康："儒家政治思想：德政说。"《中国儒学百科全书》。中国孔子基金会编。北京：中国大百科全书出版社，1996，页148-150.

Yuezhi, ed. *Kongzi de Zhengzhixue* [[The Political Philosophy of Confucius]. Changcun: Dongbei Normal University Press, 1990. 日知编：《孔子的政治学》。长春：东北师范大学，1990.

Yu, Jiyuan. *The Ethics of Confucius and Aristotle: Mirrors of Virtue*. Routledge Studies in Ethics and Moral Theory 7. New York: Routledge, 2007.

———. "Yi: Practical Wisdom in Confucius's Analects." *JCP* 33 (2006) 335–48.

Zhang, Bing-Nan. *Kongzi Zhuan* [Biography of Confucius]. Jilin: Literature and History, 1989. 张秉楠：《孔子传》。吉林：文史，1989.

Zhang, Ju-Zheng. *Jiangjie Lunyu* [Interpreting the Analects of Confucius]. Beijing: China Overseas, 2009. 张居正：《讲解《论语》》。北京：中国华侨，2009.

Zhang, Nie. "Lunyu de Wenben Xingshi yu Xiuyang Zhidao" [Textual Form and the Way of Cultivation in the Analects]. *Zhongguo Ruxue* [Chinese Confucianism]. Vol. 3. Edited by Wang Zhong-Jiang and Li Cun-Shan. Beijing: China Social Sciences, 2008. 张涅："《论语》的文本形式与修养之道"。《中国儒学（三）》。王中江、李存山主编。北京：中国社会科学，2008.

Zhang, Yan-Guo. *Lunyu Pingxi* [Commentary on the Analects]. Wuhan: Chongwen, 2003. 张艳国评析：《论语》。武汉：崇文书局，2003.

Zhang, Yong-Tao and Li Shu-You. *Ruxue Yuanliu* [Origins and Development of Confucianism]. Chinese Classics Series. Vol I. Beijing: China Youth, 2000. 张永桃、李书有：《儒学源流》。中华典籍精华丛书（第一卷）。北京：中国青年，2000.

Zhang, You-Chi. *Lunyu Yizhu* [Annotation on the Analects]. Taipei: Zhiyang, 1994. 张有池译注：《论语》。台北：智扬，1994.

Zhao, Dunhua. "Axiological Rules and Chinese Political Philosophy." *JCP* 34 (2007) 161–78.

Zhao, Ji-Hui. *Ershiyi Shiji Ruxue Yanjiu Xin Tuozhan* [New Development on Confucian Studies of the 21st Century]. Beijing: Social Sciences Academic, 2004. 赵吉惠：《21世纪儒学研究的新拓展》。北京：社会科学文献，2004.

Zhu, Chong-Yi. "Zhengshi di Miandui Siwang: Chuandaoshu de Shengsiguan" [Facing Death: Perspective on Life and Death in Ecclesiastes]. In *Jiejing: Shengjing Jingwen de Shiyi yu Quanshi* [Interpreting the Texts: Biblical Exegesis and Interpretation], edited by Chin Ken Pa and Philip P. Chia, 65–82. Taipei: Taiwan Christian Literature, 2008. 朱崇仪："真实地面对死亡：传道书的生死观"。《解经—圣经经文的释义与诠释》。曾庆豹、谢品彰编。台北：台湾基督教文艺，2008: 65–82.

Zhu, Rui-Kai. *Dangdai Xin Ruxue* [Contemporary New Confucianism]. Shanghai: Academia, 2006. 祝瑞开：《当代新儒学》。上海：学林，2006.

———. *Lunyu Benyi Xinjie* [New Interpretation on the Original Meaning of the Analects]. Shanghai: Academia, 2007. 祝瑞开：《《论语》本义新解》。上海：学林，2007.

Zhu, Xi. *Sishu Jizhu* [Commentaries on the Four Books]. Beijing: Beijing Ancient Scroll, 2000. 朱熹：《四书集注》。北京：北京古籍，2000。

Zhu, Yi-Ting. *Yu Kongzi Duihua: Xinshiji Quanqiu Wenmingzhong de Ruxue* [Dialogue with Confucius: Confucianism in the New Century of Global Civilization]. Shanghai: Academia, 2005. 朱贻庭编：《与孔子对话—新世纪全球文明中的儒学》。上海：学林，2005.

Zhu, Zhi-Kai, Xu Hong-Xing and Pan Fu-En, eds. *Kongzi Sixiang Yanjiu* [Studies on Confucius' Thought]. Shanghai: Ancient Scroll, 1999. 朱志凯、徐洪兴、潘富恩主编：《孔子思想研究》。上海：古籍，1999.

Zimmermann, Frank. "The Aramaic Provenance of Qoheleth." *JQR* 36 (1945) 17–45.

Index of Authors

Ames, Roger T., 103, 171
Anderson, William H. U., 56, 65-66, 86
Arnold, Bill T., 15

Beyer, Bryan E., 15
Bartholomew, Craig G., 37, 45, 88, 89
Barton, George A., 42, 44, 51-53, 60, 64, 76-77, 157, 174
Beentjes, Panc, 63-64
Benjamin, Don C., 15
Berthrong, John H., 34
Black, Anthony, 97, 106, 141
Blanshard, Brand, 5
Blocker, H. Gene, 98-99, 128
Botterweck, G. Johannes, 142-43
Bowker, John, xiv, 8
Brooks, A. Taeko, 95
Brooks, E. Bruce, 95
Brosius, Maria, 54-55, 71-72
Brown, Francis, xiii, 4, 77, 81, 142-44
Briggs, Charles, xiii, 4, 77, 81, 142-44
Brueggemann, Walter, 37, 85, 89

Ching, Julia, 32-34, 98-99, 165
Clifford, Richard, 49
Cobb, John Jr., 3
Covey, R. Alan., 54
Crenshaw, James L., 5, 7, 49-50, 52, 81, 100, 164
Cua, Antonio S., xiii, 18, 96
Cui, Jian-Lin, 114
Culliney, John, 128-29

D'Costa, Gavin, 3
Dahood, Mitchell J., 52, 89
de Bary, William Theodore, 19, 29, 34, 126, 129-32
Delitzsch, Franz, 44, 53, 74
Dobe, Timothy S., 32

Dong, Cong-Lin, 33
Dong-Fang, Qiao, 108, 120
Driver, S. R., xiii, 4, 77, 81, 142-44

Eaton, Michael A., 59, 162

Faulkner, Raymond Oliver, 13
Fox, Michael V., 7, 38, 45-46, 48-51, 59-61, 63-64, 66-67, 69-70, 74, 76, 78-82, 89, 143, 153, 157-58, 163-64
Fredericks, Daniel C., 52, 59
Fu, Pei-Rong, 34

Gadamer, Hans-Georg, 21
Gardner, Daniel K., 103, 117
Garrett, Duane A., 57, 61, 63, 65, 73, 75, 82, 85
Garthwaite, Gene R., 54
Gernet, Jacques, 3
Ginsberg, H. L., 52
Good, Edwin M., 45, 87
Gordis, Robert, 52, 62, 76, 79
Guo, Qing-Xiang, 33

Hall, David L., 130
Hallo, William W., xiii, 17, 72
Hart, Trevor, 20-21
Heard, R. Christopher, 32
Holladay, William L., xiv, 142-43
Hsü, Leonard Shihlien, 130
Hwa, Yung, 177

Ingram, Doug, 81

Jennings, William, 112, 119
Jiang, Yi-Hua, 99-100, 115, 135
Jones, David, 128-29
Jones, Scott C., 66
Jordan, Jennifer, 172

Kaiser, Otto, 44
Kallas, Enfrl, 37
Kam, Louie, 135
Khu, John B., 108, 118
Khu, Jose B. K., 108, 118
Khu, Vincente B. K., 108, 118
Khu, William B. S., 108, 118
Kidner, Derek, 59-60
Koh, Yee-Von, 47
Kittel, Rudolf, 59, 62-63, 69, 76, 82
Kramers, Robert P., 29
Krüger, Thomas, 72, 153, 163
Kugel, James L., 53-55, 60, 89
Küng, Hans, 33
Kupperman, Joel J., 147
Kwok, Pui-Lan, 20

Lambert, W. G., xiii, 14, 62, 141, 162
Lee, Archie C. C., ix, 7, 19-20, 25-26, 171
Lee, Eunny P., 4
Lee, Peter K. H., 34
Legge, James, 92-95, 108, 116
Leys, Simon, 105, 108, 111, 129, 131
Li, Dao-Sheng, 32
Liang, Jia-Lin, 33
Lichtheim, Miriam, xiii
Lin, Yu-Sheng, 111
Lindbeck, George A., 3
Lindenberger, James M., 15, 64
Littlejohn, Ronnie L., 95
Liu, Xiao-Feng, 34
Loader, J. A., 45-46, 62-63, 66
Loewe, Michael, 97
Lohfink, Norbert, 143, 163
Longman, Tremper, III, 38-39, 42, 45, 47, 52, 61-64, 68, 79, 88, 144, 163

Matthews, Victor H., 15
Miller, Douglas B., 86
Miller, Geoffrey D., 138
Miscall, P. D., 138
Murphy, Roland E., 7, 44, 49, 52, 62, 87, 146, 164

Nacpil, Emerito P., 24
Newsom, Carol, 52-53

Ogden, Graham S., 79, 81

Pang, Pu, 93
Perdue, Leo G., 8, 11-12
Perkins, Dorothy, 103
Perry, T. A., 38
Pinker, Aron, 80-81
Porten, Bezalel, xiv, 15-16, 64, 71
Pritchard, James B., xiii, 14-15, 62, 141, 162

Rosemont, Henry, Jr., 92, 103, 108, 116, 171
Rowley, H. H., 28-29
Rudman, Dominic, 79
Russell, James R., 56
Ryken, Leland, 45

Schoors, Antoon, 51, 76
Schwartz, Benjamin I., 99
Seow, Choon-Leong, viii, ix, 8, 14, 16, 28, 38, 42, 45-46, 50-53, 59-60, 63-64, 69-71, 73-74, 77-81, 84, 89, 140, 143, 145-47, 152-53, 175
Sharp, Carolyn J., 87-88
Shaughnessy, Edward L., 92, 97
Shi, Heng-Tan, 31
Shuo, Dongfang, 133-34
Slingerland, Edward, 102-03, 105-06, 109, 113-14, 116, 120-23, 125-26, 171
Soanes, Catherine, 5, 100
Sparks, Kenton L., 1, 13-14, 61
Sugirtharajah, R. S., 22
Swidler, Leonard, 5

Talmon, Shemaryahu, 15
Tang, Yi-Jie, 34
Taylor, Rodney L., 133, 164
Thompson, Kirill O., 111
Toorn, Karel van der, 47-48
Torrey, Charles C., 52, 81

van Norden, Bryan W., 94-95, 174
von Rad, Gerhard, 5, 15, 50-51

Waley, Arthur, 118, 131, 133

Waltke, Bruce K., 142
Walton, John H., 1
Weisman, Ze'ev, 79, 81–83
Whaling, Frank, 34
Whitley, Charles F., 52, 56, 62–63, 76
Whybray, R. N., 37, 52–53, 56–57, 64, 78, 144–45
Wu, Ming-Chieh, 33

Ya Se, 103, 105, 108, 114–16, 121–22
Yao, Xinzhong, xiv
Yardeni, Ada, xiv, 15–16, 64, 71
Yeo, K. K., ix, 30–31, 166, 170, 177
Younger, K. Lawson Jr., xiii, 17, 72
Yuan, Zhi-Ming, 31

Yuezhi, 91
Yu, Jiyuan, 113

Zhang, Ju-Zheng, 105
Zhang, Yan-Guo, 9, 94, 104, 106, 112, 114, 118
Zhang, Yong-Tao, 93, 107, 110–11, 165
Zhang, You-Chi, 103
Zhao, Dunhua, 106, 116, 135
Zhu, Xi, 18, 94–95, 102–03, 109, 115–16, 125
Zhu, Yi-Ting, 123–24
Zhu, Zhi-Kai, 127
Zimmermann, F., 52

Index of Subjects

Agape, 34, 137
Ahiqa, 13, 15–16, 64–65, 70–71, 145–55
Allah, 2, 25
Ankhsheshonqy, 13, 61, 145
approach
    comparative, 3–4
    complementary, 3
    confrontational, 3
    dialogical, 4, 17, 35
    transcending, 3
Aramaic, 15–17, 51–56, 62, 64, 69
aristocrat, aristocratic, 73, 77, 128, 131, 132
Asian, Asians, Asia, Asianized, viii, 7, 8, 17, 19–28, 31, 33, 33–35
Axial Age, 2, 4, 24, 29

biblical interpretation, 19, 22, 24–26, 178
Book of Rites (*Liji*), 18, 92
Buddhism, 3, 33, 91, 121

China, 3, 8, 17, 27–29, 31, 33, 92, 94, 97, 99, 100, 103, 121, 135, 165, 166
Chinese Christian, xi, 22–26, 30–32, 173–75
Chinese classics, ix, 1, 27, 29, 92–95, 108, 116, 178
Cheng (sincerity), 18, 109
Christianity, 3–4, 32–34
Classic of History (*Shangshu*), 18
commoner, 58, 77, 79–81, 83–85, 98, 108, 112–13, 116–17, 127–29, 131–33, 146, 157
Confucius, xi, 7–10, 18–19, 22–23, 25, 28 30, 35, 91–99, 102–36, 139–41, 143–49, 151–57, 159, 161, 165–72, 174–77
Confucian, Confucianism, 3, 8, 18–19, 22–23, 29–34, 91–93, 95–104, 107–121, 126–140, 144–48, 151, 164–70, 175
Criticism, 4, 22, 46, 69, 71, 94, 148, 150, 167
cross-cultural, 1–3, 17, 23, 28, 31–32, 35
cross-textual, 1–36, 46, 137–139, 176
cross-textual hermeneutics, ix, xi, 7, 20, 24, 26–27, 30–32, 34, 137, 171–72, 176–78

Dao, dao, 17, 31–34, 102, 105, 115, 119, 139, 156–57, 164–67, 171, 174
Daode Jing, 17, 32, 13
Daoism, Daojia, 17, 33, 91, 121
Darius I, 55, 88
De (virtue), 3–12, 102, 104, 134
disordered world, 18, 91, 112, 123
Doctrine of the Mean (*Zhongyong*), 9, 35, 137, 139, 169–71
Duke Zhou, 118, 128, 130

Egypt, Egyptians, vii, 5, 11–15, 18, 55, 71, 78, 141
Elephantine, 15–16, 64, 71, 155
Ĕlōhîm, 28, 44, 150, 163–67, 175

Fools, the, 40

ḥakam (the wise one), 4, 5, 46, 83
hermeneutics, 7, 20–31, 34, 37, 88, 137, 176

intersect, intersection, 23, 29, 36

junzi (exemplary person), 9, 18–19, 29, 94–98, 113, 116–17, 125, 130–36, 143, 145, 147–49, 154, 159, 161–162, 168, 175–76
justice, 9–10, 13–14, 19, 27, 29, 58–62, 73–75, 86–90, 98, 111, 119, 138, 141–47, 150–53, 157–58, 163–64, 167, 172

kingship, 15, 40, 43, 47, 61–62, 64, 71, 88–89

Laozi, 16, 53, 56
li (propriety), 30, 92, 96, 101–102, 112, 118, 127, 131, 133, 165
lingua franca, 17, 31–32, 92

Malaysia, ix, 2, 3, 14, 24–25, 31, 172–73, 175
Mencius (Mingzi), 17–18, 28–30, 90–92, 113–14, 137
Mesopotamia, vii, 12–15, 56, 61, 62
Mozi, 18, 28

oppressions, oppressed, oppressors, 9–10, 27, 40, 42, 47, 58–59, 61–62, 65–66, 73, 76–78, 85–86, 88–90, 97, 104, 129, 135–36, 139, 141–42, 144, 150, 152–55, 158, 164, 167, 169, 172–73

parallels, parallel reading, ix, 4, 11–13, 15–17, 23, 27, 30–31, 38, 47–48, 53, 64, 70, 110, 112, 137–38, 143, 160–61, 165, 170
Persians, 54–56, 71–72, 82, 85, 104–6, 108, 110, 112–13, 115–17, 119–20, 126–27, 130–36, 139–40, 142–44, 148–52, 154, 158–59, 162, 164, 168, 172–73
political leader, 10, 12, 37, 60–61, 70, 81–82, 85, 104, 106, 108, 110, 112–13, 115–17, 119–20, 126–27, 130–36, 139–40, 142–44, 148–52, 154, 158–59, 162, 164, 168, 172–73
political satire, 6, 10, 70, 79, 81–84, 147–48, 167, 170, 195

political wisdom, 1, 4, 6–12, 16–18, 23, 25, 32, 35, 37–39, 46, 57–59, 66–68, 75, 78, 82, 85, 87, 90, 94, 97, 100–101, 126–29, 133–139, 146, 148, 155, 160, 169, 172–73, 176
power structure, 37, 66–68, 70, 78, 85, 97, 129, 141–42, 148, 169, 172
post-colonial, 22
Proverbs, 5, 12–13, 15–16, 39–40, 49, 64–65, 70–71, 85, 137, 145–46, 152, 155, 162
Proverbs of Ahiqar, 15, 16, 64, 65, 70, 71, 155

Qoheleth, vii, xi, 7–10, 12, 16, 22–23, 25, 32, 35, 37–71, 73–90, 139–57, 160, 162–64, 167, 169–71, 174–76

ren (humanness), 18, 30, 91, 96, 101–2, 109–14, 126–34, 151, 153
righteousness, 10, 17, 30–31, 42–43, 59–62, 73–75, 86, 89, 111–14, 124, 130–31, 135–36, 138, 141–45, 147, 150, 152, 157, 159, 168
ruler, rulers, rulership, 9, 11–15, 18, 27, 37, 54, 56–58, 61, 66–68, 73, 80–82, 84, 88–89, 99, 105–06, 109–11, 114–23, 126–31, 134–35, 139–41, 146, 149–50, 153–54, 160–63, 165, 169–67

Shangdi, Shen, YHWH, 27, 28, 33, 64, 163
Shijing (Book of Songs), 18, 26, 27
society, xiv, 10, 17–19, 30, 37, 47, 61, 66, 68, 71, 75–78, 84, 97, 99–100, 104, 117–18, 120, 125–29, 131, 133, 135–36, 139, 141, 157, 169, 173–76
socio-political, xi, 2, 6, 11–12, 24–26, 35–37, 56–58, 73, 75, 84, 86, 89, 94, 96–97, 100–101, 115, 117, 120, 128–29, 131, 138–39, 148, 153, 167, 169–75

texts, cultural, 3, 19–20, 25
text, biblical, viii, ix, xi, 1, 7, 11, 17, 19–20, 22–26, 56, 137, 176, 177
Tôb-Spruch, 76, 79
tyranny, 6, 65–66, 98, 109, 136, 144, 148, 154, 163, 167, 170

Wise, the, 5, 18, 40, 46, 49, 64–65, 80–81, 84–86, 107–08, 131, 160–62, 167, 173
wuwei (non-action), 17, 103, 116, 125

xiaoren ("minor person"), 31, 112, 116–17, 131–33, 159, 161–62
xin (trust), 18, 31, 109, 110, 112, 151–53
yi (righteousness), 18, 101, 130–31, 133, 138, 142, 154

Zhou, 18, 97, 99, 114, 117, 118, 121, 128–29

Index of Ancient Documents

The Old Testament

Genesis

6:1–4	27
10:10	60
11:1–9	27
41:33	4
41:39–40	4
47:6	60

Exodus

15:6	77
28:3	4
31:3–6	4
35:25	4
36:1–2	4

Numbers

14:41	64
22:18	64

Deuteronomy

4:6	5
8:18	77
16:18	5

Joshua

17:17	77

2 Samuel

13:3–5	5
15:12	5
16:20–23	5

1 Kings

2:1–9	11
2:6	12
2:9	12
2:43	64
7:14	4
10:6	5
13:21	64, 155

1 Chronicles

22:15	4
28:21	4

2 Chronicles

7	4
13–14	4
14:10	77

Ezra

2:55	4
2:57	53

Nehemiah

7:57	53
7:59	53

Psalms

29:4	77
78:12	60
107:43	5

Proverbs

20:26	5

Ecclesiastes

1:1–11	38
1:1–2	38, 153
1:1	39–41
1:2–11	39–41
1:2–9	vii
1:2	vii, 43, 81
1:4–11	46
1:4–7	157
1:12—6:12	39–41
1:12—2:28	41
1:12—2:26	39–40, 47, 56
1:12	54, 64
1:14	41–42, 49, 146
1:17–18	41
1:18	44
2:1–11	40–41
2:3	46, 52, 77, 146
2:5	53
2:11	41, 46, 158
2:12–17	40, 41, 162
2:12–16	162
2:12	16, 54, 89, 146, 162
2:13–14	44, 162, 174
2:13	44, 83, 87, 146, 164
2:15–16	44, 48
2:16	47
2:17	75, 81, 86
2:18–26	40–41
2:22–23	162
2:24	13, 42, 49
2:25	64
2:26	44, 140, 164
3:1—6:12	39–41, 58
3:1–15	40, 42, 51, 139
3:1–9	52
3:1–8	74, 82, 140
3:1	77, 140, 144
3:2–8	46, 160, 162
3:6	140
3:9–15	140
3:10–15	174
3:10–11	44, 164
3:10	42, 44, 49, 73–76, 146, 158, 164, 175
3:11	44, 46, 50, 75, 144, 158, 164
3:14–15	41, 44, 140, 164
3:14	44, 51, 164
3:15c–17	57, 73
3:15c	73
3:16–22	40, 42, 58, 73, 88
3:16–17	8, 10, 47, 58, 73, 75, 77, 85–86, 142, 145, 147, 150–53
3:16	73, 74, 76, 86, 143, 152, 157
3:17	16, 44, 74, 86, 150, 164
3:21–22	41, 64
3:22	42, 43, 75, 78
4:1–16	40, 42, 79, 160
4:1–3	8, 10, 35, 57–58, 76, 78, 85–86, 88, 145, 152, 160
4:1	47, 58, 76, 77, 142, 146, 157, 158
4:2–3	77
4:2	162
4:3	75–77, 86
4:4	41, 64, 75
4:6	160
4:7–8, 9–12	152–53
4:11–12	41
4:13–16	8, 10, 47, 56–57, 76, 79–88, 146–47, 150, 153, 156, 160, 162
4:13–14	79
4:13	157–58
4:14–15	80
4:14	79, 80
4:15–16	79
4:15	42, 49, 80, 158
4:16	81, 82
5:1–9	164
5:1–7	38, 40–42, 44, 164
5:2	62, 158, 161–62
5:5	75, 158
5:6	41, 44, 164
5:8–10	8, 10, 35
5:8–9	54, 57, 61, 85–88, 139, 142, 145–50, 164
5:8	46–47, 60, 86, 142, 143, 157
5:9	12, 41, 60–61, 81, 157
5:13–17	47, 56–57
5:13–14	48
5:17	78
5:18–20	41, 46
5:18–19	44, 164
5:19	174

INDEX OF ANCIENT DOCUMENTS 209

Reference	Pages
6:1–12	40, 42
6:1–2	44, 47, 152–53, 175
6:2	44, 158, 164
6:11–12	41, 44, 162
6:12	64, 81
6:9	41
7:1–14	39–40, 42, 46
7:1	162
7:4–7	162
7:7	162
7:9	62
7:11–12	44
7:12	46, 162
7:13–15	146
7:13	45, 64, 75, 146
7:14	44, 46, 164
7:15—12:7	39–40, 42, 58
7:15–25	43
7:15–22	40, 58–59
7:15–18	163
7:15–16	48
7:15	16, 42, 48–49, 86, 146
7:16–18	144
7:16	16, 46, 143–44
7:17	67, 94, 143
7:18	44, 158, 164
7:19	58, 84
7:23–25	146
7:23	48
7:24	50
7:25	46, 50, 163
7:26—8:1	43, 64
7:27–29	163
7:27	38, 52
8:1–17	63
8:1–9	63
8:1	44, 46, 63–64, 146
8:2–9	8, 10, 35, 43, 57, 62–64, 67, 86, 88, 146–48, 150, 155
8:2–6	47
8:2–5	64–65, 86, 144, 146
8:2–4	16
8:2	16, 58, 63–67, 154–55, 158, 164
8:3	64–67, 86, 154–55, 158
8:4	16, 65, 66
8:5	16, 63–66, 87, 144, 155, 158, 175
8:5b–6	65
8:6–8	86
8:6	66, 67, 140
8:7–8	67
8:7	63–65
8:8	58, 62, 65, 86, 157
8:9	42, 49, 66–67, 75, 86
8:10—9:10	40, 43
8:10–13	163
8:11	53, 75
8:12	44, 60, 164
8:14–15	48
8:14	16, 162
8:15	vii, 44, 87, 158, 164
8:16–17	44, 50
8:16	46, 146
8:17	13, 44, 46, 75, 144, 163–64, 174
9:1	46, 146, 158, 162, 174
9:2–3	152
9:2	38, 86, 162, 164
9:3–16	86
9:7–9	162
9:9	44, 83, 158, 164
9:11—10:20	40, 43
9:11–12	40, 43, 48, 58–59
9:13—10:3	83
9:13	42, 157
9:13–16	8, 10, 35, 40, 43, 56–57, 82–87, 146–47, 150–51, 153, 156, 173
9:13–14	83
9:14	58, 83, 84
9:15–16	48
9:15	46, 83, 84
9:16	84
9:17—10:15	162
9:17—10:3	40, 43
9:18	84
10:1–3	46
10:4–7	8, 10, 35, 40, 43, 57, 67, 86, 88, 146–47
10:4	58, 68, 87, 154
10:5–7	47, 48, 68, 139
10:5	42, 49, 58, 68, 146, 158
10:6–7	68
10:6	68, 86
10:7	68, 157

210 INDEX OF ANCIENT DOCUMENTS

Ecclesiastes (continued)

10:8–11	40, 43, 157
10:12–15	40, 43
10:12	40, 43, 143, 160
10:14	46, 64, 158
10:16	70, 160
10:16–20	8, 10, 35, 47, 57, 68–69, 86–87, 147, 150, 160
10:16–19	71
10:16–17	56, 69, 81, 148, 150, 157–58
10:17	69, 160–61
10:18–19	70–71, 148, 150
10:18	70, 151, 158, 161
10:19	69–70, 150
10:20	14, 16, 58, 71–73, 150, 157–58
11:1–6	41, 43
11:1–2	153
11:3–4	157
11:5	44, 75, 164
11:6	158, 162
11:7—12:14	88
11:7—12:7	41, 43, 46
11:7–8	162
11:9	44, 89, 143, 158, 164
12:12	16, 83, 89
12:13–14	44, 174
12:13	44, 83, 87, 164, 174
12:14	75, 143
12:1–7	157
12:2, 3–4	157
12:5	157–158
12:6	157
12:7	44, 87, 164
12:8–14	39, 41, 43
12:8–13	44, 83, 87, 164
12:8–11	46
12:8–10	46
12:8	43
12:9–14	38
12:9–11	146
12:9	46, 50, 89, 146

Isaiah

3:3	4
7:18	60
10:13	5
19:11–12	5
29:14	5
40:20	4

Jeremiah

4:22	5
8:8–9	5
9:17–18	85
10:9	4
10:12	77
25:20	60

Ezekiel

27:8	4

Daniel

1:20	4
8:22	77

Hebrew Text [MT] of Ecclesiastes

4:17—5:8	164
4:17—5:6	41, 164
5:5b–6	41
5:7–9	8, 10, 35
5:7–8	55–61, 75, 86, 139, 142, 145, 147–49, 164, 178
5:7	41, 58, 60, 86, 142–43, 157
5:8–9	47
5:8b	60

Ancient Near Eastern

Ancient Egyptian Literature	
Babylonian Wisdom Literature	
Counsels of Wisdom	14
Dialogue of Pessimism	48

INDEX OF ANCIENT DOCUMENTS   211

Harper's Songs	48	3:5	118, 121, 122
		3:10	120
		3:12	166
Gilgamesh Epic	12, 62	3:14	118
		3:18	122–23, 166
Instruction of King Amenemhet I for His Son Sesostris I	11	3:19	119, 149, 161
		4:3	123, 161
		4:8	161
		4:10	122
		4:11	132, 159, 161
Instructions of Ankhsheshonqy	13	4:13	118, 133
		4:16	113, 159
		4:26	123
		5:7	113, 157
Instructions of Any	48	6:2	124
		6:8	133, 149
		6:11	157
Proverbs of Ahiqar	15–17	6:13	132
		6:17	157
6:80	16	6:18	123, 124
6:81–86	15	6:22	175
6:84	16, 64	6:23	156
93	16, 64	6:30	110
6:87–88	16, 64	7:8	110, 147
6:91	15	7:11	113, 125
7:103–104	16	7:23	165
11:171	16	7:30	126
12:187	15	7:37	132, 159, 161
		8:13	125, 142, 160
		8:14	120, 127
Analects		9:8	124
		9:16	161
1:4	147	9:17	156
1:5	107–8, 149, 151	9:19	156
1:10	134	11:12	161
1:12	122	11:18	159
2:1	115, 140	11:24	114, 154–55
2:3	102–4, 117, 141, 148–49, 156	12:2	108
2:5	161	12:5	161, 165
2:15	147, 161	12:7	108, 149, 151, 173
2:18	161	12:9	149
2:19	102, 104–5, 115–17, 132–33, 145, 149	12:19	115
2:20	126, 149	12:11	119, 133, 161
2:21	124–25, 149	12:13	103
2:24	113, 144, 166	12:14	133
3:1	120	12:16	132
3:2	120	12:17	104, 105, 133, 142, 149, 156
		12:19	104, 115–17, 132, 145, 149

Analects *(continued)*

12:22	104, 109, 110, 149, 151
13:1	133, 149
13:2	106, 149
13:3	120, 133, 149
13:4	111–12, 118–19, 144, 149, 152
13:6	105, 149
13:9	149
13:11, 12	135
13:13	105, 149
13:16	152
13:18	161
13:21	124
13:23	132
13:26	159
14:1	125
14:3	125, 160
14:10	161
14:23	132, 161
14:35	161
14:36	166
14:41	118–19, 149
14:43	161
15:3	133
15:7	125
15:9	111
15:10	149
15:17	131
15:18	111–13, 143
15:25	157
15:27	161
15:28	123
15:34	159, 161
15:40	115
16:1	114, 154–55
16:2	125, 139, 160
16:6	116, 132
17:4	116, 132
17:19	165
17:23	111–13, 143–45
19:3	149
19:13	159
20:1–3	149, 151, 173
20:1	127

www.ingramcontent.com/pod-product-compliance
Lightning Source LLC
Chambersburg PA
CBHW070253230426
43664CB00014B/2519